ARSON INVESTIGATION

ROBERT E. CARTER

GLENCOE PUBLISHING CO., INC.
Encino, California

Collier Macmillan Publishers
London

Glencoe Publishing Co., Inc.
17337 Ventura Boulevard
Encino, California 91316
Collier Macmillan Canada, Ltd.

Library of Congress Catalog Card Number: 74-6612

3 4 5 6 7 8 9   80

ISBN 0-02-472400-9

ARSON INVESTIGATION

GLENCOE PRESS FIRE SCIENCE SERIES

Bryan: **Fire Suppression and Detection Systems**
Bush/McLaughlin: **Introduction to Fire Science,** Second Edition
Carter: **Arson Investigation**
Clet: **Fire-Related Codes, Laws, and Ordinances**
Erven: **Fire Company Apparatus and Procedures,** Second Edition
Erven: **First Aid and Emergency Rescue**
Erven: **Handbook of Emergency Care and Rescue,** Revised Edition
Erven: **Techniques of Fire Hydraulics**
Gratz: **Fire Department Management: Scope and Method**
Meidl: **Explosive and Toxic Hazardous Materials**
Meidl: **Flammable Hazardous Materials,** Second Edition
Meidl: **Hazardous Materials Handbook**
Robertson: **Introduction to Fire Prevention**

Consultant:

CHIEF DAVID B. GRATZ

Fire Management Associates, Inc.
Silver Spring, Maryland

To My Family

Contents

PREFACE   xi

1. TODAY'S ARSON PROBLEM   1

   Facts and Figures   4
   The Causes of Increased Arson   7

2. MOTIVES   18

   Defrauding an Insurance Company   18
   Achieving a Personal Goal, Aiding a Cause, or Protesting   23
   Arson by the Mentally Afflicted   27

3. ROLE OF THE FIRE DEPARTMENT IN ARSON
   SUPPRESSION   35

   Importance of the Fire Fighter's Role   36
   Fire Department Involvement   36

4. CHEMISTRY OF FIRE   44

   Definitions   44
   The Fire Triangle   48
   Classes of Fires   51
   Methods of Heat Transfer   51
   Spontaneous Heating   54

5. DETERMINING ORIGIN AND CAUSE   59

   Preserving the Fire Scene   62
   Authority to Search   65
   Investigators and the Fire Scene Search   65
   Arriving at the Fire Scene   71

6. FIRE SCENE SEARCH   **81**

Point of Origin   **81**
Fuel Supply   **83**
Heat Source   **93**

7. SCIENTIFIC AIDS   **103**

Arson Pattern Recognition System (APRS)   **103**
The Combustible Gas Detector (Sniffer)   **109**
Gas Liquid Chromatography   **111**
Ultraviolet Light   **111**

8. ELECTRICAL FIRES   **114**

The Panel Board   **114**
Fuses and Fuse Boxes   **115**
Circuit Breakers   **116**
Wiring in the Fire Building   **117**
Overload or Short Circuit   **118**
Aluminum Wire   **120**
Summary   **122**

9. RURAL FIRES   **124**

Revenge or Spite Fires   **125**
Fires in a Series   **128**
Insurance or Fraud Fires   **132**
Goals of the Investigation   **139**

10. URBAN FIRES   **141**

Personnel Problems   **142**
Equipment   **147**
Records and Data   **148**
Developing Public Awareness   **150**

11. AUTOMOBILE FIRES   **153**

Motives for Motor Vehicle Fires   **155**
Methods of Car Burning   **156**
Immediate Investigative Procedure   **157**
Role of the Insurance Adjustor   **168**
Investigator's Salvage Examination   **172**

12. EXPLOSIONS   183

Definitions   183
Types of Explosions   184
Investigation   190

13. THE JUVENILE FIRE PROBLEM   195

Childhood Development   195
Juvenile Age Groups   197

14. INTERVIEWS, NOTES, STATEMENTS, AND REPORTS   209

Interviews   210
Notes   216
Statements   217
Reports   220

15. INTERROGATION   224

Landmark Decisions   226
Interrogator Profile   228
Meaning and Importance   230
Preparation for Interrogation   231
Interrogation Procedures   237
Summary   245

16. PRESENTING YOUR CASE   246

Evidence   246
Preparation for Court   248
The Investigator in Court   249
The Expert Witness   253

APPENDIX

A. Building Construction Terminology and Definitions   257

B. A Glossary of Insurance Terms   268

INDEX   275

Preface

The original purpose of this volume was to serve as a text on arson investigation for fire science students in universities and community colleges. In its completed form, however, the text goes beyond this objective, and will prove useful to fire fighters, fire officers, inspectors, and investigators, as well as to local and state investigators and representatives of the insurance industry.

After an overview of today's arson problem, the text begins by discussing arson motives, the role of the fire department, and the chemistry of fire—topics that provide the basic background for a study of arson investigation. Specific arson investigation techniques, including determining origin and cause, conducting fire scene searches, and using scientific aids, are the subject matter of the next group of chapters. After a discussion of various types of arson problems—electrical fires, fires in rural and urban settings, automobile fires, explosions, and the juvenile fire setter—the text concludes with a series of chapters on interrogation and on recording and presenting evidence.

The information collected here was acquired by the author in a number of ways during eighteen years as an arson investigator. Most important was the expertise gained through field experience both as a supervisor and active participant in many investigations. Attendance as a student and as an instructor at fire and arson seminars throughout the United States broadened this base of knowledge, not only through the formal instruction but also through informal discussions with knowledgeable people in the field who have devoted their lives to combatting the arson problem. Almost every bull session eventually resolved itself into a discussion of some phase of investigation in which information on interesting cases, investigative techniques, and special problems was exchanged.

Another method by which knowledge for this text was acquired was the study and restudy of arson literature. The work of the official publication of the International Association of Arson Investigators in providing information on this subject is unsurpassed by publications of any other such professional organization.

The author recognizes subject areas in which neither experience nor seminars nor study qualify him to write authoritatively. Material on electrical fires (Chapter 8) was provided by H. Ray Vliet, Chief, Edison, New Jersey, Fire Department, who is nationally recognized for his expertise on this subject. Much of Chapter B, "The Juvenile Fire Problem," was prepared by J. Charles Wilson, Chief (retired), Greenville, South Carolina, Fire Department, who has been for many years a leader in the IAAI's program to combat the juvenile fire problem, serving as Chairman of the Juvenile Committee.

Reliance on experts was particularly necessary in the chapter on scientific aids. At the request of the author, David J. Icove, Arson Investigator for the State of Tennessee, and James R. Carter of the Department of Geography, University of Tennessee, Knoxville, Tennessee, prepared the portion of the text on arson pattern recognition. In addition, excerpts from several articles that have appeared in the *Fire and Arson Investigator* were used in the chapter. These include an article on ultraviolet light by Charles M. Lane, Special Agent, General Adjustment Bureau, Incorporated, Investigations Division, Gainesville, Georgia; an article on the combustible gas detector (sniffer) authored by Charles L. Thomas and Robert I. Hilliard, Crime Laboratory scientists, Michigan Department of Public Health, Lansing, Michigan; and material from a paper on gas liquid chromatography prepared by Charles R. Midkiff, Jr., of the National Office Laboratory, Alcohol, Tobacco, and Firearms Division, Internal Revenue Service, U.S. Treasury Department, Washington, D.C. To each of these gentlemen, and to John E. Stuerwald, editor of the *Fire and Arson Investigator,* my sincere thanks.

Thanks is also due to the National Fire Protection Association for the use in the text of excerpts from several of their publications.

Though this text does not pretend to provide answers to all the day-to-day problems which face fire and arson investigators, if it assists them in any way, this will be ample reward to the author for the three-year effort of preparing it.

1 Today's Arson Problem

The crime of arson is no doubt as ancient as mankind's discovery of fire. Malicious burning of other people's property and possessions has occurred for so many thousands of years that society has accepted the fact that there will be incendiary fires resulting in loss of life and property. Even law enforcement and fire service agencies, along with others directly affected by these fires, have viewed the situation with resignation as unavoidable and made only token corrective efforts.

This apparent indifference to the problem of incendiary fires has continued unabated until the last few years, when there has been an obvious surge in interest on the part of law enforcement, fire service, and insurance personnel. Only the general public continues to ignore the situation, perhaps because of a lack of awareness of its critical seriousness.

At this point, let us examine the developments that have resulted in a vigorous effort to study and prevent arson by law enforcement, fire service, and the insurance industry. The blue ribbon National Commission on Fire Prevention and Control, in a report submitted to the President of the United States on May 4, 1973, entitled *America Burning*, had this to say concerning arson:

> In contrast to the fire accidents difficult to prevent are the fires set on purpose. In 1971, among fires reported to the National Fire Protection Association, about 7 percent were classified as incendiary; an additional 17 percent were "of unknown origin." Arsonists pick expensive targets: Among the 1971 fires in which losses exceeded $250,000, 27 percent were classified as incendiary, another 47 percent

as of unknown origin. In many large cities, fire chiefs believe that almost half of all fires in their experience have been deliberately set.

Fire has always held an attraction for demented thrill-seekers. That fire is a way of attacking authority is indicated by the fact that in 1971, 26 percent of the large-loss school fires and 44 percent of the large-loss church fires were incendiary.

Not all deliberately set fires stem from malice or thrill-seeking; an increasing number are set for profit. A number of building owners have been setting their properties afire to reap insurance benefits and tax write-offs in excess of market value, delinquent taxes, or demolition costs. In the troubled city of Newark, N.J., where the number of vacated buildings increased by 300 percent between 1965 and 1971, the number of fires in these structures increased by over 500 percent. There is evidence that the Fair Access to Insurance Requirements (FAIR) plan, designed to provide insurance on properties not qualified under normal company standards, is being used by some owners of deteriorating buildings to burn for profit.

The International Association of Arson Investigators, a worldwide organization generally recognized as the focal point of arson investigation, unanimously approved the following resolution at its 26th Annual Meeting in Lincoln, Nebraska, in April 1975:

WHEREAS: the IAAI, after thorough analysis of all available statistics, including the latest publication of the National Fire Protection Association, and after conducting surveys throughout Canada, the United States, and some foreign countries, concludes that the total overall monetary loss affecting the health and welfare of these nations in 1974 due to the widespread effect on their overall economies resulting from fire bombings, incendiary and suspicious fires, amounted to billions of dollars, and

WHEREAS: the rate of arson has increased 12% over 1973, and

WHEREAS: the loss of life and personal injury resulting from these criminal offenses has become appalling, and

WHEREAS: all indications point to further increases in arson due to the economic trend and the activities of organized crime, and

WHEREAS: the IAAI realizes that there is serious need for more extensive training of fire services and insurance personnel in detecting or determining that the crime of arson has been committed, and

WHEREAS: the IAAI is aware that the majority of fire and law enforcement agencies do not have sufficient assigned, trained, and properly equipped personnel to investigate the crime of arson, and

WHEREAS: the IAAI realizes that a successful prosecution for the crime of arson usually results from a joint investigation by well-trained and equipped fire, insurance, and law enforcement agencies, and

WHEREAS: the IAAI recognizes that a serious lack of communication exists between most insurance industry representatives, investigative agencies, and within the public safety agencies themselves, and

WHEREAS: the IAAI recognizes that statistics relating to the crime of arson is not included in the Class I category of the FBI Uniform Crime Reports and therefore does not receive the fullest attention of the news media and federal, state, and local fiscal agencies, and

WHEREAS: the IAAI recognizes that over-insurance coverage encourages arson for profit.

THEREFORE BE IT RESOLVED THAT: the IAAI, convened in annual session on the 23rd day of April, 1975 in Lincoln, Nebraska, does hereby pledge continued assistance and cooperation with the National Fire Prevention and Control Administration; the Joint Council of National Fire Service Organizations; the International Association of Chiefs of Police; the Canadian Association of Chiefs of Police; the International Association of Fire Chiefs; the National States Attorney Association; all law enforcement and fire service agencies and the insurance industry. . . . (Reprinted by permission.)

The National Fire Protection Association in its annual report commented as follows on incendiary and suspicious fires:

In reviewing the summary of fire losses by causes of fire, one notes that the most startling increase [from 1971 to 1972] is in incendiary and suspicious fires. The number of fires in this category has increased 16.8 percent, and the losses from such fires have increased by 22.6 percent. Some experienced fire chiefs feel that half the fires of unknown cause are of incendiary origin, too. If this is true, over 156,000 building fires, causing $769,400,000 loss, were purposely set. This would be only one-seventh of all building fires, but nearly one-third of the loss from building fires. Such losses call for action. One state fire marshal is so concerned over the rapid climb of incendiary fire losses that he is forming a special group of deputy fire marshals in his state to combat the problem. Incendiary fires have been particular problems in schools, churches, restaurants, and taverns. ("Fire and Fire Losses Classified, 1972," *Fire Journal* (September 1973), p. 23.)

The NFPA report of 1975 reflects no improvement in the situation:

Incendiary and suspicious fires continue to increase and to cause increased property loss. The number of such fires increased [from

1974 to 1975] 25½ percent, and the resultant damage increased by 12½ percent. ("Fires and Fire Losses Classified, 1975," *Fire Journal* (November 1976), p. 19.)

Obviously, the resolution and reports cited convey a growing concern on the part of national and international bodies. Let us examine further facts and figures to determine whether such concern is justified.

Facts and Figures

The figures listed in the table, taken from the National Fire Protection Association's annual reports on estimated United States building fire losses by cause, indicate year-to-year trends. Of these figures, the *Fire Journal* (November 1976, p. 17) said: "While they are reasonable approximations based on experience in typical states, they should not be taken as exact records for each class. The figures by themselves do not show the relative safety in use of various types of materials, devices, fuels, or services, and they should not be used for that purpose." Figures are not given for all years, but the selection emphasizes the dramatic increase in the number of fires and losses therefrom, especially in the last ten years.

Fires Classified as Incendiary or Suspicious*

YEAR	NUMBER OF FIRES	MONETARY LOSS
1950	5,600	$ 15,000,000
1953	7,500	22,000,000
1956	11,500	25,000,000
1958	21,000	32,000,000
1960	23,900	31,000,000
1963	30,000	55,000,000
1965	33,900	74,000,000
1968	49,900	131,000,000
1969	56,300	179,000,000
1970	65,300	206,000,000
1971	72,100	233,000,000
1972	84,200	286,000,000
1973	94,300	320,000,000
1974	114,400	563,000,000
1975	144,100	633,900,000

(*Reprinted by permission of the National Fire Protection Association.)

The question must be asked, Do these figures reflect accurately the seriousness of our national arson problem? First, consider the fact that the table contains information only on building fires; not included are fires involving aircraft, ships, boats, motor vehicles, and forests.

Second, the number of fires classified under unknown causes in the NFPA report of 1975 increased dramatically from 52,500 in 1962 to 137,300 in

1975. Certainly many of these would also be classified as suspicious or incendiary if more were known of them.

Third, the figures do not reflect actual reports of incendiary/suspicious fires from involved agencies nationwide; the NFPA emphasizes that the figures are "estimated." Let us examine the NFPA's method of compiling data.

> The data used in compiling this summary of fires and fire losses were obtained from an annual survey of 2,000 fire departments in the United States. The departments that responded protect populations ranging from 500 to nearly 8,000,000 and are located in all 50 states and the District of Columbia. Additional information was obtained from reports of state fire marshals and other fire departments. The information obtained from these sources was projected by recognized analytical techniques to develop the national summary. Allowances were made for unreported fires and losses. ("Fires and Fire Losses, 1975," *Fire Journal* (November 1976), p. 19.)

There is need for an accurate system of reporting by all agencies of all sizes throughout the country, which may be met by the National Fire Data Center to be established by the National Fire Protection and Control Administration.

Fourth, a problem must be resolved by the National Fire Data Center before any figures submitted from agencies nationwide will be accurate: When is an arson case determined to be an arson case? This determination varies from locality to locality. Some jurisdictions do not list a fire as incendiary until someone is convicted of the crime of arson. How are convictions on reduced charges such as malicious mischievous and malicious destruction of property to be reflected in arson figures, then? What about the juveniles who receive what is sometimes referred to as "unofficial discipline" or "official discipline" in arson cases? What about arsonists who are committed to mental hospitals, either public or private, for observation prior to sentencing and are not released for trial?

Other jurisdictions report a fire as incendiary when a person is charged with violation of arson or unlawful burning statutes. If this person is never tried or convicted, no arson has been proved. Some jurisdictions are much more likely than others to bring arson charges against individuals. A wide variance in interpretation of what constitutes reportable arson means that questionable and inconsistent figures are all that is currently available.

Some localities rely upon the report of the investigating officer to determine whether a fire should be reported as incendiary. But, since some investigators regard any case which they do not solve and on which they do not get a conviction as a reflection on their investigative ability, there is a temptation to list the probable cause of any unsolved case as undetermined or unknown, although the unsuccessful investigator may know it to be incendiary. The probability of accurate figures under such a system is minimal.

In some organizations the ultimate decision on the reported cause of any fire under investigation is made by the supervisor of the agency. Occasionally, even though the investigator's report may conclude that the cause of the fire was other than incendiary, the chief of the agency may list the fire as incendiary, or at least suspicious, basing this conclusion on motive, opportunity, and other circumstances which are indicators of an arson case.

This last procedure perhaps produces the most accurate results, but again human nature makes for considerable variation. Some supervisors consider it essential to compile figures and prepare reports which indicate a phenomenal annual increase in the number of suspicious fires and investigations. A larger budget, an increase in manpower, more sophisticated equipment, and a more prestigious position for the supervisor of the agency are the result if superiors can be convinced that there is an arsonist or a would-be arsonist behind every tree, stump, and bush.

A prime example of this kind of escalation is a case in fact in which a barge tied up at a loading dock was obviously set on fire. The fire spread to four other barges and the loading dock. The investigating officer was ordered by his supervisor to write six separate reports: one on each barge, and one on the loading dock. If the culprit is charged and convicted, the apprehension, arrest, and conviction record of this agency would show that six arson cases have been solved and that six convictions have been gotten.

In a situation where four, five or more people are charged with burning one building, the report may stress the number of individuals convicted rather than the single investigation report, and the agency is credited with solving as many cases as there are reported convictions. The final cumulative report is unlikely to show plainly that there have been more arrests than there were investigations.

A theory has been advanced that the growth in reported incendiary/suspicious fires results from improved detection methods and an increased awareness of arson as a potential cause of fires. Undoubtedly, there have been improvements in both areas, but this fact cannot account in full for the rapid increase in reported arsons. Several jurisdictions report a substantial rise in this type of fire in spite of the fact that investigative personnel and record-keeping procedures have not changed.

In spite of the questionable accuracy of the figures pertaining to incendiary/suspicious fires in the United States annually, there is absolutely no disputing the fact that the number of such fires and the resulting loss have increased at a phenomenal rate, particularly in the last ten years. Let us now go beyond the facts and figures and examine the outward and underlying causes of this dramatic increase.

The Causes of Increased Arson

Increase in Crime Generally

No effort will be made in this text to analyze the factors contributing to the spiraling crime rate in this country. Criminologists have been attempting to determine where the fault lies: in the home, in the schools, with the courts, with law enforcement. That the answer has not been found is attested to by the fact that the billions spent to assist law enforcement stem the tide of crime have resulted in dismal failure. The FBI Uniform Crime Report for 1973 indicates that major crime rose noticeably again that year, reflecting a continuing increase during each of the prior seventeen years, with the exception of 1972.

Can the increase in crime generally account for the increase in arson? Apparently not, according to a report by the Stanford Research Institute prepared for the U.S. Justice Department's National Institute of Law Enforcement and Criminal Justice. This report, prepared by Kendall D. Moll, states that arson is growing at a faster rate than other types of fires and even faster than most other crimes. Despite a general slackening of violent incidents nationally, arson is occurring at a rate ten times as high as in 1950 and is spreading to the suburbs. The study recommended that arson investigative efforts be tripled, especially in small suburban and rural communities.

Moll said that while arson rates are rising faster than other types of fires, only one percent of arson cases result in conviction, according to best estimates. Statistics compiled by the FBI and the National Fire Protection Association show that arrests for arson declined six percent in 1972 while arson went up 17 percent.

Lack of Recognition on a National Level

The failure to appreciate the enormity of the arson problem and to react aggressively to this problem certainly plays a major part in the continued increase in arson and incendiary fires. The FBI Uniform Crime Report, for example, fails to stress the alarming rise in the rate of arson by not mentioning it, along with murder, rape, armed robbery, burglary, and car theft, among the major problems faced by law enforcement nationally.

Law enforcement over the years has made great strides in the fight against arson with federal and state grants and funding for training, education, and equipment, but only one state has a two-week course to train full-time police officers in arson investigation. In recent years much attention has been directed to crime in the streets, violence, and civil rights agitation, but the general public and government officials at the federal levels fail to recognize that arson should also be a major concern in the fight against crime.

A recent article by Robert E. May, Executive Secretary of the International Association of Arson Investigators, Incorporated, discusses the indifference to arson in comparison with other crimes.

> A bank robbery takes place in a small community. One man enters the bank, passes a note to a teller and demands money. Say the teller passes over $5,000 in cash and the man flees. Immediately an alarm is given and all local police go into action. County Sheriffs, State Police and FBI descend on the scene. The news media cover this crime with reporters for radio and television coverage. The robbery becomes headline front page news, top spot on the evening news for TV, and remains in the news for days to come. However, let a business establishment suffer a fire with a loss in excess of $100,000 and you will be lucky to read of the fire in the front section of the newspaper, and it is only news within the community itself for that one day. Yet this same fire could put the firm out of business, cause the loss of jobs for some fifty citizens, loss of income to these employees, loss of tax income to the community, and possibly the loss of the business firm even reopening for business in the same community.
>
> In my recent years of experience I have yet to hear of a bank going out of business as a result of a robbery. Business firms in general will continue to operate and function within a community following their being a victim of just about any crime other than arson.
>
> To sum up, far too little attention is being given to fire and its related problems. Little is done about accurate determination of the cause of fire, and even when a cause is determined to be suspicious or incendiary, there are too few men devoting any high degree of attention to the investigation that is needed. I believe it is quite correct to state that the arson fire or the suspicious fire presents a situation where everyone concerned hastily assumes a position in a circle and each "passes the buck" to another without the circle ever being broken, and in the vast majority of cases seldom do we see a case being solved. (Robert E. May, "Arson—A Most Neglected Crime," *Fire and Arson Investigator* 24 (April–June 1974): 7–8. Reprinted by permission.)

Until national agencies recognize arson as a major crime and a major cause of the loss of property, effective investigative procedures will not be implemented. It is encouraging to note that the news media seem to be becoming alert to the problem of arson and may begin taking a look at what action is being taken to combat this problem.

Lack of Recognition on a State Level

While a number of states do approach the investigation of suspicious fires realistically and aggressively, there are many which only now are becoming aware of and involved in the investigation of this major crime. Although responsibility for fire and arson investigation rests with the fire service, the fact remains that the crime of arson is listed in the penal code of every state and classified as a major crime. Therefore, law enforcement agencies have a continuing legal duty to investigate arson cases—ideally in cooperation with the fire service—and to enforce laws on arson. Why, then, do decision makers in many jurisdictions continue to neglect to classify arson in the same priority grouping as other major crimes such as murder, rape, aggravated assault, burglary, and auto theft?

In analyzing this problem further, it appears that nationwide the principal obstacle encountered by state agencies investigating incendiary fires is lack of manpower. This was pointed out quite graphically in a talk given by Dan Econ, past president of the International Association of Arson Investigators:

> In 1970 there were 8,000 arson fires in Ohio. During the first eight months of 1971, there were 8,000 arson cases, 9,000 fires classified as undetermined, and 1,500 fires designated as suspicious. How many arson investigators does Ohio have? About eight, excluding Cincinnati, Cleveland, and Columbus, which conduct their own investigations. Is it possible for eight people to investigate 8,000 arson fires in a year? Of course not. And the same is true in a number of other states such as Michigan, where the state arson investigators cover all arson cases except those in Detroit. (Dan Econ, "Fire Marshals on Duty," *Fire Journal* (September 1974), p. 81. Reprinted by permission.)

Another factor contributing to inadequate investigation by some state agencies is that those charged with the responsibility of investigating incendiary fires are not vested with police power. A police officer charged with the investigation of murder, rape, or robbery has the authority to arrest, issue warrants, and bear arms; an investigator charged with the responsibility of investigating the serious crime of arson has no such authority.

In several states, all personnel in the state fire marshal's office—investigators, inspectors, and those charged with the responsibility of enforcing the state building codes—are involved in the investigation of arson. The investigator probably does not feel comfortably competent in a situation involving building inspection or enforcement of state building codes. Likewise, the inspector and enforcer of codes do not have the experience, background, and education to perform competently as investigators. An arson investigator is generally considered to be a special breed whose activities require special skills, experience, and knowledge. The answer to this problem is quite simple: the arson investigator must be assigned the responsibility for investigating incendiary/suspicious fire losses and must not have any other duties which interfere with this responsibility.

Several states now assign the investigation of arson cases to a state police agency or a state bureau of investigation. Under certain circumstances this can be a workable procedure. Unfortunately, in many cases the number of people assigned the duty of investigating incendiary fires is small; and they are very often pulled off these assignments and involved in other activities, leading to neglect of their principal duty and resulting in an ineffective operation through no fault of the individuals themselves.

Political factors often influence the ability of state agencies to function in the arson investigative area. While the situation has recently improved tremendously, only a few years ago some states had as many as fifty or sixty fire marshals, a number of whom were appointed by a political party grateful for their efforts on behalf of the party in local, state, and national elections. These appointees had neither the qualifications to serve in the capacity of a fire marshal nor the desire or ambition to become qualified. As a matter of fact, some were fire marshals in name only, receiving compensation while continuing with their normal employment. This situation has been almost completely corrected; but in states whose investigations were conducted for many years by the mere handful of individuals who were actually working fire marshals, the negative results of this type of operation will not be erased overnight.

To a lesser degree, politics also affects the investigative efforts in those states where each change in administration results in a wholesale housecleaning in the fire marshal's office and the appointment of a new fire marshal is usually followed by appointment of new deputies to serve under him. Even if new personnel are qualified and competent, the fact that the marshal will only be in office for four years means that there is scarcely time to organize the agency effectively before the term of office reaches its conclusion. The effect of temporary appointments on personnel is certainly negative, and high morale and dedication to such an organization would be unusual. Nonetheless, such administrative turnover continues in a number of states, contributing to an unstable, unsatisfactory effort to control arson.

Switching the responsibility for arson investigation back and forth between agencies is a final factor contributing to the arson problem. It must be emphasized that this situation exists only in a very few states, but the effect of this on competent investigation is devastating.

In summary, the crime of arson and unlawful burning is in the penal code of every state. Each state *must* accept the responsibility of enforcing these laws by developing an organization which can carry out investigations as well as spearheading arson suppression. This can be accomplished only through the training and education of appropriate fire and police agencies.

Lack of Recognition on a Local Level

Almost without exception municipalities have some procedure for investigating arson and some organization to carry out this procedure. Unfortunately, in many cases they are simply not working. In jurisdictions where arson investigation is a joint effort of police and fire personnel organized into an arson squad, the police members of the squad are often called away from fire investigations to serve in other capacities, disrupting the entire investigative effort. Many police administrators are not willing to allow detectives to devote the time which is required to function effectively as members of the arson squad. This leads to dissension within the squad, which ultimately becomes an operational unit on paper only, with the fire personnel carrying out the major responsibility for fire and arson investigations. In other municipalities, members of the fire department or fire prevention bureau are assigned the responsibility for investigation. Since these people in many instances lack police power, they must at some point in the investigation turn over their findings to the police department for follow-up. Oftentimes this cannot be accomplished effectively, and the investigations reach no successful conclusion in the majority of cases. Fire department officials resent what they perceive as a lack of effort on the part of the police department. In those areas where the responsibility for arson investigation is vested totally in the police department, fire officials are often dissatisfied with the efforts of the police department to apprehend arsonists who may be running rampant and causing wholesale loss of property.

A recent newspaper interview with Joe Lamphear, Arson Investigator in the city of Santa Ana, California, elaborates on the problems connected with handling arson investigations:

> Police and Fire Departments are arguing over who should handle arson. Here, [in Santa Ana] we have pretty good cooperation with the police. In most cities the police believe they should handle it because it involves a crime and the fire department believes they should handle it because it involves a fire. (*Santa Ana Register*, 14 April 1974, p. 1.)

That something can be done to correct this situation is suggested in Dan Econ's address to the Fire Marshals' Association of North America:

> St. Louis, Missouri, is an example of what can be done when the arson problem is given the attention it deserves. Arson for profit had taken such a heavy toll of property in and around the city that a grand jury, two years ago, investigated and found that: (1) the city fire marshal's office was not being properly utilized; (2) there was a poor allocation of manpower; (3) the record of achievement of the arson squad was poor; (4) leadership was lacking; and (5) there was no cooperation between the police and fire departments. All of those factors worked in favor of the arsonists. Furthermore, the grand jury stated that the insurance industry showed on real concern about the arson problem. It relied on a general rate increase to cover the losses,

rather than setting up adequate machinery to stop the over-insuring of property and excessive claims, or resorting to litigation to oppose fraudulent claims. The grand jury also took the banks and financial institutions to task. In effect, it said that those who make loans to individuals with heavy loss records on high-risk properties are aiding and abetting the arson problem.

. . . There are arson bureaus in fire departments, police departments, and at the state level. Yet why is it that police and fire investigators are not communicating with each other? Why is there a lack of communication and cooperation between these agencies? As the St. Louis grand jury stated, such lack of communication is an advantage for the arsonists. When a fire department squad, which has the responsibility to determine whether or not a fire was of incendiary origin, finds evidence of arson, why isn't this information turned over to the police for investigation? And in the few cases where the fire department does present the police with evidence, why don't the police follow through with an investigation? In cases where the police department has primary responsibility to investigate, why don't they inform the fire department of their findings and conclusions. Whose fault is it that there is such a lack of communication? The fault lies at a higher level than the field investigators. If such problems are going to be solved, it must be done by top-level management—by a concerted effort on the part of police chiefs, fire chiefs, and state fire marshals. (Dan Econ, ''Fire Marshals on Duty,'' p. 82.)

Just as with state efforts, municipalities must accept their responsibility for arson investigation and develop procedures and organization to effectively investigate all suspicious fires, or the increase in incendiary fires will continue unabated. This cannot be a superficial effort on paper only, but must consist of down-to-earth plans which can bring about a decrease in incendiary fires through thorough, vigorous, coordinated investigations.

Failure in the Courtroom

The ultimate in frustration for an investigator is to spend days of extensive effort preparing a complete case for prosecution, only to have the case thrown out of court or token sentences handed down. The prosecution of an arson case is a most demanding task, and there are those prosecutors who are not willing to make the effort. Lawyers regard the defense of an arsonist as a far easier job, but experience has proved that the attorney who knows the legal requirements involved in successfully prosecuting the crime of arson can secure convictions.

Another cause of failure to convict in the courtroom is the lay witnesses.

Even law enforcement officers dread testifying and often tremble at the prospect, in spite of years of training and long experience. Consider, then, the apprehension which grips the average lay witness as his day in court approaches. Yet what attempts are made to assist the witness to prepare for this ordeal? Almost without exception, the only instructions are "Be at the courtroom at 9:00 A.M." Should we be surprised when this person, completely uninformed on courtroom procedure and demeanor and the responsibilities of a witness, makes a poor witness? We should rather be surprised that the witness shows up at all.

This brings us to another point: What can be done about the great number of prosecution witnesses who refuse to appear or simply do not show on the trial date? How great is the problem of the reluctant witness? In a recent speech to the New York State District Attorneys' Association, Donald E. Santarelli, the Law Enforcement Assistance Administration Administrator, referred to a study showing that 42 percent of the criminal cases in Washington, D.C., in 1973 failed to reach trial because prosecution witnesses refused to cooperate.

> They were people who at least initially were willing to make themselves known to the police as witnesses. And we know from surveys going back to the President's Crime Commission report of 1967 that a large percentage of victim-witnesses are unwilling even to report crimes.
>
> Though the project has not yet been completed, it already demonstrates incisively what heretofore has only been suspected.
>
> What it says, in part, is that witness cooperation is a crucial aspect of the successful prosecution of criminal charges—a crucial aspect of crime reduction. . . .
>
> District attorneys and others in state and local criminal justice agencies can ignore these findings—but only at substantial risk to their communities.
>
> . . . Thirty-seven percent [of witnesses] wanted better protection for themselves; 38 percent wanted fewer postponements by the prosecutor; 44 percent wanted speedier trials; 33 percent wanted tougher punishment for criminals; and 49 percent wanted more pay for witnesses.
>
> Think of it! Thirty-seven percent of those witnesses even willing to come forward were so afraid of what might happen to them that they felt they needed protection.
>
> Analysts are still looking at the data from that survey. But they predict they will find that perhaps as many as one-third of non-cooperating witnesses fail to appear in court because they are afraid of retaliation.

There is a strong message here for all of us. It is that we must foster in witnesses a confidence that they will be safe before we can fully succeed in making the streets safe for all of our citizens.

Something has to be done about that—and now.

And 38 percent of the witnesses thought that prosecution postponements should be reduced. I think all of us interested in the welfare of the nation's state and local criminal courts must take that fact to heart.

I am not suggesting that a case should never be postponed. As a lawyer I know the tendency of courts to grant postponements, and I deplore it. What I am suggesting is that if there is going to be a delay, witnesses should not be brought into court that day and then told the case will be tried sometime later.

If a court system is properly organized it will have a witness coordinator in the courthouse working with the court, the district attorney, and the defense who will be responsible for getting the right people to the right places at the right time. (Donald E. Santarelli, "Citizens Won't Testify," *Fire and Arson Investigator* 24 (April–June 1974): 15–17. Reprinted by permission.)

Judges deserve some criticism too. We hear much concerning the impact of landmark decisions such as *Miranda* and *Escobedo*, but it is not these decisions alone which have affected law enforcement efforts so significantly. Many rulings of the Supreme Court under the leadership of Justice Earl Warren seemed to law enforcement people to favor the criminal without regard to the safety of the public. These rulings in numerous cases reversed decisions handed down by the lower courts and freed convicted felons to return to the streets. These reversals often were based on entirely new interpretations of the law which conflicted sharply with previous decisions. As more and more appeals to the Supreme Court resulted in rulings favorable to the criminal, lower courts grew increasingly cautious, fearing reversal of their decisions. Therefore, the impact of the highest court in the land was felt in the lowest courts in the land, causing judges to lean in the direction of the criminal. Every motion by counsel for the defendant has to be carefully considered so as to protect the rights of the accused.

On occasion a judge will render a decision in an arson case which is incomprehensible to fire investigators. Mr. Econ's address to the Fire Marshals' Association of North America cites two examples of irresponsible action by the courts.

One judge suspended the prison term of an arsonist who had been found guilty by jury and sentenced to three years imprisonment, plus a $2,000 fine, for burning to defraud an insurance company of

$300,000. The court said that the accused had no prior involvement with the law, and that his background was exemplary, and that no one was hurt in the fire. Another case involved an unusual decision by a family-court judge; he freed three youths charged with setting a fire that killed six persons on the condition that the youths "get out of town." (Dan Econ, "Fire Marshals on Duty," pp. 82–83.)

Arson in most jurisdictions is by statute a felony or high misdemeanor. In any case it is a heinous crime of the most serious nature, costing our citizens property loss in the millions annually and jeopardizing the lives of many. Courts must recognize these facts and deal with the arsonist realistically with a genuine concern for the average citizen whose financial well-being and safety are so influenced by the fire setter.

The Insurance Industry's Lack of Concern

The insurance companies have been blamed for many fraud fires on account of three insurance practices: (1) insuring bad risks; (2) overinsurance on property and contents; and (3) too prompt payoff on questionable fires. Any arson investigator can cite case after case in which one or more of these conditions existed. The stories are so similar it is almost as if all the storytellers had investigated the same case: "The insurance agent wrote $100,000 for old man _____ on that warehouse, which was nothing but a tumbledown ruin. The so-and-so has had seven fires in the last five years, and five of them were suspicious. On top of all that, they paid off before we were halfway through our investigation. The insurance people set aside a certain amount they are going to pay out on losses and they could care less about arson."

In answer to these charges the insurance industries say that there is no national or state information center which keeps fire statistics or records of known arsonists and that coverage may therefore be written on a bad risk without the agent's knowledge. Concerning overinsurance, the companies claim the amount of insurance placed on a building is usually determined by replacement value and not the current market price of the property. Furthermore, in some states insurance is assigned to companies by a controlling state agency. Under this setup the company cannot refuse coverage to bad risks or in high-risk districts, although it may set premiums higher in some areas than others. Industry officials maintain that the cost of investigating every person seeking insurance and inspecting every piece of property to be insured would be prohibitive. They claim also that salespersons are more careful now in their underwriting practices than a few years ago.

Insurance men maintain that they generally have little choice but to pay off on policies within a reasonably short time after the fire even when arson is suspected. The reason given is that the chance of getting a conviction in an arson case is remote, partly because of jury prejudice against the insurance industry. A major concern of insurance men is defending themselves against a defamation of character lawsuit if they even hint that there is a suspicion of arson.

There have been positive signs in recent months that the insurance industry is now deeply concerned over the arson problem. In Illinois, Michigan, and Massachusetts government–industry organizations have been formed to spearhead full-scale attacks on arson. The areas in which these groups are functioning are explained by Mr. Ralph A. Schafer, Jr., Director of Claims, State Farm Fire and Casualty Company, Bloomington, Illinois, in a talk to the International Association of Arson Investigators Annual Conference in Austin, Texas, in March 1974.

> During the past year, my Company has launched a nationwide effort in the fight against arson, and we are committed and dedicated to do, in the public interest, whatever we can to control and suppress the crime of arson and the attendant loss of life and property.
>
> It is our opinion that the insurance industry should be heavily involved with your organization in the effort to control and suppress arson. In the absence of insurance coverage, many arson fires would probably not occur. To borrow an old phrase, we would rather be part of the solution than a part of the problem.
>
> We believe that this effort must begin with establishing good communications between all interested groups, such as the fire fighters, arson investigators, police and law enforcement people, prosecutors, and the insurance industry.
>
> In Illinois, we have organized a state-wide committee whose purpose is to coordinate, communicate, and perpetuate the efforts of all of these organizations and individuals in the fight against arson.

In an arson seminar held at Illinois State University, Mr. Richard Aaberg, Vice President—Claims, State Farm Fire and Casualty Company, spoke as follows:

> [There was] a general feeling of apathy on the part of many insurance companies toward the problem of arson. It was recognized that each of these groups; the fire service, law enforcement, arson investigators, prosecutors, and the insurance companies, actually all had common goals in relation to this problem. They were all pursuing their goals with a high degree of expertise and energetic dedication, but on somewhat divergent courses. It appeared that all we needed to do was harness this great energy and knowledge.

The insurance industry is to be commended for assuming the role of leadership in combating the arson problem. However, we must all accept our responsibility and join the battle against this crime, putting an end to arson indifference on the part of national, state, and local officials, to petty jealousies among investigators and investigative agencies, to animosity between police and fire personnel, to political interference with enforcement agencies, to coddling the convicted arsonist in the courtroom, to incompetent investigators who blame others for their poor results, to public failure to comprehend the magnitude of the arson problem. If we do not dedicate ourselves wholly to accomplishing a coordinated, cooperative effort to curtail arson, we can anticipate the continuation of runaway increases in incendiary fires.

2 Motives

Motive may be defined as "some inner drive, impulse, intention, etc., that causes a person to do something or act in a certain way." In relation to crime, motive is the "why."

While establishing motive for an incendiary fire is not a necessary element of the crime and proof is not required by law, it is nevertheless an essential part of the investigative process. Development of a motive will often determine the direction in which an investigator will concentrate his efforts. An equally important reason for establishing motive is to provide the prosecuting attorney with this vital evidence so that he can effectively present the case to the judge or jury. Without the establishment of motive, the chances of a conviction, particularly in a circumstantial case, are remote.

Motives may be divided into six general classifications. In the following paragraphs we will discuss most of these major areas; the rest will be covered in other chapters, in particular, those motives associated with urban blight, which will be included in Chapter 10.

Defrauding an Insurance Company

In an insurance fraud case, the perpetrator of the fire knows that in the event of a fire insurance monies collected will equal or exceed the amount obtainable by disposing of the property in any other way, such as through sale, auction, or bankruptcy. The investigator, realizing this, must seek to determine the *immediate* idea, need, or emotion which may have caused the individual to commit the act of incendiarism. Let us examine some motives.

Fraud Fires Involving Dwellings

Quick Profit   Individuals may buy or rent a structure, move in a limited quantity of inexpensive furniture, obtain the maximum amount of insurance possible, and burn for immediate cash return. Because of the limited insurance involved, no inspection is likely to be made of the property by the agent prior to the fire or by the adjustor following the fire. Insurance payment may be based on the inflated claim submitted by the insured. Insurance frauds of this type have been repeated successfully by the same individuals moving about within a state or across state boundaries.

Need for Ready Cash   The property owner may be motivated to burn his home for profit because of a critical cash need in his business, the loss of a job, reduction in work time, or illness in the family.

House No Longer Wanted   The migration from farms to the city resulted in many surplus rural houses. Efficient farms nowadays are large, mechanized operations; therefore, small farms are decreasing in number, and the need for the tenant house or small farm dwelling is being eliminated. The recent trend of migration to the suburbs has also made many urban dwellings unmarketable, either for sale or rent.

Settlement of an Estate   Residential property may be left to a group of heirs, none of whom want to occupy the property. If a fire occurred, insurance monies paid could easily be distributed among the parties involved.

Domestic Dispute   Problems connected with property settlement as a result of a separation or divorce can often be solved without complication by dividing the cash collected on fire insurance policies.

House Damaged or in Generally Poor Condition   Damage due to massive attacks by termites, high water, or other acts of nature may not be covered by insurance, but the building in question is probably insured against loss by fire.

New House of Inferior Construction   The wrath of a new homeowner who becomes aware of the shoddy construction of his "dream house" may cause the irate party to "sell it to the insurance company," particularly if the builder provides no satisfaction.

Excessive Operational and Maintenance Costs   With the drastic increase in the costs of many services, including repairs to plumbing, painting, replacing roofing and guttering, many families have found it impossible to continue ownership of their home. A major contributing factor is the increase in the cost of utilities, particularly those related to providing heat. Whether heating is done by electricity, oil, or gas, homeowners now find this financial burden increasingly unbearable. In some instances, costs of utilities may exceed the monthly house payment, a condition very few families can handle financially.

Financial Overextension   Many purchasers of homes do not realize the full extent of their commitment at the time of purchase. Anticipated promotions and salary increases may not have been forthcoming; increases in income may not cover the acceleration in the cost of living; sharp increases in property taxes and insurance premiums may add to the amount of monthly payments. In short, homeowners may realize that they have bitten off more than they can chew and that it is financially impossible to continue to own, operate, and maintain their homes.

Decline in Property Value   Changes in zoning regulations may allow industries to move into a residential community. In anticipation of decline in value of all residential properties in the affected area, homeowners may decide to dispose of their property to the insurance company. Migration into the community by groups considered undesirable may also prompt homeowners to burn their property to (1) escape from the neighborhood or (2) get a fair return before property values fall.

Miscellaneous Causes   Unusual motives may prompt individuals to dispose of their property by fire. For example, there is a case on record of a property owner evicting a tenant who was infected with syphilis and then burning the property to make sure the premises were uncontaminated.

Liquidation of an Obviously Failing Business

A variety of reasons for failure of a business may prompt its owner to commit arson for the sake of insurance monies.

Uncollectable Accounts Receivable   As the volume of a business decreases and the profits decline, the owner, in an effort to keep his enterprise going, may increase credit limits and terms of payment or extend credit to individuals and firms which are poor risks. This may salvage the business temporarily, but eventually many of these accounts become first delinquent and then uncollectable.

Generally Poor Economic Conditions   During periods of recession, some businessmen, fearing a depression, may decide the time is appropriate for a fire, especially if economic conditions decline to the point where the business may no longer operate at a profit.

Competition   A business which has operated profitably for years may suddenly become a liability because of a competitor whose new and modern plant, more attractive merchandising, greater variety of goods and services, and lower prices because of greater volume put the older establishment at a disadvantage. Many downtown businesses have been wiped out by the competition from suburban shopping centers, whose convenience, parking, and year-round protection from the weather are attractions they cannot match.

Obsolete Merchandise   In placing orders, the merchant of today must accurately anticipate the public taste and project what will sell and to what extent. In the clothing trade, for example, an incorrect guess on what will appeal to the public can result in an accumulation of merchandise which is almost immediately obsolete because of constantly changing styles.

Excessive Inventory   A manufacturer may convince a merchant that a certain item will sell rapidly and that a large order would be advisable. If it does not sell, the merchant is stuck with a large inventory of unwanted merchandise. This situation can also develop when a supposedly "hot" item hits the market. The public clamors for the product, and the merchant begs the manufacturer for all he can deliver. Unfortunately, by the time of delivery, weeks or even months later, the demand may no longer exist.

Seasonal Business at an End   In resort areas particularly, a businessman may realize that the season is over and potential customers are gone for six, seven, or eight months. However, creditors will not wait that long to be paid.

New Business Venture Unsuccessful   An individual, perhaps inexperienced, may open a new restaurant, paint store, tire distributorship, or other business. Initial expenses of stocking, advertising, and promoting the venture far exceed estimates, and the business does not succeed. If there is no purchaser for the failing business, arson for insurance monies may seem the only way out.

Failure to Receive Expected Orders   Manufacturers in a small industry may "hold on" in anticipation of a large order from some department or chain store. When this order does not materialize, the business may be faced with failure.

Obsolete Machinery   The manufacturer who must replace machinery often may not have the capital to accomplish this. The situation can develop without warning and catch the businessman completely unprepared. For example, many tire recapping plants were hard hit several years ago when tire widths and rim sizes were changed.

Damaged Machinery   Plants can be burdened with excessive and unexpected costs of machinery repairs, sometimes because of improper maintenance or acts of sabotage during labor disputes.

Absence of Material for Manufacturing Process   During the oil embargo of 1973, industries dependent on petroleum derivatives to manufacture their products were forced to close. Many reopened when the raw materials again became available; some did not.

Inability to Fulfill Contracts   On occasion a manufacturing firm may guarantee delivery of an order by a certain date and agree that if delivery is not made on time, it will pay a monetary penalty for each day past the deadline. Also, there may be a provision cancelling the contract if timely delivery is not made. As the deadline approaches, the manufacturer, realizing that fulfilling the contract is impossible, may further realize that he may obtain an extension or be released from the contract entirely if the plant is struck by fire.

Labor Problems   Two kinds of labor problems may tempt the businessperson to arson. First, a lengthy strike may cripple production and bankrupt a business. Second, the manufacturer may realize that if he pays the wages demanded, he will not be able to operate at a profit.

Liquidation of a Business for Some Specific Purpose

Let us now examine a second category of motives for business fires.

Dissolution of a Partnership   Either or both partners in a business may want to terminate the association.

Settlement of an Estate   A business left to heirs who cannot agree on an equitable division or who are not interested in continuing the operation may be set on fire, for insurance monies can be distributed easily.

Disposal of Vacant, Unrentable, Unmarketable Property   Ownership of certain types of property, such as large warehouses and old buildings, is often undesirable. Shopping complexes in the suburbs have caused many in-town buildings to become vacant and completely useless, with no market value. This condition will continue as newer and finer shopping centers make old shopping centers obsolete and useless.

Relocation of Business   (1) Present quarters may be outgrown. Business growth, projected expansion, or desire for more modern quarters may make moving necessary. The insured may believe it is more expedient to burn and rebuild than to remodel. (2) The building may be condemned. Premises found to be in violation of health and/or fire regulations require extensive and expensive corrective actions. (3) The business may be declining because of location. The business decline of many establishments located in the downtown section of large metropolitan areas is a cause of concern not only to city leaders, but also to the business people affected. Although efforts are being made in some areas to restore, renovate, and salvage the "central city," many merchants see a move to suburban shopping centers as a requisite for survival. (4) There may be problems due to crime. Some merchants have found their present locations untendable because of shoplifting, breaking and entering, armed robbery, protection shakedowns, and damage resulting from civil disturbances.

Sale of Land without Building   A windfall comes to the businessman occasionally from an unexpected source, government. When property is being acquired for an expressway, a property owner in the right of way may be offered $50,000 for a plot of land with the building standing thereon, and $75,000 for the same plot with the land cleared. A bonanza is realized when the structure burns, thus providing insurance monies, clearing the land, and earning the extra $25,000.

Desire to Terminate a Lease   A lessor who realizes that loss of a present tenant would mean difficulty re-leasing the property may refuse the request of the tenant to terminate a long-term lease. A complete and total fire will normally free the tenant from such a lease unless the property owner rebuilds, which is unusual.

Achieving a Personal Goal, Aiding a Cause, or Protesting

The motives which fall under this classification are so many and varied that it is possible only to cite some typical examples. Since some motives are self-explanatory, a brief comment is sufficient.

Personal Goals, Financial

Insurance Adjustor   An insurance adjustor may commit arson to secure a contract to adjust the loss.

Insurance Agent   A series of losses in a community causes people to become more fire conscious, resulting in increased amounts of coverage and new policies. If the agent has settled his claims promptly, he will benefit greatly from the fire awareness of the citizens.

Building Contractor   A building contractor may profit from arson by securing the contract to wreck or to rebuild.

Conspiracy   On rare occasions a carefully designed scheme involving an assured, an insurance agent, and an insurance adjustor is contrived. The agent writes insurance on the property and contents far in excess of actual value. After the fire, the adjustor finds the claims in line with the excessive coverage. All three parties split a bountiful insurance payment forwarded from the unsuspecting home office.

Competitors   Arson may be committed to stifle competition.

Watchmen and Security Personnel   There have been cases in which watchmen or security personnel commit arson to secure employment or to justify their positions.

Personal Goals, Nonfinancial

Police Personnel   Police may commit arson to obtain recognition.

Security Personnel   Security personnel may commit arson to obtain recognition.

Fire Fighters   Volunteer fire fighters may commit arson to collect the small amount of money paid during fire-fighting activities or to demonstrate the need for paid fire department personnel in the community.

Students   Students may commit arson to avoid attending school or to protest real or imagined mistreatment.

Defendant in Impending Trial   The accused may wish to frighten an adverse witness into altering testimony or failing to appear at the time of trial.

Aiding a Cause

Labor Disputes and Strikes   Strikers may wish to damage the plant involved or to intimidate strike breakers.

Racial Conflict   (1) Sometimes, when a black family moves into an all-white community, neighbors will set fire to the house, burn crosses in view of the occupants, and commit other acts of violence in an attempt to force the family out of the area and avoid integration. (2) Property may be set afire by members of the owner's race because his or her racial views are contrary to theirs. (3) Schools are occasionally set afire to promote integration. The fire setters in these situations reason that if an all-black school is destroyed school authorities will have to allow these students to attend a previously all-white or predominantly white school. (4) Schools and buses are sometimes burned in protest of integration and/or forced busing. The arsonists reason that if there is no school building, there can be no integration; if there are no buses, there can be no forced busing.

Protest   (1) Arson and fire bombing may be committed against corporations and institutions which are participating in some phase of an unpopular cause. (2) A festival crowd can become a violent mob in protest of police action which restricts their freedom. This can result in attacks on law enforcement officers and massive destruction of police cars, concession booths, and the like by fire. (3) Minority groups resort on occasion to arson to protest alleged mistreatment of a member of their group by police, a storekeeper, or other parties. Additionally, fire settings may occur on the anniversaries of the death of revered minority group leaders.

Revenge, Spite, or Anger

This broad area of motives for arson covers many possibilities. We will confine our coverage to the incidents most frequently encountered by investigators.

Domestic Quarrel   (1) A violent argument between a husband and wife or a man and a woman living together may result in one seeking immediate revenge by setting fire to the other's clothes, automobile, or other personal possessions. The cause of this problem is often another woman or another man. (2) Fires have been set by a woman to arouse sympathy or to prove to a man how much she needs his protection. This motive may be identified by an utterly fantastic version of the fire, replete with details of strange people in the house, being tied up, locked in the closet, and whatever else springs from a fertile imagination. (3) The same motives may induce a homosexual who fears the breaking up of a relationship to set a fire. (4) In domestic conflicts, it is frequently the man who becomes the fire setter. A court award of children, home, car, and alimony payments to the wife may trigger the ex-husband to seek revenge. This is particularly likely if the wife remarries happily or if she takes the husband to court for nonpayment of alimony.

Conflicts between Groups   (1) A family may resort to setting fires to another family's property during disputes over a variety of issues involving property lines, damages done by children or dogs, and other seemingly minor matters which have led to long-lasting and bitter feuds. (2) A community can become sharply divided over issues which vitally affect the future of its citizens, such as rezoning, location of industries or public institutions, support of public office seekers or officeholders, and school bonds. One faction may resort to arson in such disputes.

Personal Grudge   (1) When a family is ejected forcibly from a house or apartment for nonpayment of rent, the head of the household may react violently, feeling that if he cannot occupy the house or apartment, nobody will. (2) An employee whose anticipated promotions, increases in wages, and other recognition have not been forthcoming or who has been fired or otherwise disciplined may resort to fire as a means of revenge against the employer. (3) Holocausts have been created by individuals setting fires in bars and taverns where they feel they have been ill treated. Sometimes a person who has been refused service and physically ejected from the premises returns, throws a container of flammable liquid into a crowded room, and prevents escape by blocking exits with chains and bars on doors. One such incident recently resulted in 26 deaths in a crowded tavern.

Arson to Conceal or Commit Another Crime

Obliterating Evidence   The arsonist may wish to (1) cover up the fact that a stock shortage exists; (2) destroy records which might reveal embezzlement, forgery, or fake records or reports; (3) conceal a murder, burglary, or larceny.

Diverting Attention   A fire may divert law enforcement officers and watchmen, allowing looting and burglary at another location in the community.

Escaping from Jail or Some Other Institution   Arson to allow escape is another form of arson for diversion.

Vandalism or Malicious Destruction

Fires which are set for no apparent motive are constantly increasing. These wanton acts are committed by individuals or groups with no stronger motivation than destruction for destruction's sake, like defiling and destroying paintings, statues, monuments, and other works of art. Public buildings are often the targets for such actions.

No doubt one cause for this is the breakdown of accepted and shared standards of behavior on the part of many people. With respect for our nation's leaders eroded by their conduct in office, it is small wonder that many segments of our society use this as an excuse for their own misconduct.

Arson by the Mentally Afflicted

When a community suffers a series of fires, a great hue and cry inevitably arises from the news media and the public: "We've got a pyromaniac on the loose in our city." "This firebug is going to burn our whole town to the ground." "If this pyro isn't caught pretty soon, there isn't going to be a barn left in the county." There is no doubt in anybody's mind that there is a maniac on the loose.

Actually, this may be the fact of the matter, but many times it is not. The investigator must not be caught up in the hysteria and set his sights entirely on apprehending a pyromaniac. The person or persons setting fires in a series may have a motive for these acts which has absolutely nothing to do with any mental disorder. The motives may fall into several categories, such as spite, revenge, or to attain some other personal goal.

A medium-sized city recently was stricken by a series of incendiary fires, with buildings of all kinds set on fire. Terrified citizens demanded apprehension of this firebug on the loose. Information from an informant/accomplice led to the apprehension, arrest, and conviction of a young man in his twenties. His motive for the fires? His father was a fire department officer who had served his community well for ten or twelve years. When the fire chief retired, this man believed his father should have been appointed chief. Instead, another fire department officer in his early 60s was promoted. This young man reasoned that if the new chief had to respond to many fires his health would fail, and he would elect to retire, thus opening up the chief's job to his father. There was no evidence of mental or emotional disorder of any kind. The motive was definite and distinct—to accomplish a goal, the appointment of his father as head of the fire department.

Another series of fires involved the burning of fourteen late model cars in a sixteen-month period. The owners of these vehicles had no motive for burning the cars. In fact, one fire was set on the parking lot at an auto dealership and another was torched on the showroom floor. From all indications, the authorities were dealing with a firebug with a penchant for burning cars.

A young man interviewed previously was picked up again and questioned. After a lengthy interrogation, he confessed to setting the fires. His motive? Being on the effeminate side, he was ridiculed by his peers and had problems competing with his colleagues for the affections of the opposite sex. His pride and joy was his late model automobile, which helped him endure the ridicule and compete with his rivals for female companionship. He burned newer model cars of his tormentors and rivals so he could have "the newest car on the block." The cars burned in the dealership had been casually examined by two friends shopping for a new car.

To summarize, the investigator must avoid jumping to the conclusion that every series of fires is caused by a firebug. The fire setter may have any of the common motives to commit arson.

Productive research on the firebug by psychiatrists and psychologists has so far been unimpressive, yielding only relatively meager results. Admittedly, pathological fire setting is an extremely complex problem; yet it is difficult to understand why psychiatrists and psychologists disagree in so many areas related to these fire setters. Some researchers maintain that all pyromaniacs are enuretic. One reknowned psychologist categorically stated at a recent conference of investigators that all fire setters were mentally ill or emotionally disturbed at the time they set a fire. Investigators in attendance challenged this belief, citing fires set to collect insurance as one obvious exception. The "expert" refused to be persuaded and repeated his statement several times during the session. If those with expertise obtained through education and experience have such widely varied opinions, can the investigator successfully cope with situations involving pathological fire setters?

Another area of concern is the fact that assistance from the psychiatrist and psychologist comes after the fact. When a fire setter is apprehended, perhaps after many fires and months of investigation, the psychiatrist and psychologist conduct extensive research on the individual, revealing perhaps that the subject was enuretic, overly protected by his mother, antisocial, inclined to suicide, resistant to discipline, and given to feelings of extreme hostility following any act of rejection by those upon whom he was dependent. Mother/father conflicts often surface during the course of the study, and male fire setters often have a history of unsatisfactory sex relations with their wives or women in general.

The results of a case study of this individual may be quite fascinating, but does the investigator really benefit from such studies? Seldom if ever is the person conducting such a study willing to discuss the individual or the case with investigators, who might profit from such a discussion by being better able to identify some trademarks of the type of individual being sought in a similar series of fires.

The psychiatrist and psychologist could be of material assistance to an investigative team coping with a series of fires. The trained, experienced investigator develops skill in recognizing the insurance fraud fire. He knows some characteristics of the juvenile fire setter and can come reasonably close to pinpointing the age group involved. The female fire setter may also be recognized by certain key factors, particularly the items which are burned. Identification of the pathological fire setter, however, requires expertise attained only through extensive and specialized education which the majority of investigators lack. Investigators are inclined to feel that a psychiatrist or psychologist presented with detailed facts related to a series of fires should be able to provide some indication of the type of person setting the fires. Certainly such assistance would be far more beneficial to the investigator than a study of the fire setter after he is apprehended, particularly if the results of such a study are not shared with the investigator.

Perhaps the most practical, down-to-earth approach to the problem of pathological fire setting has been made by William D. Rossiter, former Fire Marshal for the State of Wisconsin and a nationally recognized arson investigation expert. Mr. Rossiter speaks as a law enforcement officer rather than a psychiatrist, a psychologist, or a social worker. He divides the pathological fire setters into four groups: (1) the mental defective, (2) the psychotic or insane, (3) the psychoneurotic or neurotic, and (4) the psychopathic personality or sociopath. Admittedly overlapping exists between these groups, and individual fire setters may possess characteristics of more than one group.

The Mental Defective

The severely feebleminded do not present a major problem to the investigator, as they are seldom involved in fire setting. The lowest classification of mentally defective persons can be trained only to a limited extent, for their mental development ranges from that of an infant to that of a two-year-old child. These individuals are not capable of deliberately setting a fire.

The mentally defective whose mental development ranges from that of a two-year-old to that of a seven-year-old are capable of setting fires for the same reasons as children within this age range. For example, an individual with a mental age of six or seven might set fires to get even with his or her parents, just as a six- or seven-year-old child would.

The third classification of mental defectives, whose mental age is eight to twelve years, may be a more serious fire-setting problem. Without exploring further the difference between high feebleminded, low and dull normal, and other subclassifications, we must recognize a problem encountered with this entire group. An individual whose mental age is eight may have thirty or forty years of experience, depending on chronological age. During these years of experience he has learned many things the eight-year-old youngster would not learn. If such people have often been in trouble with the law, they have picked up "on the street" a degree of cunning to deal with law enforcement officers. They know their rights, know the stock answers, and, most important, know that the less they say the better.

While it must be recognized that there are many exceptions, generally speaking, mental defectives will act in the same manner as normal children of the same mental age.

The Psychotic or Insane

In our discussion, psychosis and insanity will be considered to mean the same thing, though actually, psychosis is a medical term and insanity a legal term. Coverage of insanity will be confined to those manifestations which most frequently result in fire setting.

There are four types of schizophrenia: simple, hebephrenic, catatonic, and paranoid. The hebephrenic and catatonic are not fire setters, but the other two may often be. The simple schizophrenic is the ne'er-do-well who feels his life has been wasted and blames the world in general for his situation. Included in this group are many professional bums, lazy, shiftless, drifting from job to job. These people are most difficult to apprehend, as they are constantly on the move. Individuals who fit into this group have set fires all over the country for years before being caught.

The most dangerous of all the psychotics is the paranoid schizophrenic, who is deluded and may suffer from hallucinations. The most dangerous delusions are those of persecution, for these people may feel compelled to strike back at their "persecutors." Hallucinations, involving both auditory and visual senses, result in these people hearing voices and on occasion seeing nonexistent things.

Rossiter tells us that the paranoid schizophrenic may go through three stages of the disease or may remain in the first or second stage. The first is a retreat stage during which the schizophrenic tries to avoid and escape from a nonexistent enemy. The second is a defensive stage, during which the schizophrenic seeks help in combatting his imaginary enemies and may attempt to involve law enforcement officers as well as other high officials in his problems. In the attack stage, the schizophrenic becomes a real danger: nobody will listen to him or help him, so he will take care of his enemies himself. Attacks on political figures are often committed by paranoid schizophrenics, who will also burn a building to get rid of his enemies without the slightest degree of remorse or concern for the lives of others.

Another form of insanity, manic depression, is most common among women. During the manic phase, this person is on a terrific high, belligerent and likely to set fires; otherwise, she is in the depths of depression during which she may kill herself and others, even her own children.

Another type of insanity is paranoia, or paranoid psychosis, which is similar to paranoid schizophrenia with one important difference: in schizophrenia the delusions are changeable, while in paranoia they are fixed. The paranoiac's delusions develop around one fixed idea, and as long as nothing interferes with the delusions there are no problems. An example is the so-called mad bomber of New York, a paranoiac whose fixed delusion that the utility company for which he once worked was plotting against him prompted his bombings for the sake of revenge when he could get satisfaction in no other way. Such people are particularly dangerous for two reasons: first, they are often successful people who appear to function normally in every way; second, they are capable of careful and ruthless planning.

The Psychoneurotic or Neurotic

There are numerous fire setters within this grouping, including the pyromaniac, who is a rare bird. Some experts contend that the pyromaniac is both neurotic and psychotic; others make a clear distinction, feeling that a subject may be either neurotic or psychotic, but not both. Pyromania may be defined as an uncontrollable compulsion to set things on fire. The pyromaniac *must* set a fire; nothing else will do. He sets fires when the urge arises, regardless of where he may be.

The Psychopathic Personality or Sociopath

This group includes the sex psychopath, who is the most dangerous type of chronic or compulsive fire setter, as the sex drive is the most powerful drive in our behavior pattern. The sex psychopath's need to set a fire is closely allied with sexual gratification, which may be accomplished by masturbating while watching the fire, although in some cases ejaculation is attained without any stimulus other than viewing the fire. Since the setting of fires is an integral part of such a person's sex life and sex is an important facet of the total motivation pattern, his whole existence may revolve around sexual gratification and the means by which this satisfaction is attained. The effect that fire setting has on those around him does not concern the pyromaniac at all, at least not until he has an orgasm. His behavior from this point on will vary from helping the fireman and rescuing victims to simply walking away from the fire scene.

Oftentimes the activities which accompany a fire also stimulate the sex psycho. The excitement at the fire scene, the sirens, the flashing lights, the crowd, the fire itself may be enough to cause ejaculation without need for masturbation. This person may set dozens or even hundreds of fires in his lifetime. Even after being apprehended, his compulsion to set fires will continue.

One case on record involved a series of fires occurring shortly after midnight in the basement storage and laundry rooms of a large apartment complex. The fires were set in such a way that flaming combustion was minimal, but much smoke was created. The occupants fled from their apartments in various stages of night dress, wrapped in sheets, bathrobes, or whatever was available. Local authorities conducted stakeouts, attempted to establish patterns, patrolled the area extensively, and followed the normal investigative procedures without success. Particular attention was directed to the crowd; pictures were taken with the hope of picking out a familiar face. The fires increased in frequency and still no progress was made towards identifying or apprehending the perpetrator until at one fire an off-duty fire fighter was standing under a tree observing the scene when something overhead attracted his attention. There seated on a limb watching the entire scene, particularly the women in various stages of undress, was the arsonist masturbating to the stimulus of the scene below him.

Other Mental Afflictions

There are several other types of mental afflictions which account for a number of fires: (1) senility, (2) epilepsy, and (3) delirium tremens. The elderly person in a confused state will set fires for a variety of illogical reasons, but primarily to gain attention. The epileptic may set fires during a seizure as part of a pattern of violent behavior. Delirium tremens, the DT's, is a result of excessive use of alcohol which causes victims to "see" things that are not there. In one such case, an individual was pursued day and night by a figure with the body of a snake and the head of his mother-in-law. To rid himself of this creature, he would enter a vacant house, closely followed by his delusion, lead it into a closet, slam the door quickly and thus trap his tormentor. Then the building was set afire to destroy it. Interestingly, after a period of treatment some improvement was noted: the body of the figure changed from a snake to a horse, but the head of the mother-in-law steadfastly resisted removal.

Investigative Procedures

Having accomplished a broad coverage of the chronic or compulsive fire setter, let us now consider the fire setter's apprehension.

As a background to investigative procedures, it seems appropriate to trace the development of the chronic fire setter. Such a person does not ordinarily become a fire setter overnight, but rather follows a development process which may take months or years. Initially, satisfaction, whether sexual or otherwise, may come from the sirens and blinking lights of responding apparatus whether or not there is actually a fire. Therefore, at this stage a false alarm satisfies the fire setter's needs.

In the second stage, fire department activities have become old and just don't provide enough excitement. Some actual fire setting is done: sheds, garages, and similar structures.

The third stage involves setting bigger and more frequent fires. At this point there will be no turning back, even though there may be periods of several months during which the subject sets no fires. Larger buildings will be burned and the rate of fire setting will accelerate. The only way to stop it is by the apprehension of the fire setter.

It has been said that the chronic fire setter reacts immediately to an urge to set a fire, but there are certain traits, habits, and trademarks which he unconsciously develops. The investigator must capitalize on this fact to develop a pattern which will lead to apprehension of the fire setter.

First, the chronic fire setter often will "discover" and report the fire. "Discovering" his own fire apparently gives him some pleasure, which is increased when he is on the spot waiting when the fire department arrives. He may actually participate in the fire-fighting activities, entering the building, manning hose lines, and even giving instructions to the fire fighters. Any individual, regardless of occupation and reputation in the community, who discovers an unusual number of fires is a prime suspect. Anyone hanging around the fire station, asking questions and displaying an undue interest in the situation, should be considered a suspect.

Second, a fire setter will not leave the scene of the fire in its early stages, since the reason for setting the fire is to obtain some gratification or satisfaction from watching it. The sex psychopath may leave the scene after he has ejaculated. Every effort, therefore, must be expended by the investigator to observe the crowd of bystanders at a fire in order to find familiar faces. The cooperation of fire department personnel in this endeavor is necessary. Pictures of the crowd taken either by investigators, the news media, or others should be enlarged and studied in detail. The arsonist may act peculiar, appearing to enjoy the fire, laughing, joking, and in general conducting himself in a manner sharply contrasting with the rest of the crowd.

Third, in spite of the fact that the fire setter sets a fire on the spur of the moment and uses whatever material is at hand, a pattern of some sort develops.

Type of Building Involved   The arsonist may be attracted to certain kinds of buildings: warehouses, churches, schools, or vacant buildings.

How the Fire Is Set   The chronic fire setter normally uses whatever material is available, so the set may be rather crude. As a general rule, accelerants are not used, for the fires are not planned in advance. Once the fire setter discovers a method which produces good results and avoids detection, he may stick to this method.

Where the Fire Is Set   The arsonist also falls into an unconscious pattern of setting his fires in certain places either inside or outside of structures.

Time   Normally, fires set by pyromaniacs occur at night.

Dates and Days of Week   Some believe that psychopathic arsonists become more active during phases of the full moon. While this seems to smack of superstition, there are documented cases which substantiate this belief. Fires set on certain days of the week may reflect non-working days or payday. A lengthy stay in the local tavern on certain regular days of the week may put the subject in a state of drunkenness which stimulates his fire setting tendencies.

Questioning Techniques

Investigative efforts conducted in cooperation with involved agencies may lead to a suspect, who must then be questioned. The techniques used will vary with the age or mental age of the person. The mentally retarded suspect whose mental development is that of a twelve-year-old should be questioned like a twelve-year-old, keeping in mind the cunning which can be attained through the experience of his or her actual age.

As a general rule, the hard-nosed approach with the chronic fire setter is the least effective technique. The interrogator should project an attitude of sympathy and understanding concerning problems which may have caused the suspect to set a fire. The suspect may appear to the investigator to be stupid, but this may be a deliberate act to convince the interrogator that the person is not smart enough to plan a fire.

Questioning the chronic fire setter is perhaps the most difficult assignment faced by investigators, comparable only to a similar encounter with a ring-wise professional torch. While each case is different, there are certain characteristics such people have in common which the skilled interrogator must understand and utilize effectively in his line of questioning. Such understanding can be developed through a combination of experience and extensive study of the pathological fire setter.

The pressure on investigative agencies to apprehend the perpetrator in a series of fires is tremendous. A fraud fire case is usually a one-time shot: the building is destroyed, the owner collects, and that's it. The public is seldom interested in such cases because these fires do not affect them directly and are not a threat to their property or safety.

In a series of fires the investigators must utilize every means at their disposal to apprehend the arsonist. He must be caught because he will not quit. The public demands it, local government demands it, the news media demand it, professional pride demands it, and the threat of destruction to property and loss of life demands it.

3 Role of the Fire Department in Arson Suppression

Without the assistance and cooperation of the fire department, the arson investigator's chances of success are minimal. At the outset it is important that we identify the extent of the fire department's involvement in investigation at the fire scene.

In most jurisdictions suppression personnel in the fire department confine their efforts to two key actions, (1) observation and detection, and (2) determining the origin and establishing the cause of the fire. Our coverage in this chapter will be limited generally to (1) above, although some very basic actions at the scene directed towards (2) are included. More extensive discussion on determining the origin and establishing the cause is included in later chapters.

In some jurisdictions the fire chief assumes personal responsibility for conducting arson investigations. This situation may be the result of unavailability of arson investigative personnel on a local or state level. Even when such personnel are available, two factors can, in the judgment of the fire chief, dictate that he and other fire department personnel conduct the investigation. First, the chief may figure that the requirements placed on the fire department for substantiating the fact that arson exists are so stringent that if they have to do all this work they might as well complete the investigation without outside assistance. Second, the long delay in response by investigative agency personnel after receiving a request to enter the case makes it illogical and unreasonable to delay the investigation until they do arrive on the scene. In all probability both of these situations occur because of lack of adequate investigative personnel on a local or state level.

The fire chief who assumes full responsibility for conducting the investigation must react positively and aggressively to this challenge.

Importance of the Fire Fighter's Role

Many incendiary/suspicious fires are not investigated because no one detects the questionable nature of the fire and requests an investigation. It is, at least in part, a responsibility of the fire department to request such a probe in the event department personnel observe circumstances which indicate the fire may be incendiary.

Fire department personnel can gain information of value to the investigating officers concerning the fire. Observations on which fire fighters may be questioned are discussed in the remaining portion of this chapter.

Members of the fire department can contribute to establishing the incendiary origin of the fire by their testimony in the courtroom. Normally, the fire officer and fire fighter do not testify specifically that the fire was of incendiary origin. They relate their observations at the fire scene, and this evidence becomes an important facet of the prosecution's case.

Need for Continuous Training

It cannot be assumed that periodic sessions in arson detection will meet fire department needs. This type of training must be continuous because of turnover in personnel, particularly in volunteer departments, but also in paid departments.

We must further recognize that since the principal responsibility of the fire department at the scene is saving lives and property, arson detection may be overlooked. There must be continuous refresher training in this vital investigative activity or it will be forgotten.

Motivation for Fire Fighters to Cooperate

The possibility of appearing in court as a witness or otherwise becoming involved in the legal aspects of an arson case is not a pleasant prospect to the majority of fire fighters. Therefore, motivation must be provided for their participation in arson investigation activities. Perhaps the principal motivating factor is the fire fighter's own safety. It must be pointed out that the incendiarist, regardless of motive, has little concern for the safety of those responding to extinguish the fire. Incendiary fires often involve large quantities of an accelerant distributed throughout a building. While fire fighters are engaged in suppression in one area, such liquids may unexpectedly ignite with an explosive force, causing serious injury or possibly death.

Fire Department Involvement

At the Station

The time the fire was reported can become very significant as the investigator develops the sequence of events. How the fire was reported, whether by box alarm, phone, or other means, is also important. If the fire was reported by telephone and the conversation is recorded, the recording could prove valuable to the investigator and might lead to the identity of an individual turning in false alarms.

The identity of the person discovering and reporting the fire is important to the investigator. In many instances the discoverer and reporter are the same individual, who can furnish information concerning the fire in its early stages and help develop the fire story. Even more significant is the possibility that this individual may be the fire setter. Particularly in the event of a series of fires, any person who reports and discovers an unusual number of fires in a given period of time should be suspected as the incendiarist, regardless of the individual's position in the community. It is not reasonable to suppose that any one person would discover a number of fires in any specific period of time. The possibility that this person is responsible for setting the fire cannot be overemphasized.

En Route to the Fire

Fire department personnel should observe the general weather conditions. If the weather is cold, it would be unusual to find all the windows opened upon arriving at the fire scene. Conversely, if the temperature reading is high, it would be unusual to discover the furnace or other heating appliance in use.

Observation should be made also as to whether it was clear, cloudy, or stormy. The incendiarist may try to blame the fire on lightning, but if the sky is cloudless with no indication of a storm, lightning is a very unlikely cause of the fire.

Fire department personnel should note the direction and approximate velocity of the wind. The person who discovered the fire may inform the investigators that it was burning on the outside of the structure at the right front corner and that in a matter of minutes the entire building was fully involved. This would be an unusual circumstance if the wind was blowing from the point of origin away from the structure.

Natural conditions which delay arrival of the fire apparatus at the fire scene should be reported to the investigator, conditions such as heavy snow, ice on the highways, and possibly flooding. This might indicate, particularly in the case of a fraud fire, that the arsonist deliberately waited for such conditions before setting the fire so that the destruction of the building along with all evidence of incendiarism would be complete.

In proceeding to the fire scene, man-made barriers or obstructions delaying the arrival of the fire equipment should be observed. Any effort to hinder the fire trucks in their progress to the fire scene indicates a desire to assure a total loss. Such man-made barriers might include barricades, trees felled across the highway, cables stretched across the road or street, and whatever other obstacles might occur to the arsonist.

People are ordinarily attracted to the scene of a fire. Therefore, people leaving the fire scene either by car or on foot should be observed by the fire fighters as closely as possible under the circumstances. The investigator can expect little more than a general description of a car leaving the scene, such as the color, make, and model. Any description of the occupant or occupants would be helpful, but the difficulty of making this observation is understandable. The dress, appearance, and general description of individuals leaving the scene by foot should be noted. Observations concerning people leaving the scene either by foot or by car increase in importance in the event of a series of fires. It is often through such information furnished by fire department personnel that a suspect or suspects are developed.

Arrival at the Fire Scene

The *time of arrival at the scene* should be noted for several reasons. The fire department must defend itself against public criticism based on frequent allegations of a long delay between the time the fire was reported and the time of arrival at the scene. Additionally, the elapsed period between the time the fire was reported and the fire department's arrival at the scene is most important to the investigator. From the person discovering the fire, the investigator will obtain a description of the appearance of the fire in its early stages; from the fire fighters he will obtain a description of the fire as it appeared on their arrival. If the fire progressed to an unusual degree during this period, the presence of an accelerant to increase the rate of fire spread is probable.

The fire department personnel's *means of gaining entry* into the building is important to the investigator for several reasons. A building open and readily accessible to anyone prior to the fire somewhat complicates the investigation. If the building was securely locked and there were no indications of forcible entry prior to the fire, the owner or occupant or others who might have keys in their possession may be suspected. On the other hand, evidence of forced entry (Figure 3-1) prior to the arrival of the fire department indicates the involvement of persons other than those who have keys to the building. In any case, it is essential that the investigator establish the means of entry by the fire department so that he can consider the various possibilities.

On occasion the arsonist, particularly in fraud fires, will cover the windows and doors with blankets, screens, or other material, obstructing the view into a structure. This prevents observation of his activity prior to the fire and delays detection of the fire after it is set.

Perhaps the most important information that can be furnished to the investigator by fire department personnel is the *exact location of the fire*. This information is vital for the investigator faced with the task of determining origin and cause of a fire which has completely destroyed a large structure, for it allows concentration of fire scene examination efforts at a particular point or area of the structure. The importance of this information cannot be overemphasized.

FIGURE 3-1. Evidence of forcible entry is rarely this obvious.
(Courtesy Commonwealth of Virginia Arson Investigation Division)

Observations concerning the *color of smoke* are significant. We know, for instance, that petroleum-base products give off a heavy black smoke, particularly if combustion is incomplete. The presence of smoke of this description where no petroleum-base products would normally be found would interest the investigator. It should be pointed out that in fires where an accelerant was present, it may burn off in the early stages of the fire so that the color of the smoke will be normal when the fire department arrives.

The same principles apply to observations of *unusual flame color*, for we know that different materials burn with different flame colors. Of particular interest is the bright orange flame which accompanies the burning of an accelerant and other petroleum-base products. The existence of flame of this color without a logical explanation is a suspicious circumstance. Once again it must be pointed out that accelerants may burn off prior to the arrival of the fire department so that the color will be normal when they reach the scene.

The presence and detection of separate and unconnected fires in a structure is in many instances the principal means by which the incendiary origin of the fire is established. The observation of this condition by fire fighters and testimony to this effect in the courtroom are vital in the prosecution of arson cases.

The detection of "streamers" in a structure is another indication of an incendiary fire. Material used to cause the fire to spread rapidly from room to room and floor to floor in a structure may consist of paper, a flammable liquid, or other highly combustible material. The fire fighter may also observe other preparations to assist the spread of the fire: interior doors propped open, holes punched in the walls from room to room, plaster pulled down to expose the wood lathing.

The investigator is interested in the behavior of the fire—not only rapid increases in fire size and intensity, but also any burning contrary to normal fire behavior. An example would be fire moving against the wind after openings exist in a structure.

Fire fighters know that water will normally reduce the size and intensity of fire. When water is applied and burning increases rather than decreases, the presence of an accelerant is indicated. A fire that rekindles several times in a particular spot also indicates the presence of an accelerant.

The observations of fire department personnel concerning the presence or absence of furniture, clothing, and personal effects in a house are significant to the investigator, particularly in fraud fires. In a normal fire of accidental origin in a dwelling, we would expect to find a reasonable quantity of household effects. Their unexplained absence leads to the distinct possibility that preparations for an incendiary fire were made and that these items were removed from the dwelling prior to the setting of the fire. The absence of irreplaceable personal effects of sentimental value, such as family pictures, the family Bible, and other mementoes, is especially significant. An additional consideration would be the absence or presence of family pets at the time of the fire. Loss of life to any pet, such as a dog, cat, or bird, might indicate that the fire is accidental, for many people would think twice before starting a fire which might cost the life of a family pet. By the same token, the absence of such animals at the time of the fire when their presence would appear to be normal could be considered a suspicious circumstance.

The investigator will question fire department personnel concerning their observations of any large pieces of furniture, appliances, kitchen accessories, quantity of clothes, linens, etc., outside the dwelling. If there are only a few people at the fire scene when the fire department arrives and items such as those mentioned above have already been saved, it may be that they were removed before the fire was set.

In mercantile and manufacturing losses, fire fighters should note any absence of stock, fixtures, and items of machinery, which may indicate that preparations had been made by removing them prior to the fire. The investigator will question fire fighters concerning any tampering with fire doors and sprinkler systems. In structures where these items exist, if the fire doors have been propped open and the sprinkler system has been rendered inoperative, this would indicate an obvious desire for a complete and total burning.

During the Later Stages of the Fire

Fire department personnel should observe the manner and dress of occupants. People react in different ways to fires which involve their family and their property, but normally a person will show signs of being upset by such an event. If an occupant appears unusually calm at this time, there may be some grounds for suspicion. The dress of the occupant may also prove significant. If a family were reportedly roused out of bed by fire at three or four o'clock in the morning and were fortunate to escape with their lives, it would seem unusual for any member to be fully clothed, with socks and shoes on, in which might be considered normal dress for a person during daylight hours.

The presence at the fire scene of individuals who appear or act unusual is an item of interest to the investigator. One such person is the "eager beaver," who has no particular involvement with the fire department or any fire-fighting activity but seems to take a great deal of interest in what is going on. The eager beaver may become actively involved in the fire-fighting activities even though he lacks experience and make a real effort to prove his value to the members of the department. He may be waiting for the department when they reach the fire scene, very anxious to lead them to the exact location of the fire. Later this person may appear frequently at the fire station to discuss the fires taking place in the community. Any individual who seems to be reacting in an unusual manner while the fire is in progress should be closely observed by fire department members. In the event of a series of fires, the fire fighters should look for repeated appearances by the same individual. If fires are occurring at late hours of the night and the same individual or group continue to appear, this information should be conveyed to the investigator without delay.

After the Fire Is Extinguished

Unless there are provisions for immediate fire scene examination by other personnel, selected members of the fire department should examine the premises to determine origin and cause. This is not a complete and thorough examination, but an immediate effort to look for evidence of multiple fires, streamers, unusual odors, unusual and uneven burning, and other indications of an incendiary fire. The presence of accelerant containers should be noted at this time, particularly in an illogical location. Containers capable of containing an accelerant would not be unusual in a garage or storage room, but in the living room, dining room, or den area they would be suspicious.

The heating system should be examined, including the position of the draft controls. The fire box should be checked for indication of a recent fire when warm weather would not dictate the necessity for heat. The flue and exhaust pipes should be examined for defects which might have been deliberately created to ignite the structure. Oil and gas lines should be closely scrutinized for breaks, either accidentally or deliberately created. The incendiarist will initiate burning in an area which would not create suspicion, such as near any heating unit; therefore, this area must be examined carefully to eliminate suspicions of a "deliberately accidental" fire.

While no complete effort can be made at this time without interfering with any future investigation, routine examination of wiring should be made, particularly at the point of origin. The condition of the wiring and burn pattern in relation to the wiring might well reveal a fire of accidental origin. The fuse box should be checked for blown and oversized fuses, pennies behind the fuse, and fuses "jumped" by other methods. Generally speaking, if an overload has caused the fuse to blow, only the element will be burned in two. Where there has been a dead short or a short of severe intensity, the interior of the fuse will be severely discolored and the contact point may be pitted.

At this point further efforts should be made to note any absence of furniture, clothes, and personal effects in a dwelling fire loss. Outbuildings should be searched to locate any items removed prior to the fire. When legal problems arise during such a search, it can be explained that the purpose of the examination was to eliminate the possibility of hidden fires.

In the case of mercantile and industrial fires, further observation must be made to detect the absence of stock, fixtures, and machinery. The removal of stock in a mercantile fire is evidenced by empty or near-empty shelves, clothes racks, counter tops and counter interiors, and various types of display racks. The removal of fixtures is indicated by the illogical location of the remaining fixtures, as well as large, open floor spaces. In a manufacturing or industrial fire, removal of machinery is indicated by unexplained open spaces and possibly by markings on the floor which show that machinery was at one time located at this point.

Fire department personnel should look for the unusual, which requires some explanation. For example, in a dwelling fire loss, are there several "For Sale" or "For Rent" signs displayed on the premises? Is there a notice that the property will be auctioned off on a date several days after the fire? Are there inspection and condemnation notices on the building? Is the property in a rundown or dilapidated condition which makes it almost uninhabitable? If such a condition exists, we must keep in mind that insurance on all ten-room houses will be the same, regardless of condition, so the insurance carried on such property far exceeds the actual value of the property, thus providing the owner with a strong motive for arson.

In both dwelling and industrial fires, the location of vehicles at the time of the fire must be observed. At the dwelling fire, if there are indications that the owner's car or cars are normally parked close to the house, either in a driveway or carport, why then, at the time of the fire, would such vehicles be parked some distance from the house? In an industrial fire, why would delivery trucks or other vehicles be parked some distance from the loading doors or dock, perhaps as far removed from the involved structure as a fenced-in area would permit?

There are other factors which somehow indicate to the alert fire department officer that something is suspicious about the fire. When this nagging suspicion exists, the total circumstances of the fire must be considered. Does the fire have a reasonably acceptable cause? Is there a motive on the part of the owner? Was the conduct of the owner normal or unusual under the circumstances? Was he or she under the influence of alcohol? Do other members of the family or occupants seem upset by the fire? If not, could this indicate they were all involved in the burning of the property? If the total circumstances of the fire arouse the fire officer's suspicions, the time has come to call for outside assistance in whatever form it exists in the locality.

The owner and occupants should be informally interviewed by fire department personnel exhibiting a sympathetic approach to the owner with no indication that there is any suspicion as to the cause of the fire. Perhaps a good opening would be "Mr. or Mrs. _____ , this is a terrible thing. What happened here?" Then the interviewer may let family members or occupants talk without interruption. This is their first opportunity to either tell the truth or make up a story about how the fire occurred, a task they may not be prepared for. The interviewer should mentally note everything these people tell him.

The purpose of these interviews becomes more apparent as the investigation proceeds. A thorough investigator will question fire department personnel about any conversation with the owner at the time of the fire. At some later time the insurance adjustor will take a detailed written statement from the owner and possibly others. By this time the owner may have decided to change the story, either because it does not sound plausible or because he or she has forgotten what was told the fire fighter. When the investigator questions the owner/suspect further, discrepancies may appear between what was told the fire fighter, what was told the adjustor, and what version of the fire is being given the interrogator. Pointing out these discrepancies to the suspect is an invaluable weapon which may be the catalyst for securing a confession.

Every effort must be made to secure the scene as far as possible in the exact state that existed when the fire was extinguished. This requirement will be discussed elsewhere in the text, but its importance dictates repetition. When complete salvage and overhaul operations are conducted at a fire scene, the probability that the investigator will make any definitive determinations as to origin and cause are reduced to near zero. The fire department must therefore disturb the entire fire scene as little as possible. It has been said that an arsonist's best friend is the tidy fire fighter. We must not make the investigator's difficult fire scene examination an impossible task.

Occasionally evidence in a very obvious physical form will be discovered by the fire fighters, for example, glass, metal, or plastic containers in areas where such items would not normally be found. If at all possible, such evidence should be photographed exactly as it is found with whatever photographic equipment is available. When moving a container from its original location, care should be taken not to smear any fingerprints. This can be accomplished by holding the container by the edge of the top and bottom surfaces. Above all, don't pass the container around from one person to another to sniff the contents! Since most accelerants will dissipate rapidly, it is essential to pour any liquid residue into an airtight container, either a mason jar or metal can. This should be sealed and labeled on the exterior as to when, where, and by whom it was found. A portion of the liquid can be left in its original container if this container can be sealed or if a large quantity of liquid is present. Rags, papers, wood, soil, or any material suspected of containing an accelerant must also be placed in an airtight container. Such samples may require a larger container, for example a lard or flour tin, which must be sealed and labeled.

There are certain general instructions which the fire fighter must follow. First, if physical evidence of arson materials is detected, secure a generous portion so that laboratory technicians will have a sufficient quantity to make positive identification. Second, in handling physical evidence, the chain of custody must be established immediately. One person must assume responsibility for the evidence. Its value is negated if a container is thrown up on the fire truck, taken back to the station, and placed in the open apparatus bay. Any defense attorney can have such evidence ruled inadmissible with a minimum of effort because of failure to preserve the chain of custody.

Further action by fire department personnel at this point will depend upon the standing operating procedure in the jurisdiction involved. In some localities, if the fire department is satisfied with their determination of origin and cause, no further action is necessary; in others, the fire prevention bureau examines all fire scenes. Frequently, such examination is made only when no satisfactory origin or cause determination can be made by the fire department. If fire department personnel have a basis for believing a fire is incendiary/suspicious, request for investigation should be made to the appropriate agency without delay. A close working relationship between fire and police personnel is absolutely necessary to combat incendiary fires effectively. This applies equally to the volunteer departments in rural areas and the paid metropolitan departments.

4 Chemistry of Fire

In this chapter we will discuss the chemistry of fire on a fundamental level, providing concise, understandable definitions and practical explanations of terms commonly used in the fire service. The ability to recite a definition of some fire-related term word for word is absolutely valueless, however, if the definition is not understood. Also, this understanding must be accompanied by an ability to put this knowledge to practical use. Moreover, certain information important in fire fighting is not pertinent to fire investigation: for example, while the tetrahedron of fire may influence not only immediate but also long-range fire-fighting tactics, strategies, and practices, it is of little significance to the investigator.

Definitions

What Is Fire?

Can you imagine a situation where the outcome of an arson trial hinged on the ability of a key witness to satisfactorily answer the question, what is fire? One witness qualified as an expert, based on experience and training, had given excellent testimony for the prosecution. On cross-examination, the defense attorney extolled his investigative skills and lauded his outstanding testimony. After lulling his victim into a false sense of well-being, counsel asked this simple question: "What is fire?" The response—it is hot, is yellow or orange in color, and will burn you—was hardly expert testimony. After hopelessly entangling himself in wordy definitions which he could not explain because he did not understand certain terms, the witness was thoroughly confused and his testimony was discredited. As a result, the prosecution's case collapsed and a probable arsonist was released.

We can escape such a predicament by remembering and understanding a very simple definition: "Fire is rapid oxidation accompanied by heat and light."

What is Oxidation?

Oxidation may be defined as the chemical union of a substance with oxygen. Generally speaking, oxidation is classified either as slow or rapid. Examples of slow oxidation are the drying of paint, the rusting of iron, and the decaying of wood. Slow oxidation is not accompanied by noticeable heat or light; the great majority of substances do not react to or unite with oxygen in any noticeable manner. Rapid oxidation is accompanied by noticeable heat and light. Heat is produced at a rapid rate which results in combustion or burning; the heat serves to increase the rate of oxidation, thus speeding combustion.

What Is Combustion?

Combustion is the chemical union of a fuel with oxygen at a rapid rate, liberating light and heat energy. Combustion cannot take place until a substance has reached its ignition temperature.

What Is Ignition Temperature?

Ingition temperature of a substance, whether solid, liquid, or gaseous, is the minimum temperature required to initiate or cause self-sustaining combustion independently of the heating or heated element. The ignition temperature of a specific fuel is only approximate because it is affected by a number of conditions, such as the presence and nature of adjacent substances and the state of the substance itself. For example, the ignition temperature of shredded wood is much lower than that of a solid block of the same wood. The ignition temperature of steel wool is much lower than that of a solid block of steel. Thus the ignition temperature of wood, generally listed in the 400°F range, is obviously an approximation.

Determining what outside source of heat caused a substance to ignite may be difficult. It is important to keep in mind that moderate heat applied over a long period of time will more readily raise a substance to its ignition temperature than high heat applied briefly to a combustible. For example, a heating pipe which makes near contact with wood will eventually ignite the substance, whereas more intense heat from a blowtorch applied momentarily will not cause ignition.

Some Common Substances and Their Ignition Temperatures

Gasoline	700 to 800°F, with higher octane having a higher ignition temperature
Kerosene	450 to 490°F
Turpentine	464°F
Butane	864°F
Propane	871°F

What Is Flash Point?

Flash point is the lowest temperature at which a flammable liquid will give off vapor in sufficient quantities to form an ignitable mixture with the surrounding air. There is a line of distinction between the flash point and the fire point of a liquid. Flash point means that this ignitable mixture will flash but will not continue to burn; fire point, normally a few degrees higher than the flash point, will support continuous combustion. In theory, all combustible liquids and solids have a flash point, but the term is used almost entirely in reference to liquids. Knowledge of the flash point and fire point of common liquids is essential to effective investigation of fires where these liquids are present.

Some Common Liquids and Their Flash Points

Gasoline	−45°F
Kerosene	115°F
Ethyl Alcohol	55°F

What Is Meant by Explosive (Flammable) Range?

The difference between the upper and lower flammable limits, expressed in terms of percentage of vapor or gas in air by volume, is known as the explosive or flammable range. This means that if the quantity of a flammable vapor, expressed in terms of percentage by volume of gas in air, is below the lower flammable limits there will be no ignition of explosion. If the quantity of a flammable liquid is above the upper flammable limits, there will also be no ignition or explosion.

Let us take as an example gasoline, a liquid with which we are quite familiar. The flammable range of gasoline is 1.4% to 7.6%. This means that if we have a vapor composed of 1.4% gasoline and 98.6% air we have a flammable mixture. Any mixture in which gasoline vapor is below 1.4%

will not ignite because it is too lean. If the gasoline vapor content is above the 7.6% upper explosive limit, the vapor will not ignite because it is too rich.

The most rapid burning takes place in the center of the explosive range. For gasoline a mixture of 3½% gasoline vapor to 96½% air will produce maximum efficient burning. Often adjustments to the carburetor of an automobile are made to correct a situation in which the mixture of gasoline and air is either too lean or too rich.

Explosive Range of Some Common Vapors

Gasoline	1.4% to 7.6%
Kerosene	0.7% to 5 %
Acetylene	2.5% to 81 %
Natural Gas	6.5% to 17 %
Butane	1.8% to 8.4%
Propane	2.2% to 9.5%

What Is Meant by Vapor Density?

The weight of a vapor or gas compared with an equal volume of air is known as the vapor density of that vapor or gas. If air is the standard of 1, a figure less than 1 indicates a vapor lighter than air; a figure greater than 1 indicates a vapor heavier than air. Air movement must also be taken into consideration when examining a fire scene, but it is essential that the investigator understand vapor density and know the weight relationship between common vapors and air.

Vapor Density of Some Common Vapors (Air = 1)

Gasoline	3–4
Kerosene	1
Ethyl Alcohol	1.6
Natural Gas	0.8
Butane	2
Propane	1.6

The Fire Triangle

New knowledge of the tetrahedron of fire will materially affect fire fighting in the future, but an understanding of the basic fire triangle will suffice for the investigator in most instances. The fire triangle consists of oxygen, fuel, and heat, pictorially illustrated as follows:

Normally the elements of oxygen and fuel are always present; therefore, determining the source of heat is the principal problem facing the investigator. Taking into consideration some facts discussed earlier in this chapter, let us examine the elements of the fire triangle and how they may affect the task of the investigator. Fuels normally exist in one of three different physical states:

1. solid, such as wood, paper, cloth, rubber, etc.;

2. liquid, such as gasoline, kerosene, or alcohol;

3. gas, such as natural gas.

The physical condition of these fuels, particularly wood, affects their ignition temperature and rapidity of burning. Fibrous woods will ignite and burn much more rapidly than others; bulk wood's ignition temperature is much higher than when shavings and chips are present. When liquids are the fuel source, we must ascertain whether the temperature of such fuel would have allowed the liquids to give off flammable vapors. Flammable gases are easily ignited, and the principal problem faced by the investigator in dealing with them is their source, since they are normally confined and controlled.

Often insufficient attention is given to the second element of the triangle, oxygen or air. The quantity of oxygen in the burning area can have a fantastic effect on the rate of burning and the intensity of the fire, a fact often overlooked by the investigator. Oxygen makes up about 21% of the air around us. Any amount less than this will slow down burning; any amount more than this will accelerate it. When the oxygen content is below approximately 16% by volume, burning will cease. When fuel and heat exist in a tightly closed area little or no burning may take place because the oxygen content is reduced below 16%; when the fire is vented and oxygen can reach it, intense burning immediately results. This condition has caused injury to fire fighters who may have opened a door to such a charged area while standing in front of the door rather than to one side.

Another fact the investigator should be aware of is that life also will cease when atmospheric oxygen content reaches a level below 16%. This is particularly significant in investigating fatal fires where actual burning of the victim has been insignificant. Often it is not the heat which kills but a smoldering fire in a confined area which consumes the available oxygen, causing loss of consciousness and eventually death. This is typical of fires which occur as a result of careless disposal of smoking materials. The victim did not wake up when he or she felt the heat from the smoldering mattress or upholstery in an overstuffed chair because lack of oxygen caused loss of consciousness and then death, and the burning of the body occurred only after the victim was already dead.

Extensive efforts are made by fire prevention personnel to minimize the hazards accompanying oxygen use in hospital operating rooms and wherever pure oxygen may be present. Devastating fires have resulted from burning accelerated by the presence of oxygen above the 21% normally present in the atmosphere.

An example occurred several years ago during our space program efforts when ignition took place in a ground test capsule. A closer look at this tragic event may give insight into the effect on fire of an above-normal oxygen level. The incident occurred in a spacecraft mounted atop the rocket which would propel it into the initial flight stages. Three astronauts in the capsule at the time of the ground test were in an atmosphere of 100% oxygen. For our purposes, the cause of the fire is immaterial, as our concern is only with burning rate in an oxygen-charged atmosphere.

Events occurred in the following sequence. The first indication of trouble was a report over the intercom within the aircraft by one of the astronauts: "Fire—I smell fire." Two seconds later, there was a cry, "Fire in the cockpit," silence for three seconds, then a shout, "There's a bad fire in the spacecraft." For seven seconds there were signs of confusion in the capsule, with sounds of frantic moving about and cries of alarm. The last words spoken, four seconds later, were "We're on fire—get us out!"

Technicians watching the flight on closed-circuit television observed only a ball of fire flashing across the screen. Rescuers, only a few feet from the spacecraft when the fire broke out, were unable to help because of the terrific heat. The fire penetrated the aluminum shell and surrounded the exterior. Efforts to control the blaze were futile, but twenty-seven people suffered smoke inhalation in the attempt. When the hatch was opened, about five minutes from the start of the fire, the bodies of the astronauts were found near the escape hatch.

Conditions within the spacecraft indicated the inferno-like intensity of the heat: almost all wiring was melted, most of the communication system received extensive damage, elaborate control devices were destroyed, the interior was a black charred mass. The astronauts were almost completely destroyed, with little but their bones remaining. It was later estimated that the temperature in the capsule may have reached 2500°F.

In summary, the investigator must clearly understand the effect that oxygen content has on the rapidity of fire spread and the completeness of burning.

Classes of Fires

The most important use of the classification of fires is for selection and application of the proper extinguishing agent. It is also necessary for the investigator to be familiar with these classifications so that he may communicate with fire department personnel.

The following classifications are recognized nationally in the United States:

Class A - Fires in ordinary combustible materials, such as wood, cloth, and paper

Class B - Fires in flammable petroleum products or other flammable liquids, gases, or greases

Class C - Fires involving energized electrical equipment

Class D - Fires in combustible metals, such as magnesium, titanium, and sodium

The investigator must understand, however, that a Class C fire becomes a Class A fire when electrical current is eliminated and only Class A fuels are burning. Likewise, a Class C fire in a transformer filled with oil becomes a Class B fire when electric current is shut off.

When a fire department officer describes the fire on the motor of a vehicle as a Class D or magnesium fire, the investigator must know that this fire would burn with fierce intensity. Further, in some instances the fire department would not have the proper extinguishing agent to control a fire involving this material. These two factors would account for extensive destruction of the vehicle which would not ordinarily result from a motor compartment fire.

Methods of Heat Transfer

Since transfer of heat is responsible for most fires, we must understand the basic methods of heat transfer: conduction, convection, and radiation. To these three methods is sometimes added a fourth, direct flame contact. If the investigator is to successfully determine the origin and cause of a fire and why it spread as it did, he must understand each of these principles.

Conduction

Conduction is the transfer of heat from one body to another either by direct contact or through a heat-conducting solid, liquid, or gas. A simple example of this is a hot iron on an ironing board, or a stove pipe in contact with wood. Insulating material will not totally stop the transmission of heat, but will slow it. If the rate of heat conduction is greater than the dissipation rate from the combustible material, the material may reach ignition temperature, particularly when conditions of conduction exist over a long period of time.

Convection

Convection is the transfer of heat by means of moving gases or liquids. It is convection that can cause the investigator the greatest problem if he does not understand this principle. Most fire fighters have encountered situations in which the primary burning is confined to a basement or lower floor at the time of their arrival. Then a brownish smoke appears around the eaves of the roof and suddenly the cry goes up "She's burning in the attic." No flame actually reached from the fire burning below to the attic, but superheated gases traveling upward caused the ignition of combustible material in the roof area, showing that movements of superheated air or gases can cause ignition of material with a low ignition temperature that is removed from the actual burning itself. Upon examination of the structure after the fire is extinguished, the investigator who does not understand convection may mistakenly analyze these separate points of burning as the separate and unconnected fires which normally are associated with incendiary fires.

For example, in one dwelling fire it appeared that seven separate fires had occurred in different areas of this one-story structure. The point of origin of the fire was traced to a mattress in one bedroom. In other areas, curtains, paper, and furniture which had the lowest ignition temperature had caught fire, not from direct flame, but from superheated gases which had reached a probable temperature of 500°F as they circulated through the building. These same superheated gases, usually brown in color with wisps of flame appearing occasionally, account for what is called "flashover." When the room temperature reaches 600°F to 700°F these gases ignite and the entire room appears to burst into flame at once. This can also account for eyewitness descriptions of flames spreading down a hallway with fantastic speed.

If the accumulation of these superheated gases is sufficient in quantity, what may appear as an explosion occurs when they reach ignition temperature. A case on record illustrating this principle involved a fire in a large metal building used as a manufacturing plant for wood products. Floor space in this building was approximately the size of a football field. The building had no windows and was almost airtight, so superheated gases had no means of escape. When temperatures in the interior reached nearly 700°F, these gases ignited with phenomenal results: the structure appeared to explode, not outward but upward. The roof and sides held firm, and the entire massive structure rose three to four feet off the ground and then dropped back on its foundation. The conditions on the interior, however, had not materially changed; accumulation of gases was extensive, as was the heat buildup. When the gases re-ignited, the results were again sensational: this time the entire roof blew off the building and great masses of ignited gases spewed 100 to 200 feet into the air. Witnesses described the spectacle as resembling an atomic blast.

In summary, a clear understanding of the principle of convection is a must, for the investigator without this understanding will be unable to reach any conclusions as to origin and cause of many fires and unable to explain the fire spread or the resulting burning pattern.

Radiation

Radiation is the transfer of heat by heat rays through intervening space. A prime example of this is heat from the sun which reaches us through millions of miles of space. Radiant heat causes problems for fire fighters, since many times buildings adjacent to an involved structure ignite strictly from radiant heat, when conduction, convection, and direct flames are not involved.

The investigator must understand some facts connected with radiation. First, because the sun's rays reach us normally in a vertical or near vertical manner, it is erroneously assumed that radiant heat rays only move vertically or near vertically. Any experienced fire fighter knows better, having observed ignition of one building from another by means of radiant heat moving horizontally. Second, heat radiation is not a one-way process. Heat reaching a wall by radiation from a stove in turn radiates heat in all directions. Third, heat transferred by radiation spreads in all directions from its source and not just in one direct line. Fourth, situations can occur which involve transfer of heat by a combination of radiation and conduction: for example, radiant heat from one source can heat a wall, pass by conduction through the wall, and emerge from the other side where once again heat may be transferred by radiation.

Without a clear understanding of heat transfer by radiation, the investigator may find explanation of the fire spread from one point to another extremely difficult. This is particularly true if the fire has moved from one room to another with no indications of the convection process or direct flame in evidence.

Direct flame is sometimes listed among the methods by which heat is transferred. No explanation of this phenomenon is necessary, for it is quite obvious that direct flame applied to any combustible material will ultimately result in ignition of this material.

Another method of heat or flame spread which is of major importance to the investigator is falling burning material. These materials can fall down through wall space, utility cores, laundry and trash chutes, and elevator shafts. Wood and other combustible material which falls from the ceiling or through burned-out flooring from the floor above can create fire patterns puzzling to the investigator. This is particularly likely when such materials burn extensively in the area where they have fallen, creating significant damage such as holes in the floor, and perhaps leading the investigator to the conclusion that this lowest point of burning was the point of origin of the fire. This method of heat and flame spread must be given full consideration by the investigator when examining burn patterns.

Spontaneous Heating

Spontaneous heating is the process by which a material increases in temperature without drawing heat from its surroundings. Spontaneous heating of a material to its ignition temperature results in spontaneous ignition or spontaneous combustion. The fundamental causes of spontaneous heating are few, but the conditions under which these fundamental factors operate to create a dangerous condition are many and varied.

Spontaneous combustion is perhaps the most overworked of all fire causes, along with careless smoking. When a barn is destroyed by fire and determination is made that hay was placed in the building recently, the cause almost automatically is listed as spontaneous combustion. Many fires in confined areas, such as broom and mop storage closets, are immediately classified, Cause—Spontaneous Ignition of Oil Soaked Materials. While it cannot be denied that numerous fires are thus caused, careful investigation would reveal that spontaneous combustion was not the actual culprit in many cases.

Fermentation, the most common type of spontaneous ignition, occurs in vegetable matter such as hay, straw, grain, and other silage. Moisture content is a prime consideration; well-cured hay, with low moisture content, will not ferment and thus will not reach ignition temperature by itself. By the same token, if it is too wet, hay will not ignite spontaneously. Partially cured hay has just the moisture required for spontaneous ignition. Sawdust in large piles will ignite spontaneously on occasion, but the depth of sawdust and its moisture content must be considered before listing this as a fire cause.

Richard G. Koegel, Research Fellow, and H. D. Bruhn, Professor of the Agricultural Engineering Department, College of Agricultural and Life Sciences, University of Wisconsin, Madison, conducted extensive studies of spontaneous ignition, particularly as it relates to barn fires. In their report on these studies, they comment as follows:

> There appears to be a very narrow range of moistures from which the process leading to spontaneous ignition can start. Microorganisms need moisture to multiply. However, if moisture is too high, the heat they generate will be dissipated. The critical initial moisture may vary with different materials. However, it is not necessary that the material in question always be precisely between the critical limits. If, as frequently happens, material which is below the critical moisture is mixed with material above the critical moisture, moisture will be transferred from the more moist to the less moist material resulting in a moisture gradient near the interface which will include material at the critical moisture. In addition, cases have been recorded where thoroughly dry material was wetted either by a leaking roof or by flood

waters and somewhere in the materials, a moisture content developed that led to spontaneous ignition.

Spontaneous ignition could be prevented if all materials stored were well below the critical moisture level (or in the case of silage, if all the material was well above the critical moisture). In agriculture, even though the farmer realizes that excessive heating of stored material will result in losses, he may, on occasion, due to weather conditions, be forced to store materials which have a moisture content other than the desired one. This could be the case when impending rains force the farmer to weigh the alternatives of a certain loss due to an almost dry hay crop being severely damaged by rain as compared to a possible loss due to overheating caused by storing at high moisture. Or it could come about on a day when drying is very rapid so that the first material to be stored is more moist than desired while the last material to be stored is dryer than desired. There is a particular danger, as mentioned earlier, when relatively dry material is placed in close proximity to relatively moist material, since a region of critical moisture can form near the interface of the two materials. The situation is further complicated by the fact that most farmers rely on experience and observation to determine the moisture content of hay. This, at best, is relative and under unusual drying conditions can be in considerable error. (Koegel and Bruhn, "Causes and Indicators of Spontaneous Ignition in Organic Materials," *Fire and Arson Investigator* 22 (July–September 1971): 30–31. Reprinted by permission.)

Oxidation heating, another type of spontaneous heating, is most often associated with vegetable oils, materials containing vegetable oils, or by-products thereof. Factors creating oxidation heating must be ideal, with good insulation and near perfect oxygen supply essential. If the heat created is not contained, it will normally dissipate; however, if some insulation material such as cardboard or cloth is present to confine the heat, ignition temperature may be reached.

For example, a large oil-soaked mop used in cleaning a gymnasium floor may be placed in the corner of a small storage room with other cleaning paraphernalia, such as brooms, wiping rags, and other mops packed around it. Often such storage rooms are small, tight, and quite hot both summer and winter; heating ducts frequently run through these areas, with no means provided for lowering the temperature. These conditions are ideal for spontaneous ignition: fast-drying oils, good insulation, proper oxygen supply, and high external temperature. School fires frequently result from these conditions after the room has been closed and the building has been closed for several days, perhaps for a holiday or weekend.

Fires may also originate from various products used in connection with painting activities. A painter's wiping rag containing linseed oil and other oils to speed drying has sometimes actually ignited in the painter's pocket. Conditions are ideal: insulation by body and pocket, proper oxygen, external heat from the body, and the moisture of perspiration from the hands. Fires associated with painting operations more typically result from improper storage of equipment at the end of a working day. Often this equipment is stored rather haphazardly in a corner, with oily rags, brushes, coveralls, cans of linseed oil, turpentine, and thinners piled on top of each other. To compound the problem, this mess may be covered over with several thicknesses of drop cloths. Such ideal conditions do indeed cause fires.

Spontaneous ignition by fermentation or oxidation may require several hours or several months; but since buildup of heat accelerates the buildup of heat, as the temperature rises within the mass the process of oxidation increases its pace. When temperatures in the material reach 160°F, the rate of oxidation will be approximately 32 times faster than at 70°F. If the temperature is raised to 190°F, the rate of heat production will double two more times so that it is 128 times the rate at 70°F.

The third type of spontaneous heating, by chemical action, causes few fires because of the precautions ordinarily taken in using and handling chemicals.

A few substances that are not combustible themselves may generate sufficient heat to ignite combustible materials present. Unslaked lime, the most common example, generates considerable heat when water is added to it. Other substances in this category are sodium hydroxide, potassium hydroxide, and calcium oxide.

Hazardous substances which ignite or explode on contact with either water or air are found principally in chemical laboratories where proper safeguards are normally taken. Among these substances are sodium, sodium peroxide, potassium peroxide, and phosphorus. Sodium and potassium oxidize rapidly but generate little heat when exposed to air; contact with water produces an extremely rapid chemical reaction, generating great heat and highly flammable hydrogen which ignites immediately.

Another material subject to spontaneous ignition is charcoal. The widespread use of charcoal briquets means that fires from this cause occur frequently in boxcars, trailers, and warehouses. Charcoal is most susceptible to spontaneous heating when it is (1) fresh, (2) has absorbed moisture, (3) is pulverized, (4) is subjected to outside heat, and (5) has some insulating cover.

Wood can be transformed into a substance called pyrophoric carbon. The constant heat from a steam pipe, for example, lowers the ignition temperature of the surrounding wood until it assumes the characteristics, and sometimes the appearance, of charcoal, which is notorious for its spontaneous heating quality. At this point a slight rise in temperature of the steam pipe will cause the wood (pyrophoric carbon) to ignite spontaneously. Wood reaches this state not in weeks or months, but over a period of years. Fires resulting from this type of ignition can prove particularly puzzling to the investigator.

The NFPA *Fire Protection Handbook* has this to say about this subject:

Section 3-5. Most commonly, the ignition temperature of wood is quoted to be of the order of 392°F. Wood in contact with steam pipes or a similar constant temperature source over a very long period of time may undergo a chemical change resulting in the formation of charcoal which is capable of heating spontaneously. It has been suggested that 212°F is the highest temperature to which wood can be continually exposed without risk of ignition.

Section 3-5. Ignition will occur when a material is heated above its ignition temperature. Thus, moderate heat may cause ignition if applied for a long enough period of time to raise a combustible to its ignition temperature, whereas high heats applied momentarily to a combustible may not cause ignition. For example, over a period of time, a steam pipe in contact with wood may result in ignition, whereas a gas-fired blow-torch held momentarily on a painted wood surface may blister the paint but not ignite the wood, despite the fact that the torch flame temperature is higher than the ignition temperature of the wood. Because the reaction in both cases cannot be determined in advance, it is common practice to avoid direct contact between steam pipes and adjacent combustibles and to condemn as unsafe the practice of burning paint off wood surfaces. The illustrations do, however, vividly show the influence of the rate and period of heating on the ignition of the same type of combustible in roughly the same shape and form.

Section 7-50. Any source of heat is a potential fire hazard unless it is arranged to prevent the possibility of dangerous temperatures developing in adjacent combustible materials. Because of the possibility that wood and certain other combustible materials may ignite at temperatures far below their usual ignition temperatures after long and continued exposure to relatively moderate heat, and to provide a factor of safety, it is good practice to install heat producing appliances in such a manner that under conditions of maximum heat (long and continued exposure), the temperature of exposed combustibles will not exceed dangerous limits. This is done by providing clearance between the appliance and combustibles. (*Fire Protection Handbook.* 14th ed. (National Fire Protection Association, 1976. Reprinted by permission.)

Many other substances are subject to spontaneous heating. The investigator must become thoroughly familiar with these substances and the conditions which promote ignition from within these substances. A final word of caution: while many fires do result from spontaneous heating and ignition, this should not be regarded as a catch-all fire cause. It is extremely embarrassing to classify a barn fire cause as spontaneous ignition from newly stored hay only to have an individual confess later that he torched the building.

Our objective in this chapter has been to discuss the chemistry of fire on a basic level. Detailed technical information on the chemistry of fire is available from many sources. However, the understanding of the chemistry of fire and the ability to apply this knowledge will prove far more valuable to the investigator than technical information when he really "gets into the trenches" to determine the cause of a fire.

5 Determining Origin and Cause

Statistics on fire causes are prepared annually by the NFPA, based on information compiled from selected localities nationwide. Without meaning to criticize this effort, we must nevertheless ask the question, "How accurate are these figures?" Some fire departments whose figures are included in the NFPA report require that the causes of all fires be quickly determined and listed on the fire report under categories other than Unknown or Undetermined. The result of this policy is that the listed cause of many fires is based on a calculated guess rather than a true determination, for there are fires whose true cause may never be determined and others which require weeks of intensive investigation to pinpoint the cause. The demand that fire department officers make an instant determination of cause on the spot at the fire scene and never list a fire cause as undetermined can lead to two unfortunate situations: first, the figures reported will be inaccurate; second, and more important, this policy can cause serious problems later in the investigation. Assume the fire department officer required by regulations to list the cause of a fire ascribes it to Careless Smoking, Cigarette-Ignited Sofa, when he is not at all sure of the true cause. Later on, after a complete investigation, someone may be charged with deliberately setting fire to the sofa, a charge based on circumstantial evidence and perhaps the testimony of a well-qualified investigator concerning burn patterns and intensity of burning. The defense attorney, having acquired the fire report, will ask the fire officer on the witness stand, "What did you list as the cause of this fire?" The officer can either admit to not knowing what caused the fire, much to the detriment of his reputation and that of the department, or else stand his ground, insist that careless smoking was the cause of the fire, and thus destroy the prosecutor's case.

Another factor which affects the accuracy of fire cause figures is slipshod reporting. Is it proper to list a fire cause as Electrical if a plugged-in iron is left unattended face down on an ironing board, igniting the cover and subsequently other combustibles? Is it proper to classify as Electrical a fire caused by the wind blowing a lamp into an upholstered chair where the hot bulb ignites the chair cover? What is meant when Faulty Furnace or Heater is recorded as a fire cause? What was the nature of the fault? Did the furnace or heater blow up or overheat? Were nearby combustibles ignited or did fire start in an area away from the furnace as a result of an overheated flue? Is the cause actually Faulty Heater when three or four inches of fuel oil accumulated in the bottom of a space heater is carelessly ignited? Faulty Furnace or Heater tells us almost nothing; a brief description of what took place and why it took place is mandatory for an understanding of the cause of fire.

Along the same lines, we may wonder why two cities twelve miles apart, with almost identical populations, with similar ethnic groups, and other common factors, report widely varying annual incendiary fire figures. Perhaps one locality makes no conscientious effort to determine fire causes because its fire department believes "Our job is to put out the fire; finding out how it started is somebody else's problem." There may be no "somebody else," no fire prevention officer or local fire marshal to determine cause. Perhaps in one jurisdiction the police department investigates all fires reported to them as suspicious. If there are therefore no cause determinations at all, obviously no fires would be determined to be suspicious. Under these circumstances, the city would report no arson cases, an impressive record far removed from the actual facts of the matter!

Another factor which can preclude accurate determination of fire origin and cause involves an accepted and recommended fire department practice—salvage, overhaul, or cleanup. These terms are used synonymously, but there are differences between them which should be clarified. Salvage operations during and after the fire are designed to reduce damage from smoke, water, and weather. They assist in determination of fire origin and cause provided the investigator understands salvage practices and is informed what salvage activities took place at the fire. For example, the investigator may be at a loss to explain the absence of scorch or charring patterns on certain pieces of furniture when some articles in that area are severely burned. The difference may be accounted for by fire department salvage operations during the fire, so the investigator must determine what salvage efforts were made.

Overhauling after the fire is extinguished is a twofold operation. The first phase is search of the fire area to locate and extinguish any remaining traces of fire; the second phase, closely resembling salvage, consists primarily of efforts to prevent further damage to structure and contents from the elements. Since no fire department wants to risk a rekindle, the necessity for efficient overhauling is recognized, but the extinguishing phase can create major obstacles to determining origin and cause. Such overhaul may consist primarily of the indiscriminate use of a high-pressure solid stream which tears down ceiling and plaster, moves furniture, and either washes any evidence out the door or buries it under inches of debris and water. The first phase of overhaul may also involve removing from the building furniture and/or fixtures which might cause a rekindle. This may make it difficult to reconstitute the fire scene for determination of cause, but if it protects such articles from the elements, this can be most helpful to the investigator.

Cleanup, the third of these closely related activities, can be a real headache to the investigator although its public relations value is immeasurable. By shoveling, scooping, mopping, and sweeping, the fire department makes every effort to restore the premises to prefire condition, but possible evidence has thereby been shoveled out the door, scooped into containers and carried off, mopped up and poured in a convenient storm drain, or swept out into the yard or street. Heavily damaged furniture may be thrown into a huge pile of debris where it is crushed, broken, or buried—pity the poor investigator who attempts later to reconstruct the scene and put the furniture back in its previous location. These heavily damaged items may be thrown into a growing pile in the most heavily damaged area of the structure, which is normally the area where the fire originated. Consider again the plight of the investigator: What in this great mass was there at the time of the fire and what was thrown in later during the cleanup operation? The problems of the investigator are also compounded when heavily damaged material is thrown into the area of origin when it is still burning under control and, as a result, is completely destroyed.

The more severe the fire damage and the more complete the destruction of any structure, the more difficult it will be to determine the origin and cause. We can safely assume that every fire department will conscientiously endeavor to extinguish every fire to which it responds. However, occasionally the property owner will request that the fire department let a structure burn completely so he won't have such a mess to clean up. A fire department that accedes to such a request may be legally liable if at a later date the property owner decides he was not given proper fire protection. Second, a request such as this may indicate that the owner was desirous of complete destruction to eliminate any evidence of arson, for which arson he may be responsible. Good practice dictates that every reasonable effort be expended to minimize the extent of burning in spite of any request to the contrary by the owner.

We can summarize this discussion in one simple instruction: every effort made by the fire department to maintain the scene as nearly undisturbed as possible will be of immeasurable assistance in determining the origin and cause of the fire.

Preserving the Fire Scene

Up to this point all reference to preserving the scene has been negative—don't destroy the evidence. But this is not enough; fire fighters must actively secure the fire scene during the fire, immediately after the fire, and until examination of the site is completed.

Initially, fire department personnel should not tramp through the building, particularly in the apparent area of origin, for an incendiary device or fire set may be walked on and destroyed in this manner. Further, fire fighters and/or law enforcement officers should keep all unauthorized persons clear of the fire scene. It is not unusual to find the owner or occupant probing around through the debris allegedly looking for salvageable items or valuables. It is entirely possible that he or she is trying to locate and remove any evidence of a set fire. Keeping people away from the fire scene presents no significant legal problem, except in the case of the owner. In most states, statutory authority exists for excluding all persons from the fire scene while the fire is being fought. However, we know of no authority or case history which would permit exclusion of the owner from the property once the fire has been extinguished. In some states there are statutes designating the fire chief as the individual in charge, with authority to control the fire scene by whatever means are necessary. The question is, when does this authority cease? Liberal interpretation would indicate that so long as the fire department is on the scene such authority continues, but since statutes and interpretations on this very sticky question vary among states and other legal jurisdictions, fire fighters should familiarize themselves with the policies which apply in their area of operation. In summary, every reasonable legal effort must be made to exclude all persons from the entire fire scene, including the surrounding premises.

Securing every fire scene, however, would be a nearly impossible task, especially in rural areas where volunteer departments provide fire protection. What guidelines can be offered to indicate whether securing the fire scene is necessary? The fire department can often make a quick determination that a fire has been set when any of the following conditions exist: (1) separate and unconnected fires (Figure 5-1), (2) the odor of or other indications of accelerants, (3) streamers causing the fire to spread throughout the building, (4) holes knocked in the walls to enable the fire to move from room to room more rapidly (Figure 5-2), (5) incendiary devices, varying from a candle to ingenious electrical and mechanical setups, (6) a deliberately created short circuit in the electrical service, (7) disconnected or loosened oil or gas lines, (8) unexplained holes burned in the floors in various locations, and (9) unusual conditions, such as covers over the window, the absence of furniture and clothing in a supposedly occupied dwelling, or the absence of furniture, fixtures, and stock in an operational business.

What means are available for securing the fire scene? A one- or two-day

FIGURE 5-1. Initial examination of this scene indicates two separate fires. Actually, plastic drapes on window at right ignited from the fire at left, fell to the floor, and created the burn pattern shown. (Courtesy Commonwealth of Virginia Arson Investigation Division)

FIGURE 5-2. The arsonist intended to help the fire spread into the attic area by knocking holes in the second-floor ceiling. (Courtesy Commonwealth of Virginia Arson Investigation Division)

delay in the arrival of an investigator may make it impractical for anyone to remain on guard at the scene. Under these conditions the fire department may be able to do nothing more than rope off the area and post signs: KEEP OUT, BY ORDER OF THE FIRE DEPARTMENT, or, THE SHERIFF, or STATE FIRE MARSHAL'S OFFICE. Unfortunately, this probably will not succeed in excluding the average citizen with his insatiable curiosity. Certainly the owner will not be deterred by this procedure. The best that can be said about this effort is that it is better than none at all.

Ideally, the premises should be secured by guards around the clock if necessary until an investigator arrives on the scene. More than one guard may be needed when a large building is involved, and no one should be required to stand guard for more than four hours. Specific instructions to guards should include the following: (1) no one will be permitted to enter the fire scene without written authorization from the person in charge of the investigation; (2) nothing will be removed from the premises by anyone not involved in the investigation; (3) any unusual events should be noted and reported, including names of persons who are persistent in their efforts to gain entry; (4) a list must be maintained of those who enter the premises at any time while the property is under guard. Posting guards without specific instructions as to their duties is a waste of manpower which will not accomplish the objective—to protect the fire scene.

Fire department members themselves sometimes disturb or alter the premises in such a way as to confuse the investigator. This is best illustrated by several factual case histories. A fire department responded one hot, humid night to a fire in a restaurant, and several exhausting hours were required to extinguish the blaze. After the fire was out, members of the fire department availed themselves of sandwiches, cakes, cookies, candy, soft drinks, and beer provided by the grateful owner. When the investigator arrived on the scene later, bottles, cans, and wrappers were scattered over the premises, leading to the conclusion that somebody broke in to vandalize and to obtain food and drink and then set the place on fire to cover the crime.

Another situation which can confuse the investigator occurs when members of the fire department remove any item from the premises. The owner who set the blaze may claim that somebody broke in, stole some items, and then set the fire to cover up the crime. One case history involved a blaze in a small grocery store. Investigation revealed the stock was practically nonexistent prior to the fire, but a few canned goods were removed by the fire fighters following the fire. The owner claimed that fire fighters carried out box after box of canned goods. Examination of the scene showed that the few cans on the shelf during the burning left a small, clean area in contrast to soot deposits in unstocked areas. These fire fighters endangered the good image of the fire service and caused difficulties for the investigator by removing a few cans.

Authority to Search

In many states the chief of every fire department is charged with the responsibility of determining the origin, cause, and circumstances of every fire occurring within his jurisdiction. Other states place this obligation on the local fire marshal or local fire prevention officer. State fire marshals' offices or agencies serving as the arson investigation body statewide are almost universally charged with the duty of investigating the origin, cause, and circumstances of every fire determined suspicious by such local officials.

Even when legislation assigns all of these authorities investigative responsibilities, there are cases in which the authority to search has been challenged. The Fourth Amendment to the Constitution of the United States provides that "The right of the people to be secure in their persons, houses, papers, and effects against unreasonable searches and seizures shall not be violated, and no warrants shall issue, but upon probable cause, supported by oath or affirmation, and particularly describing the place to be searched, and the persons or things to be seized."

What problems does strict interpretation of the Fourth Amendment pose to fire scene examination? If obtaining a search warrant is mandatory, during the delay in obtaining the warrant the arsonist can destroy all evidence of the crime. More important, the statutory requirements under which a judge may issue a search warrant are not usually met: the fact that a fire took place is not probable cause for search; additionally, no description of the persons or things to be seized can be made without making a search of the premises. Fortunately, the courts have in many instances realized the impossibility of proceeding under a search warrant mandate. The key word in debate on this issue is *unreasonable*. The courts have ruled in several cases that there is nothing unreasonable about a search for the cause of fire by either fire or police officials.

In spite of such favorable decisions, every fire and police official must clearly understand the legal restraints on search in his jurisdiction, for valuable evidence will be inadmissible if it is discovered during an illegal search. Worse yet, action may be taken against those conducting a search deemed to be illegal without a warrant.

Investigators and the Fire Scene Search

Investigator's Mental Attitude

To be consistently successful in determining origin and cause of fires the investigator must, first of all, have a positive mental attitude. Investigators otherwise are inclined to conduct a so-called "windshield" fire scene examination. The investigators drive to the fire scene and find complete and total destruction (Figure 5-3). The weather is probably very hot or very cold, for it seems there is no place hotter in summer or colder in winter than a fire scene. Under these conditions investigators may decide that it is not necessary to remove themselves from the comfort of the front seat, and a windshield investigation follows, usually concluding as follows: ''The fire scene was examined, and because of complete destruction no determination could be made as to the point of origin and cause of this fire.''

FIGURE 5-3. The investigator faces nothing but a pile of ashes on many occasions. (Courtesy Commonwealth of Virginia Arson Investigation Division)

Facing a fire scene where destruction is absolute and complete can be discouraging; the investigative task is more difficult, and assistance will surely be required from other sources. But no circumstances justify throwing in the towel without any effort whatsoever. After a large fire loss in a major city, the fire prevention officer, in reply to a newspaper reporter's inquiry as to the cause of the fire, stated that from what he had been able to find out, the building was completely destroyed so it would be impossible to determine how the fire started. As a result, he had not been to the scene! Fire scene examination can be frustrating, fruitless, and utterly discouraging. Any person lacking determination, perseverance, and a positive mental attitude in this vital investigative function should enter some other field of endeavor.

Investigator's Physical Condition

Second, the investigator must be in good physical condition. We read from time to time about a crew of city workers digging through the debris, sifting the ashes, and reconstructing the fire scene. More often than not, the "city workers" carrying out this task are the investigators, with occasional help from a volunteer or two. What is involved in fire scene search that requires physical exertion? Many times the investigator must spend hours shoveling, raking, and removing six, ten, or sixteen inches of debris from the area to reach the base of the fire. Removal is necessary, for otherwise debris is shoveled and raked into one section of a room by the investigator only to be shoveled and raked from that same section later, thus doubling the amount of work. If the investigator does his job properly, search in the area of origin will be done on a layer-by-layer basis down through the debris. This may require use of a very small hand shovel, such as a child might use at the beach, and probably a fine mesh screen for sifting. This relatively inactive process, continued for hours or days, can be quite physically demanding. Reconstructing the fire scene involves returning everything to its original position—furniture, flooring, studs, doors—and this work too is ordinarily done by the investigator.

It is always necessary to eliminate any possible accidental causes of the fire from electrical wiring and heating systems even though point of origin and cause may already be determined. The defense attorney on cross-examination may ask the very simple question, "Did you examine the electric wiring and the heating system in this structure?" If the investigator answers "No," the impression is immediately conveyed to the court that a thorough fire scene examination was not made. Further, the defense counsel will have a field day: "The truth of the matter is that you didn't bother to look any further because you didn't want to find anything. You were perfectly satisfied with your version of the fire cause and made no effort whatsoever to consider those factors which are responsible for so many thousands of fires annually in our great nation." The attorney is probably just putting on a show, hoping to confuse the issue, but the investigator's testimony has been damaged.

Physically checking out the wiring and tracing oil or gas lines may involve crawling on the stomach through close quarters in a low roof attic or in a sixteen- to eighteen-inch crawl space under the first floor. An investigator who is too fat, feeble, or hung over will not be able to conduct this kind of thorough fire scene examination.

Keeping an Open Mind

Third, the investigator must approach every fire scene examination with an open mind. Preconceived ideas as to the fire cause may induce an investigator to subconsciously develop evidence substantiating this cause or to jump to hasty and erroneous conclusions. Consider a case in which a fire inspector has warned a building occupant several times concerning unsafe storage of cardboard boxes in the furnace room but these admonitions have gone unheeded. A fire occurs and the same inspector is assigned to make the investigation as to cause. Human nature being what it is, the investigator inevitably thinks en route to the fire scene, "I've been telling Blivits about those boxes. Now look what happened." Under these circumstances a fair and impartial determination of the fire cause is improbable.

Sometimes an investigator can be misled by information supplied by others prior to reaching the fire scene. After a fire in a variety store in a small town, a local official called the state investigative agency and stated, "We have established that this fire started in a storage room from a light bulb hanging too close to some cardboard hat boxes, but we'd like for you to come down here and prove to folks that we are right." On first examination this conclusion seemed reasonable, but a light bulb won't get hot if there is no current running to it, and further examination revealed that the wiring stopped at the ceiling. Keep an open mind!

The Knowledgeable Investigator

Fourth, the investigator must possess knowledge and understanding in certain key areas.

The Chemistry of Fire and Fire Behavior   This subject has been dealt with in a previous chapter, but it is important enough to deserve additional emphasis by repetition.

Building Construction and Materials   The investigator may be at a loss to explain intense burning in a den or recreation room immediately adjacent to rooms which suffered only superficial damage. The fact that the den walls were plywood or untreated wood could explain this, particularly if walls in the adjacent areas were of plaster or plasterboard. The investigator must determine types and quantity of wood used in the building. Was this wood exposed? Was it treated? Were there any unusual materials such as plastics present which could contribute to intense or unexplained burning? The type of heating system must be determined, particularly if used in conjunction with air conditioning. Hot or cold air duct systems can materially affect the burn pattern. It is foolhardy for an investigator to attempt a fire scene examination without a thorough knowledge of the general design, construction, and materials involved in the structure.

Fire-fighting Operations   Perhaps the greatest problem facing the investigator with a non-fire related background and no fire-fighting knowledge or training is the inability to understand fire-fighting operations, how they influence the burning and ultimately the burn patterns. Not understanding fire department operations, procedures, and equipment also leads to serious communication problems between the fire officer and the police-oriented investigator. The officer in charge may explain to the investigator how the fire was fought, how the building was ventilated, what type of fire streams were used, how much water was required to extinguish the blaze, what exposures were protected, what areas of the structure were "written off"—all of which contribute materially to the eventual burn pattern. Sometimes the investigator nods his head wisely, attempts to show comprehension, and congratulates the chief on what a fine job his department did in containing and extinguishing the fire without the slightest conception of the true significance of the interview. An investigator examining the fire scene must have knowledge of the fire-fighting operations employed to accurately interpret what he sees.

Although every action of the fire department will have some effect on the fire, ventilation and application of fire streams probably affect burn patterns more appreciably than any other phase of the operation. Ventilation can be achieved by utilizing natural openings such as doors, windows, or skylights. When such openings cannot be used, fire fighters create their own openings by cutting holes in roofs and walls. In many cases, smoke ejectors or fans are used to speed the removal of smoke, fire gases, and heat through one or more of the openings.

When a structure is opened at the roof or uppermost portion, it is called vertical or top ventilation. This allows the upward rise of heated gases naturally without mechanical assistance. Since interior temperatures of a fire-involved structure can reach 1000° F and more, the passage of this heat accompanied by smoke will leave a path from the body of fire to the outside opening. Actual burning may take place along the route of escape if combustibles are heated sufficiently. Without any extension of fire, heated gases and moisture in the smoke will cause discoloration and cracking of plaster, plasterboard, and paneling. Paint blistering and even broken glass can result if enough heat has accumulated. Another method of ventilation, cross or horizontal ventilation, produces the same physical results as vertical ventilation. An investigator can erroneously conclude that there was a widespread fire extension when actually damage resulted from efforts of the fire-fighting forces to rid the structure of contaminated atmosphere.

Ventilation handled improperly can cause extension of fire through the introduction of oxygen to the fire. A highly heated, oxygen-deficient atmosphere ventilated to admit oxygen may cause heated gases as well as combustibles to explode in what is called a back draft or smoke explosion. To avoid this, fire fighters commonly pull down ceilings and otherwise ventilate confined areas. The investigator must consider or rule out back draft as the cause for an apparent explosion.

Fire streams can be divided according to how they are applied, hand line or master stream. Hand lines consist of hoses handled and advanced by fire fighters and of streams delivering up to 400 gallons per minute. Master streams deliver in excess of 400 gallons per minute and are supplied by multiple 2½-inch or larger hose lines. These streams can be applied in either fog or solid stream patterns, depending on the desired purpose. The fog stream has good heat absorption qualities but limited reach; the solid stream has little heat absorption capability but good reach. Hand lines and master streams equipped with fog nozzles are operated with 100 pounds per square inch pressure at the nozzle. The solid stream hand line is normally operated at 50 p.s.i. nozzle pressure, and the solid master stream at 80 p.s.i.

The investigator should determine what method of application was used in extinguishing the fire. A common practice in combatting fires in confined areas is to apply a fog stream into the heated atmosphere, thus creating steam. Water applied in this manner will expand 1,700 times in the form of steam and act to smother the fire. Additionally, the expansion will push smoke and fire gases out of the structure and cool the atmosphere. Damage is minimal, for only a limited amount of water is required and the fast removal of heat retards fire extension. The investigator will observe evidence of general heat damage in the confined space but the burned area should be clearly visible. Unless extensive overhaul operations are required, the scene should be relatively undisturbed.

Solid streams are employed on open fires or when necessary for their reach capabilities. If conditions permit fire fighters to hit the main body of fire with a solid stream of water, extinguishment will be effected. These streams have enough power to move furniture and fixtures in a structure and totally change a fire scene from its original condition.

When considering the attack and application of water, the investigator should evaluate the selection and proper use of fire streams by fire-fighting forces. A fog stream applied into too little heat or missing the body of fire will cause rapid extension as air is pulled into the fire by the spray pattern and fire is pushed away from the water. This is an all too frequent happening when hose commanders overestimate the reach of a fog stream. The solid stream which is not applied onto the body of fire will have little extinguishing properties and can cause extension. A frequent mistake of inexperienced fire fighters is application of water into heat or smoke using a straight or solid stream.

The knowledgeable fire investigator occasionally discovers that improper fire-fighting techniques may be responsible for total destruction of a building. While this is of no particular concern to the investigator it may remove some suspicion from the fire. In the case of a one-story restaurant blaze, on the arrival of the fire department the fire was confined to the front portion of the building. Without charging any lines or attempting to ventilate or make entry through other access doors, fire fighters broke out the front plate glass window. The addition of oxygen caused an immediate increase in fire intensity and extension which effectively eliminated any possibility of entering the building through the front. The total fire department action from this point was to fight the blaze from the street with high pressure solid streams, with the predictable result that the blaze was driven back through the entire length of the restaurant, causing complete destruction and leaving a burned out shell.

Several other fire-fighting operations might be mentioned, such as rescue, salvage, overhaul and exposure protection, which have an effect on the fire scene but do not cause alteration of burn patterns approaching the effects of ventilation and fire streams.

The investigator must have the proper tools and equipment to conduct a thorough fire scene search. The list below must be considered minimum requirements.

Camera
Combustible gas detector
Portable gas chromatograph
Lights (2)
Tape recorder
Tape measure
Ruler and yardstick
Shovel, short handle, square point
Rake, short handle
Hoe, short handle
Cultivator
Small hand shovel
Ax
Hand saw
Hack saw
Pry bar
Claw hammer
Tin snips
Wire cutter
Pens and pencils

Screwdriver
Wrench
Knife
Screen
Shears
Staple gun
Metal cans, various sizes
Mason jars, various sizes
Sealers
Labels
Marking pencil
Cardboard boxes
Plastic bags
Sponge
Rags
Magnifying glass
Note paper
Paper towels
Hand cleaner

Arriving at the Fire Scene

At the investigator's arrival at the fire scene circumstances and conditions encountered vary tremendously. There may be a four-day-old pile of ashes in a completely deserted and remote rural area where those people who can give information and assistance must be sought out. Another fire scene may show only slight damage and a very obvious point of origin; fire department personnel and other key witnesses are on the scene and available for immediate interview. On occasions such as the latter determining the origin and cause is a simple task.

While both of the above situations may create problems, the most challenging fire scene examination is one that combines adverse factors. Destruction from the fire is almost complete; cleanup operations have been extensive, without regard for protecting the evidence or preserving the integrity of the fire scene; dozens of "experts" have tramped through the remains, and even worse, have moved contents and furniture. The investigator is greeted by a mass of humanity composed of local officials, insurance agents and adjustors, public adjustors, representatives of the gas and electric companies, attorneys for various interested parties, reporters for the news media, "experts" there for unknown reasons, and other unidentified individuals. The pressure may be terrific, for the investigator is regarded as the expert, the authority, the person with the answers.

Entering the fire scene escorted by this mob, the investigator's every action will be observed, and unsolicited advice and guidance will be generously given. If he approaches a gas appliance, the representatives of this organization will immediately volunteer that they have checked out the gas system, which is operating flawlessly and could not possibly be responsible for the fire. The investigator must rise to the occasion by informing this gang that they are not needed, but this must be done tactfully. These people must be advised that the fire investigation, including the fire scene examination, will be a time-consuming process lasting several days or weeks. Their interest and willingness to be of service is appreciated, and if each of them will furnish his or her name, address, organization and telephone number, they will be contacted as the investigation proceeds. This action will normally break up the mass meeting; if not, the investigator should request that the fire or police officials secure the building and remove all persons except those specifically designated to accompany the investigator into the fire scene. Such firm, positive action at this juncture will get rid of the crowd and also generate respect for the investigator, increasing their confidence in his or her ability to accomplish the job.

There are no hard, fast, inflexible steps to be followed in making a fire scene examination. The suggestions which follow do not apply in all situations, and common sense may dictate another order in which certain actions must be taken. For example, if the fire chief or the first fire fighter to respond or the discoverer of the fire is on hand and available, conduct at least the initial interview while it is mutually convenient because a followup conference will probably be required.

Not all steps covered will be required at all fire scenes. It would be a waste of time to obtain an inventory and check out all insurance, mortgage, and financial information during an obvious spite or revenge fire investigation.

We must establish from the outset that an investigative examination is a

FIGURE 5-4. Exterior examination of this dwelling indicates level and extent of burning, as well as wind direction. (Courtesy Commonwealth of Virginia Arson Investigation Division)

slow, tedious, time-consuming task which cannot be rushed. Investigators sometimes are pressured to perform more investigations by supervisors who don't understand why they should spend two days at a fire scene. Such ignorance is a major reason the arson problem has reached its present proportions: the harried and hurried investigator must make a superficial examination based on sketchy information, reach a conclusion as to origin and cause that is based more on guesswork than logical deduction, and move on to the next investigation in order to keep up, to write reports, to get the case off the daily calendar. Until investigators can convince supervisors that fire scene examination requires time, hard work, and dedication to detail, the arson figures will continue to skyrocket. They must be determined that if the circumstances permit, they will do a thorough fire scene examination whether it takes three hours, three days, or three weeks.

In the case of partial destruction there is a logical procedure to follow. The exterior of the structure should be examined for clues as to the point of origin and the area of most severe burning by making a complete circle around the structure, at a distance of 35 to 50 feet from the building if possible. Look at windows, doors, and exterior walls (Figure 5-4). Above which windows and doors is the most intense burning? Note these, making a rough sketch of the building and locating windows and doors for orientation when in the interior. On which side of the windows and doors is the most severe burning? This will reveal wind direction. Examine trees, bushes, or adjacent buildings for evidence of intense heat. This too will reveal wind direction. If no wind is reported the extent of heat damage to adjacent buildings may indicate the level of burning in the involved structure (Figure 5-5). Examine the area around the structure for evidence of streamers leading up to the fire set. Check bushes, fences, and other objects at ground level to assist in determining the height of the fire in the involved building. This process must not be rushed, for every bit of information should be drained from this exterior examination. Photograph the building in a logical sequence while proceeding around it.

Heavy burning around and above a basement window clearly indicates the fire originated at this level. This exterior examination may show little damage to the structure below roof level. If the roof is burned off the entire structure and little damage is evident below the top floor ceiling level, the attic area is the probable point of origin. In the process of this circling, look also for the obvious—containers of accelerants or other indications of arson. Look for glass or other material from the building which would not normally reach such distances from the structure unless blown there by an explosion of some description.

Another recommended step which is seldom taken is to view the fire scene from above (Figure 5-6). This can frequently be accomplished by going to the roof of an adjacent building; however, it may be necessary to utilize fire department aerial equipment. In the case of only partial destruction, this overhead view will reveal exterior damage particularly to the roof, which cannot be seen from ground level or within the structure. The exterior overview will show a complete burn-through of the roof, as well as hot areas indicated by melting of the roof material. Discoloration of metal roofs will indicate the areas of most intense burning. Ventilation steps taken by the fire department which might account for the burn pattern on the interior can also be observed and noted.

In the case of a large structure, it may be necessary to overview the scene from a helicopter or light aircraft. The former is preferable because of its ability to hover, which allows photography and a longer look at the fire scene. It is particularly important to take photographs, which may be enlarged for future study. This view from some airborne vehicle also gives a clear picture of the area around the fire which may assist in planning stakeouts at a later date if this is necessary in a series of fires. In the case of two simultaneous or nearly simultaneous fires, both suspected to be incendiary, an aerial photograph will show the distance between the involved buildings and locate other buildings which would prevent fire communication from one involved structure to the other.

What are the advantages of an overview of a structure which is completely consumed? Areas of most intense burning will be indicated by a complete

FIGURE 5-5. Structures adjacent to involved buildings can assist in establishing areas of most intense burning, as well as wind direction. (Courtesy Commonwealth of Virginia Arson Investigation Division)

FIGURE 5-6. This is a total-destruction fire scene viewed from above. With assistance from early arriving fire fighters, investigators were able to pinpoint the origin and establish cause. (Courtesy Commonwealth of Virginia Arson Investigation Division)

absence of any combustibles, particularly wood. In almost every instance there are areas of a structure removed from the point of origin where there will be some undestroyed combustibles. Noting these areas will help with the fire scene examination on the ground. Additionally, the overhead view and photographs will reveal room divisions in the structure, as well as the location of major appliances and other items of furniture and fixtures which do not burn out of sight.

What is sought in both the outside and overhead examinations is to encompass the entire scene. Within the structure or the area where the structure formerly stood, the investigator is limited to observation from one point.

Let us assume now that the investigator enters a partially burned structure. The area of most intense burning is fairly confined and the area of origin is clearly indicated. Do we proceed immediately to the area of origin? Prior to concentrating on the area of origin, the entire interior of the building should be examined to observe the general characteristics of the building. What is its apparent age? How are the walls and floors constructed? What about contents and housekeeping? It may not be possible to ascertain all this information at the burned out area, but these factors will have a definite effect on the burning and may account for some unusual findings in the area of origin. For example, an old structure will be more dried out; the wood will be seasoned and will burn more intensely. If the walls are plasterboard the spread of the fire from room to room will be slower than with lath and plaster walls from which much of the plaster has fallen. If the floors are poorly constructed the fire will burn more intensely because of space between floor boards. It may at first be difficult to account for some items being in the area of origin, but if we see evidence throughout the building of furniture, appliances, and clothing scattered about like a junkyard the explanation is much easier. The ultimate reward of a complete search of the interior of the structure is to discover a previously unnoticed separate and distinct fire set which did not succeed.

Leaving the partially burned structure momentarily, let us tackle the complete destruction problem. It goes without saying that the fire scene examination under these conditions is far more difficult than with the partial loss; nevertheless, we must accept the fact that many, many times this is the situation encountered by the investigator. When there is no structure left the investigator may feel compelled to kick around in the ashes, pick up a few miscellaneous items at random, and perform certain other rituals which may convince someone, including himself, that he is examining the fire scene.

Chances of finding an incendiary device or detecting the presence of an accelerant are negligible, but the investigator must still attempt to achieve three objectives: first, to make every effort to locate indications of arson, such as incendiary devices or the presence of an accelerant; second, to eliminate the natural and accidental causes of the fire, such as electricity or heating and cooking systems; third, in the case of a suspected fraud fire, to determine the absence or presence of those items normally found in a dwelling or mercantile establishment.

Examining the remains of a structure about which the investigator has no knowledge as to contents, building construction, and materials will amount to merely probing around in the debris, picking up items, kicking the ashes, tossing shovelsful of mess about. The investigator must have outside assistance for any reasonable chance of success in reaching the three objectives outlined previously.

From what sources can information be obtained? First, recall the requirements placed on the insurance adjustor, to provide the investigator with complete data on the structure, its age, condition, construction, contents and their location. Second, the investigator's own efforts have come up with similar knowledge through the neighborhood check, including a sketch of the entire structure. Armed with this information he can now proceed with some degree of intelligence to make a fire scene search, knowing the general layout of the building, including the heating and electrical systems, and knowing the location prior to the fire of major appliances, furniture and fixtures, and any unusual items. The search begins to make sense at this point because there is some knowledge of what the burned building and its contents were like prior to the fire.

What other sources of assistance are available? One source which cannot be emphasized too strongly is fire department personnel. We outlined previously the fire department's responsibility in arson detection. Probably the most important contribution that the fire fighter can make to the investigation is to recount observations of the fire itself. The investigator who does not ask the right questions, however, may not obtain the information, because details that may seem unimportant to the fire fighter can be most vital to the investigation. Perhaps this can best be illustrated by case histories.

Three small children lost their lives in a one-story single-family dwelling fire while their father was at work and their mother was visiting in the neighborhood. The local prosecutor was anxious to determine whether charges of criminal negligence should be brought against the parents. Damage was extensive in the kitchen area, and intense heat had reached the bedrooms where the youngsters died as they slept. The point of origin was clearly in the area above the electric cooking stove. A frying pan on the stove was severely damaged, its bottom almost completely destroyed. The stove had obviously been left on, igniting the contents of the pan, which in turn caused ignition of overhead wooden cabinets. The critical question was whether the stove had been left on or had been turned on by some unknown party, perhaps one of the youngsters, after the mother left the house. The distraught mother was interviewed, and she stated that she had fried chicken for supper in the pan, that about forty minutes after supper she had put the children to bed, and that shortly thereafter she had gone next door for a cup of coffee. She stated that the oldest child, four years old, could open his bedroom door and wander through the house, that he could reach and push the control button on the front of the cook stove, and that he had done so on several occasions in spite of scoldings.

The lapse of forty minutes from the time the pan was used eliminated the possibility that the stove had been left on by the mother. It was necessary now to determine how the stove had been turned on and by whom. The fire fighter who had first made entry into the structure was interviewed at the fire scene. He recalled entering the building through the front door, which was closed but not locked, and proceeding into the kitchen area which was the center of the fire. He stated that he had little difficulty extinguishing the fire, which was confined primarily to the cabinets above the stove, and that, following the extinguishment, he then pushed the buttons on the stove to make sure it was turned off. This could easily have terminated the interview; however, he was asked to describe his actions in detail when he turned off the stove. The investigator felt he was not getting all relevant information from this key witness. The fire fighter stated that there was a small red light visible on the front of the stove, which is how he knew it was still on. He pushed the Off button on one burner but the red light was still on. He pushed another Off button but the light remained on. It was not until he pressed the third button that the light went out.

This information established that three burners were activated at the time of the fire, a fact confirmed by further detailed examination of the stove controls. The fact that the controls on three burners were in the On position eliminated the already remote possibility that the mother had carelessly left the stove on, for she had previously stated she only used the one burner.

Another case which points out the importance of the fire fighter's recollections involves a three-story frame furniture storage warehouse. Destruction was extensive, and the investigators faced a jumbled mass of household effects piled five to six feet deep. Making origin and cause determination seemed nearly impossible, but since another fire had occurred several blocks away at the same time, this fire was highly suspicious. A team of investigators, local, state, and insurance, initiated the normal investigative activities including interviewing fire fighters. Because there had been two simultaneous major fires and therefore a large manpower response, locating the earliest arriving individual was a difficult task. Three fire fighters were interviewed at the fire scene. They had attacked the fire at a window located on the first floor of the building when no fire was visible elsewhere in the structure. Examination at this point revealed deep burning and complete destruction of the sash in the area, confirming this as a point of origin. Immediately inside this window, approximately three inches from the wall, was a stack of wrapping paper piled almost to the ceiling. The area between the stack and the window was severely burned, both the floor and wall.

Most of the damage to the stack of paper was confined to the center portion, which was exposed to the window side. Fire could not have reached this point over the top of the paper because of its proximity to the ceiling. The edges of the stack were not burned as severely as the center portion, thus eliminating the possibility that the fire reached this point by burning around the edges. The examination determined that there was only one possible way for the fire to have originated and burned as it did: the fire had been set through the window. Extensive efforts failed to reveal the presence of an accelerant in this area, but the elimination of accidental causes for the fire enabled the prosecutor to establish the incendiary origin of the fire.

Information furnished by the fire fighters enabled officials to bring this investigation to a successful conclusion by directing their efforts to one area and thus eliminating days of perhaps fruitless work.

The discoverer or reporter of the fire is often a valuable source of assistance, but the investigator should realize that such information must be carefully evaluated for reliability. The average person subjected to the excitement and trauma of discovering a fire may be able to recall very little with accuracy and give responses to questions that are pure guesswork or conjecture. Nevertheless, the discoverer must not be overlooked as a possible source of information.

Another valuable source of assistance is photographs taken at any and all stages of the burning—photos, slides, and movies. Ideally, the fire department will have a photographer, but in many cases shortage of personnel precludes the creation of such a position. Many times amateur photographers and fire buffs will respond to any fire call and immediately begin taking pictures, either for their own personal use or to sell to the news media. Newspaper and television reporters with cameras of all kinds can be of material assistance to the investigator. A newspaper may publish one or two pictures of a fire, but there are normally many more which they do not use; similarly, the TV reporter may use only a small percentage of the total footage shot at the fire scene. Access to all of the pictures and all of the footage should be requested at once, for what is not used is disposed of almost immediately.

Using all of these photos, the investigator may be able to follow the development of the fire from the earliest picture through to the last. Photos taken in the initial stages of the fire are of particular value. Studying them may enable the investigator to pinpoint the origin of the fire from which its spread can be traced. Movie footage is probably even more beneficial, for it will be in sequence.

Although ordinarily the point of origin should be established before attempting to establish the cause, testimony from witnesses, fire fighters, and occupants may, on occasion, establish a fire cause which leads to the area or point of origin, as in the case of the variety store fire previously mentioned, in which the overhead light was eliminated as a cause. Damage to the structure was extensive, but there was much left to examine. The design and construction of the old building, added to and cut up many times over the years, complicated the examination. An overhead skylight, false ceilings, and the variety of materials used in modifying the building added to the problem. Careful reconstruction of the scene, study of burn patterns and depth of charring, and other indications of area of origin led nowhere. Burn patterns on the furniture, fixtures, floors, walls, woodwork, and other combustibles gave contradictory evidence. Accidental sources of ignition were checked out without any significant results. The furnace was also eliminated as a possible cause.

The store had been open, operating, and full of customers when smoke was noticed coming under the door of a large rear storage area and, at almost the same instant, the sound of breaking glass came from this room. The store manager unlocked and opened the door to the storage room, which was full of smoke but showed no flames. No one had been in the involved room for several hours prior to the fire, so the human element was eliminated.

During the course of the investigation, the secretary in the building adjoining the store was interviewed. She stated that on arriving at work she had set the thermostat on 75 so the oil-fired furnace could warm the building and noted about thirty minutes later that the furnace had never cut off even though the building was quite warm. The furnace was roaring and making other cracking and popping noises she had never heard before and the temperature reading was almost 85 degrees. She turned the thermostat back to 60 degrees but the furnace continued to burn and roar, the pipe leading into the chimney was red hot, and she could actually see fire burning fiercely in the pipe. She was actually in the process of picking up the phone to call the fire department when she heard the approaching sirens.

The rest is anticlimactic. The chimney into which the pipe led was originally in the involved building, although it was no longer used in any capacity in the store's heating system. Examination of the chimney revealed numerous holes, some large enough to stick a fist in. The wood at this point had ignited from the intense heat generated by the runaway furnace. Several broken panes in the skylight had provided a perfect draft for smoke, heat, and fire, which spread in the direction of this natural ventilation and broke out other panes (remember the sound of breaking glass?), rapidly increasing the intensity and volume of the fire. It had burned through the ceiling of the storage room and eventually involved the entire storage area.

In this case after a cause for the fire was established, the burn pattern made sense. Without this cause it is doubtful if determination of the point of origin could have been made.

6 Fire Scene Search

Point of Origin

In a search to determine the specific point of origin, take a long look at the entire area of origin, concentrating on the ceiling, for the point of most severe overhead damage may indicate the fire originated directly beneath. Consider factors which may have caused the fire to move in an unusual and abnormal direction, such as drafts. In the case of a fire starting at or near floor level, heat and possibly flame will move to the ceiling, and for a time at least, will be trapped in the ceiling area. If an opening of any kind exists in the ceiling, fire will move toward this opening. In a dwelling, heat duct vents in the ceiling or near ceiling height will draw the fire in that direction. In commercial buildings, openings in or near the ceiling will be created by heat ducts, conduits, and plumbing. Drafts created by any openings can materially affect the direction in which the fire will move.

Heat and flame will be seeking a means of escape. If no escape is found, fire will reach the ceiling, move horizontally across, and then down the opposite wall of the room, causing ignition of material on the opposite wall and almost down to floor level, thus creating another area of low burning which could be misinterpreted as the point of origin.

Having noted the most heavily damaged portion of the ceiling, retrace the heat flow downward. Take into consideration the type of construction and material involved: burned veneered and plywood paneling will take on a different appearance from a plaster or plasterboard wall; some material will ignite more readily than others and thus give a misleading impression of the point of origin. Assuming that the construction and materials involved would not cause unusual burning, fire flow can be traced by determining the area of deepest charring on the various materials involved. It is possible that the only damage between floor and ceiling will be superficial burning of the wallpaper or wallboard. The principle of convection could account for this unusual burning pattern.

Having traced the fire to its point of origin, determine the level of origin within the involved room by examining the bottom side of shelves, furniture, window ledges, molding, and all materials still in place. If the deepest charring of these items is on their top side, the fire started at a level above the burned materials; conversely, charring on the underside of these items may indicate a low point of origin.

Once the area of origin has been completely examined without altering conditions as found, the scene should be reconstructed. This involves returning everything to its prefire position, utilizing information provided by others as needed. Right any furniture turned over during the fire-fighting operations; restore doors, studs, and other materials to their original positions; return also all items of furniture and fixtures which were removed from the structure during salvage and overhaul operations and as a result of any other postfire activities. This process may involve extensive efforts, not only in actually moving the items but also in obtaining accurate information as to exactly where they were located prefire.

When this task has been completed, examine all the items in place. The surface of all materials which are facing the point of origin will be the most severely damaged, so making a complete examination of all exposed surfaces will indicate the point of origin of the fire.

Let us discuss a fire scene search involving a living room, assuming that the furniture in this area is extremely limited. Items 1 and 2 in the illustration are end tables; item 3 is a sofa; items 4 and 5 are upholstered chairs; and item 6 consists of built-in, open-front bookshelves.

To determine direction and level from which the heat originated, examine the four legs of the table, item 1. Which sides of the legs are the most

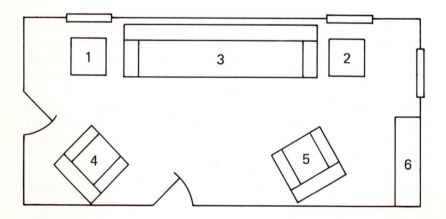

severely damaged? If the exposures which face item 3 suffered the deepest char, item 3 is indicated as the point of origin. If the legs on item 2 suffered the deepest charring on the sides towards item 3, item 3 is again indicated as the origin. The body of the table and the edges of the top itself may serve as indicators. Is the most severe damage on the edges exposed to item 3, with only slight heat damage on the opposite edge? If the areas of deepest charring on the table top are in the direction of the sofa, there is another indicator that this is our original source of heat.

The two upholstered chairs can cause some problems as indicators because of the varying ignition temperatures of materials involved, but they may be examined in the same manner. Are the areas facing item 3 the most severely damaged? Are the backs of these items away from the sofa much less damaged than the front exposures? What about item 6, the bookshelves? Examining them will give not only direction, but also some indication of whether the fire was rapid and intense or slow and smoldering. If the undersides of the shelves are uniformly undamaged down to a level of three or four feet from the ceiling, a smoldering fire with a uniform, gradual buildup of heat is indicated. On the other hand, extensive damage (deep charring) to the shelving, both top and bottom, indicates a rapid, intense fire.

The investigator next examines the walls and ceiling area. Is heat damage more intense and extensive in the ceiling area over the sofa, or is heat damage to the overhead surfaces generally uniform? If the damage overhead is noticeably greater than elsewhere in the ceiling area this indicates an intense, rapid buildup of heat emanating from the sofa. If, on the other hand, overhead damage is relatively uniform, the fire was in all probability slow and smoldering. Examination of the walls gives clues not only to the point of origin, but also the type of fire. If the damage on the walls is generally uniform down to a line three or four feet from the ceiling, most likely there was a smoldering fire; conversely, a definite line of demarcation on the wall leading away from the sofa means a rapid, intense fire.

There is nothing mysterious about any of the these steps taken. Common sense indicates that surfaces facing the point of origin of the fire will be more severely damaged than those not exposed to the original source of heat. The investigator continues this process by examining any and all exposed surfaces in the room, such as windows and door facings, and noting which exposures are most severely damaged. Surfaces facing the ceiling which have a baked appearance indicate a slow buildup of heat; conversely, deep charring in the surfaces exposed to the overhead area indicates a rapid, intense buildup of heat. The effects of convection and falling burning materials on these surfaces must also be considered in making conclusions from this examination.

In searching for the point of origin, the investigator may ordinarily assume that the lowest point of burning is probably the original source of fire. However, this is not always the case, as we shall see.

Let us assume that the lowest point of origin at a fire scene is at floor level. The deepest charring has occurred in a 2 × 3 foot section of wooden flooring. One possible cause is falling burning material. If this material burns long enough and intensely enough it will cause deep charring and may burn completely through the floor. Falling burning material may create burn patterns in the flooring which are easily identified; a piece or section of flooring falling from above should create a pattern on the floor below in the shape of the material which fell and burned. However, numerous fire scenes have been examined where the burn pattern resulting from falling burning material is almost identical to that created by accelerant being poured on the floor and ignited.

The point is that deep charring or a complete burn-through of the flooring is not per se indicative of an accelerant (Figure 6-1). Investigators have concluded and testified in court that intense burning in a certain section of flooring meant unequivocally that an accelerant was present in the area. This is not necessarily so, and the investigator must eliminate other possible causes of the deep charring and/or burn-through, such as falling burning material.

FIGURE 6-1. Holes in the floor such as these are indications of the use of an accelerant. However, the investigators must eliminate all other conditions which might cause such burning. (Courtesy Commonwealth of Virginia Arson Investigation Division)

The flooring in that specific area must be examined to establish whether any unusual conditions or circumstances exist which would have caused it to burn more readily. Perhaps the most effective method of covering this topic would be through some actual case histories.

A person of limited means began operation of a typical country store in a rural area where gasoline, soft drinks, and a limited supply of groceries were available. After several months of operation a fire occurred which caused extensive damage but not complete destruction. An investigation was requested several days after the fire by the insurance company because of (1) adequate insurance coverage and (2) a very low volume of business. The financial condition of the insured was poor; suppliers were demanding payment for goods previously delivered and for several weeks prior to the fire all supplies were shipped on a COD basis. It seemed only a question of time before the enterprise would collapse. Obviously, these circumstances pointed suspicion at the owner/assured, even though his background and reputation were spotless.

Examination of the scene revealed indications of vandalism: sandwich cases were broken open, empty soft drink bottles and candy wrappers were everywhere. Entry to the store would have been easy, for the front door could be opened with little difficulty.

Suspicion thus pointed in two directions and several members of the investigative team began to explore both possibilities while others concentrated on the fire scene. In the back of the structure in a storage area was found a complete burn-through of wooden flooring whose pattern fit perfectly that associated with the presence of an accelerant, a round hole about eighteen inches in diameter. The investigators thought they had determined the point of origin of the fire, but the burn pattern in the structure indicated otherwise, for the majority of damage was in the front of the building. Could this have been caused when the glass windows broke out in the front of the store during the fire, thus drawing the fire in this direction? Burn patterns did not support this theory. Another consideration was the fact that the most intense burning was near the ceiling level. The question was, if the hole in the floor was not the point of origin, what caused it?

The investigator cleared a larger area of the floor surrounding the hole, which incidentally should have been done in the first place. This revealed some nail holes in the flooring which were explained by examination of the ceiling in the area. At exactly the proper angle to accommodate an opening for stairs leading to the second floor was a section of plasterboard which did not match the rest of the ceiling. Inquiry revealed that for approximately fifty years the people who operated the store had lived upstairs and that about ten years prior to the fire the stairs had been removed and the opening to the second floor covered over. The only steps leading downstairs terminated at a point immediately adjacent to where the hole was burned. Constant foot traffic had almost completely worn the floor through at the bottom of the steps and altered its consistency to the point that it was much more combustible, in an almost fibrous state. The floor ignited during the fire and, because of its condition, it burned through readily, leaving a hole almost identical with what would result from a small quantity of accelerant.

The case was concluded several days later when an eyewitness contacted the investigators. On the night of the fire he was returning to his home in a nearby city when he noticed an unusual glow in the rear of the store. He drove behind the building and observed arcing in the lead-in electrical wiring, after which he called the fire department. He did not return to the fire scene and was not aware of the investigation until he read about it in the paper, at which point he got in touch with the investigators.

The apparent acts of vandalism were committed by persons in the building during and after the fire. This was substantiated by the condition of candy and sandwich wrappers, which would have been completely consumed if they had been there prior to the fire.

Not only may the thickness and consistency of flooring in areas of heavy traffic such as kitchen and entrance hall be affected, but the floor may become depressed by the weight of foot traffic, and any flammable liquid present will tend to puddle in these low areas. Deep charring or complete burn-through can occur either with or without the presence of an accelerant, leaving almost identical burn patterns. Only by careful examination of the surrounding area can it be determined that flammable liquids were used, as these will produce more extensive damage to the nearby exposures. When the presence of an accelerant is suspected, we must examine the area beneath, for some of the liquid may have dripped through and caused additional burning. Often laboratory analysis of wood and soil samples taken from the area will positively identify flammable liquids.

Previous use of a motor which might have required oiling or from which oil might have dripped in a specific area can also cause heavy charring or complete burn-through. Examples of this are the household sewing machine, refrigerators, washers, dryers, and other household appliances used in the same location for many years. In cases where oil and grease have soaked into the floor over a period of time, the edges of the burn-through will be almost vertical, as shown below.

Another possible cause of holes in the floor during a fire is termite damage, which can change the consistency of the wood, creating air spaces which will allow for increased combustion and, therefore, deeper charring or, on occasion, burn-through. Foot traffic through the building during and after the fire may cause flooring, weakened by the fire, to collapse under the weight of fire fighters, sightseers, and investigators. Where break-through from weight occurs, the broken edges will be a dead giveaway.

When the floor is burned through from topside, the major damage will be on the upper surface of the flooring. The burn pattern will appear as follows:

Conversely, when the fire burns through from underneath, the appearance at the edges of the hole will be as follows:

After the point of origin is determined the cause of the fire must be established. While there are occasions when the cause may be known or suspected from the first, normally the investigative procedure is from origin to cause. When the point of origin has been established, the cause may be obvious and many sources of accidental or natural fires can be eliminated.

After the "where" (point of origin) of the fire has been determined, the task then becomes establishing the "what" (fuel supply) and the "how" (heat source). The three requirements for combustion are heat, fuel, and oxygen and since oxygen is normally present under almost all conditions, the investigator's job is to determine the source of fuel and heat.

Fuel Supply

Sources of fuel may be generally classified in three categories:

1. *flammable liquids,* such as gasoline, kerosene, and paint thinner;

2. *combustible solids,* such as wood, paper, and rags;

3. *combustible gases,* such as natural, liquefied petroleum, etc.

Item (3) will, in all probability, involve an explosion of sorts. Explosions and gases as a fuel supply will be discussed later in the text.

The materials mentioned in item (2) are normally present in most structures. The critical point is whether these materials were in a normal location. For example, why would newspapers, clothing, and rags be piled up on the floor in the middle of a room? Were such items used to create streamers or trailers, leading from room to room, on the floor or suspended from furniture or fixtures?

In searching for evidence of such combustibles, the investigator must realize that they may be buried under inches of debris. Plaster, wallboard, and other combustibles or non-combustibles which fell on top of such items during the fire create more work for the investigator during his examination, but their presence will have protected the floor area and prevented complete destruction of evidence.

During or following the fire a huge pile of debris may have been created outside of the structure by extensive fire department cleanup efforts. On the other hand, the scene may be relatively intact, with no significant overhaul or cleanup activities undertaken during or following the fire. When the first situation is encountered, the course of action should be to examine the debris where it is found. Significant results are unlikely, unless some incendiary device which did not burn out of sight is found; and even when such an item is discovered, the problem is establishing where it came from in the structure.

When the scene is relatively intact, it would be very unwise to shovel all the materials into one big pile either inside or outside of the structure. The logical and productive technique is to examine the debris layer by layer at the point of origin, a very time-consuming and tedious procedure. Small hand tools, such as a shovel resembling a child's beach toy (but of strong metal construction) and a three-prong hand cultivator are used for this job. Materials found at each level—wood ash, plaster or wallboard, window glass, fabrics, and possibly charred or crumpled newspapers—must be examined carefully. This examination may indicate the sequence in which the materials burned at the point of origin. Are these materials in layers as one would expect to find them, or are the crumpled newspapers found under charred drapery fabric, in which case why were they in that location to begin with? The most important portion of the debris is near floor level, and extra care must be used at this point.

In a search at the point of origin for a source of fuel, the investigator will often concentrate on detecting the presence of flammable liquids. There are several technical devices on the market which aid in this search, but it has been said that the best of all detection systems is one's nose. This statement is not intended to diminish the importance of scientific aids or challenge their reliability, but unfortunately many investigators do not have access to such equipment on the scene.

In seeking to locate flammable liquids, look for any containers in the area of origin—be they milk cartons, metal cans, plastic containers, or whatever might have been available to the arsonist. Again ask the obvious question, Why were such items in the living room, or dining room, or in a clothes closet? How were these items situated in the debris? If they are on top of the mass, perhaps they were thrown in after the fire and played no part in the fire. On the other hand, if the bottom of such containers is directly on the floor, this indicates they were so located prior to the fire.

Perhaps our immediate conclusion on discovering such a container is that all traces of any accelerant would have been consumed in the fire. However, two factors must be taken into consideration. First, combustion in a metal container may not be complete, and portions of the flammable liquid may remain. Second, debris falling into the container may prevent complete consumption of the liquid, particularly if water reaches the inside. In the event the remains of such items are found, they must be photographed in their original position and precisely located by measuring distances from other fixed points in the room, such as walls, doorways, and windows. The contents of the containers should be checked carefully for odors. If equipment is available at the scene, utilize this to determine the presence of some flammable liquid; otherwise, the residue in the bottom of the container should be prepared for laboratory examination, using accepted evidence-gathering and labeling procedures. If the container was in direct contact with the floor during the burning, the bottom should be relatively free from fire damage. Photograph both the bottom of the container and the section of the floor on which it was located. Preserve the container carefully as evidence for possible introduction into court as a prosecution exhibit. It is these very items, particularly if located in several areas in a structure, that may enable us to establish the corpus delicti. The importance of these items as evidence cannot be emphasized too strongly, but slipshod handling can result in these exhibits being ruled inadmissible in the courtroom.

Assuming that no such containers are found in the debris at the point of origin, continue the layer-by-layer checking process, being alert for odors of any flammable liquids, utilizing either nature's gift (the nose) or scientific instruments, if available. When the fire setter has piled up material such as paper, wood, rags, etc., and then saturated the mass with an inflammable, odors may very well be detected (Figure 6-2). Often the arsonist will use a combination of combustibles and flammable liquids as trailers or streamers (Figure 6-3). The recidivistic arsonist may have found out from previous experience that trailers of cloth alone are not successful but that when the trailers are laid out and then saturated with an inflammable the result is quite satisfactory. Another technique employed occasionally is to strew book matches along the route of the trailer.

FIGURE 6-2. Fire "set" made up of kerosene-soaked rags and matches. (Courtesy Commonwealth of Virginia Arson Investigation Division)

When odors of flammable liquids are detected in the debris, this material must be sealed immediately. Gasoline and other liquids used by the skilled arsonist will vaporize and evaporate in a matter of minutes. If the job is done right, notes must be made concerning when and where such samples were found. An arsonist using an accelerant usually just pours the liquid out on the floor in one or more locations, in which case the presence of such a

FIGURE 6-3. "Streamers" consisting of kerosene-soaked bedspread and matches. (Courtesy Commonwealth of Virginia Arson Investigation Division)

liquid will probably not be detectable until the examination reaches floor level. Significant damage to the bottom of furniture and fixtures and deep, rolling charring (alligatoring) on exposed wood surfaces indicate a rapid, intense fire consistent with the presence of an accelerant.

When a flammable liquid has been poured on the floor and ignited, what evidence may be found? The practice of rubbing one's hand along a smooth surface and then sniffing the fingers is utterly ridiculous and completely nonproductive, for flammables poured on the floor and ignited would burn completely on these flat surfaces. More important, flammables, like any other liquid, will flow to the lowest level. The burn patterns from this flow will vary according to the type of flooring involved.

When an accelerant is used on a rug, there will be a distinct pattern where the liquid burned; burning here will be heavier than in the area around it. To determine the existence of an inflammable in a rug, it is necessary to dry it out; otherwise all that can be observed is the wet surface of a rug.

Linoleum floors, whether laid in sheets or in individual squares, will sustain the most damage at the joining edges, where flammable liquids will flow into the cracks and burn. It is at these cracks also that there is the greatest possibility of finding residue of accelerants, for flammable liquids, particularly kerosene and fuel oil, penetrate into most surfaces further than they will burn. In order to locate accelerants, it is necessary to tear up the linoleum and examine the underside and the edges for odors. Examine the sub-flooring for traces of accelerants as well as the areas beneath the flooring.

Hardwood floors may have a charred pattern which indicates exactly what the arsonist did prior to the fire. Accelerant may have splashed over into the surrounding area (Figure 6-4); in seeking its level, the fluid will have run along the cracks away from the puddle. There may be a charred, ink-blob outline on the floor, but accelerant should be sought not only in the cracks within the blob pattern, but also in those extending outside of the pattern. Look in the cracks!

FIGURE 6-4. The arsonist carelessly dripped fuel oil in his wake while moving from one fire set to another. (Courtesy Commonwealth of Virginia Arson Investigation Division)

Regardless of the type of flooring, tear out the baseboard, quarter round, and sills, for liquids will flow under these and not burn. In a normal fire involving Class A materials, the dead air corners at floor level are usually the least damaged (Figure 6-5). If extensive charring occurs at floor level in a corner, it is probable that a low spot existed into which a flammable liquid flowed and burned. Doorways are often slightly lower than the floor in the immediate area as a result of foot traffic and settling. If a flammable liquid burns in this area, it will burn under the sills and door. A wood door charred on the bottom edge is a strong indication that an accelerant burned on the floor under the door.

FIGURE 6-5. Low burning around the baseboard indicates the presence of a flammable liquid. Such intense burning in "cool" areas at floor level and in a corner is not normal. (Courtesy Commonwealth of Virginia Arson Investigation Division)

As in other phases of fire scene examination, there are no mysterious procedures to be followed in locating fuel supply. Generally speaking, the requirements for success in this area are dedication, attention to detail, time, and above all the willingness on the part of the investigator to get in and dig.

Heat Source

The most obvious heat source is open flames—matches, candles, furnace and stove pilot lights and burners, and welding and blow torches. Smoking materials such as cigarettes, cigars, and pipe ashes may also be included in this group.

In cases where matches are the suspected source of heat, the question is whether they were discarded carelessly or accidentally or whether they were used deliberately by an arsonist. Usually this determination is not too difficult to make. If a burning match tossed into a trash basket causes a fire, the investigator must then analyze the entire case, starting with whether the fire was desired. Were there indications that plans had been made for the burning? Were balled-up papers in the trash container, or were contents normal? Had items of clothing, furniture, and personal effects been removed from the premises prior to the fire? Were the matches used as part of a delaying device, such as with a lighted cigarette tied to a book of paper matches? This device gives the arsonist the opportunity to leave the scene before ignition occurs.

Matches may be used in conjunction with other mechanical devices which enable the fire setter to cause a fire when he is absent from the premises. This set-up may involve use of the telephone or doorbell as a means of igniting the tip by contact with some abrasive surface. Fortunately, the majority of these jack-leg efforts end in failure. Even when successful the destruction may be limited and the "plant," relatively intact, can be found during the fire scene search by the investigator.

Careful examination at the point of origin will often result in portions of matches being found. It is amazing how much of these items will remain even when intense burning has occurred. Such potentially valuable physical evidence must be handled carefully and preserved for examination and comparison. The suspect may have in his possession the book from which the match was torn. Under favorable circumstances laboratory examination under microscope may establish that the sample found at the point of origin came from a specific book.

Candles

When candles were used in many households as the only source of light, accidental fires from this cause were common. In today's society, with these items used almost entirely for decorative purposes, such is not the case. Nevertheless, they can be the cause of accidental fires, particularly during holiday seasons. Often a centerpiece for the Christmas dinner table may feature a burning taper in a bowl surrounded by artificial flowers or other decorative material. When the candle is allowed to burn down to the level of such decorations, ignition can occur. Since these items are often made of highly flammable material, an intense fire may result. Leaves from a holly tree allowed to dry out indoors also become highly flammable and subject to ignition from this heat source.

While the use of lighted candles on a Christmas tree is a custom long abandoned, their use for other decorative purposes is still fairly common. Often lack of proper bases can cause problems, as when people melt a small amount of wax in a flat container and plant the base of the spire in the hot wax. Vibration, wind, or other factors can cause a candle to topple over and ignite any combustibles in the area. In some cases, people put burning candles in windows where curtains or drapes are hanging. Direct exposure to the flame as a result of movements of such material can result in ignition and an intense fire which gives off toxic gases. Electric bulbs in direct contact with curtain or drape material may produce similar results. Sometimes the commercial candleholder itself will ignite when the flame reaches it. Although this problem has been reduced substantially by safety requirements imposed over the last several years, there are a number of these unsafe holders still in use in households. The fact that the majority of people are now unfamiliar with the proper use of candles contributes in large part to the problem. Fire prevention bureaus must emphasize to the populace the hazards associated with these decorative items, particularly during holiday seasons, to prevent tragic loss of life and property.

Candles have been used as an ignition source by arsonists since time immemorial. Their advantage is the delay in ignition, which gives the arsonist an opportunity to absent himself from the area. But the incendiarist's lack of knowledge relative to the chemistry of fire may trip him up. The fire setter carefully plans and executes his fire, covering the windows and doors to prevent early detection and placing a candle in the center of a pile of rags or papers on which he pours a generous quantity of accelerant. To assure total burning, he saturates the premises with a flammable liquid. Before lighting the wick, he makes a final survey of the situation, assuring himself that everything is in order. Meanwhile vapors from the flammable liquid are accumulating so that when a match is struck the accumulated vapors within the flammable or explosive range ignite. Either of two things can occur: the entire building is either immediately engulfed in flames, or an explosion blows the structure apart, seriously injuring or killing the perpetrator. Oddly, under either condition, the fire-set may be relatively intact and salvageable as evidence.

The incendiarist may fall into another trap involving the use of a candle by assuming that ignition will not take place until flame comes into direct contact with the set and overlooking the distinct possibility that the vapors from the flammable liquid may fall within the flammable or explosive range at any time during the burning of the candle. Again a premature fire or explosion occurs and once again the incendiary device may be left in place and only slightly altered from its prefire or pre-explosion condition.

Candles will burn at various rates, depending on composition and size. The thicker the candle the slower the rate of burning. A candle 3/4 to 13/16 of an inch in diameter will burn at the rate of an inch per hour. To be accurate, the investigator must locate a specimen of similar size and composition and conduct experiments under similar conditions, realizing that several inches of the taper may have been cut off by the arsonist.

Candles generally leave a deposit of wax which may soak into a wooden surface such as flooring or tabletop. In the process of melting, the wax will protect the spot where the object rested so that charring at this point will be less severe than in the immediate surrounding area. A careful search of the scene can result in locating the holder, which may be fire resistant.

Cigarettes

Fire Marshal C. W. Stickney of Oregon conducted extensive experiments on cigarettes as a heat source, the results of which were published by the National Fire Protection Association in a pamphlet, *How to Identify Fire Causes*. His coverage of this subject is so comprehensive that we have reproduced it at this point in the text.

> A cigarette at the surface of the burning tobacco, without draft has a temperature of about 550° F.; with draft, 800° F. Insulated as it would be after burning into a mass of combustible material, the temperature is about 950 degrees F. A cigarette will burn for 15 to 25 minutes.
>
> With this low surface temperature, a cigarette lying on a smooth-surfaced board with only a small portion of the burning coal touching the surface has little chance of doing more than char the surface. The same usually occurs when a cigarette burns on a flat thin surface of more combustible materials such as paper or cotton. A cigarette will usually burn out even when completely covered with very light, loose material, such as cotton cheesecloth, since the heat is dissipated through the loose cloth and does not build up to ignition temperatures.
>
> To cause flaming combustion a cigarette requires a fairly good insulation. Dropped on upholstered furniture, it usually rolls in between cushions and arm or backrest. After burrowing in and finding insulation, the temperature will rise to about 900° F. This action is slow, and flaming combustion of the furniture usually will not start for at least 1½ hours. The first 45 minutes usually results in a smoldering area of about 6 in. to 8 in. in diameter. When furniture has been 30 to 70 percent destroyed by a cigarette fire the coil springs of the cushions, and often the main springs, will be heated to a degree which causes them to anneal and collapse of their own weight. A temperature of about 1,150 degrees F. or above is required to make furniture springs collapse of their own weight. After a fire is extinguished, springs are seldom annealed or soft. They are usually much harder than normal, even though collapsed, due to the rapid quenching or cooling action of the fire streams. If springs should be found in an annealed condition after a fire it would only indicate that the temperature of the springs rose to above 800 degrees F. and then slowly cooled. It may be possible to gain some idea of the temperature of the fire by running a Brinnell or Rockwell hardness test on the

involved springs. During controlled tests it was noted that the cigarette fire usually burrowed in between the padding of the coil springs and then smoldered from the inside until the padding was reduced to ash. This smoldering was found to continue for as much as three hours; and thermocouples in the cushions indicated the heat ran from 1,400 to 1,600 degrees F.

Where fire from other sources in the room burn upholstered furniture to the same extent (30 to 70 percent) the padding is burned from the surface in, and the temperature around the springs usually does not run high enough or long enough to cause their collapse. Tests with crumpled papers burned on upholstered furniture also failed to collapse the springs—as did tests with up to one quart of gasoline. This type of fire burning on the surface of padded furniture has a high enough temperature to collapse the springs, but as the heat is mostly on the top of the spring it does not affect the main body. Also, springs are ideally designed for dissipation of heat applied to one end only. Large quantities of flammable liquids on upholstered furniture will soak in and create high enough temperatures around the body of the spring to cause collapsing if allowed to burn long enough. In actual fires in protected areas this seldom happens, since a flammable liquid fire will usually flare up with intense heat and break the windows in one to two minutes. It is usually discovered, reported, and extinguished with a total burning time of only 10 to 20 minutes, which is not long enough to heat the springs to the collapsing temperature. Flammable liquids or any other burning material on the floor beneath the springs will usually cause them to collapse, since the heat will bank up under the top padding and the temperature will rise rapidly.

If the furniture is completely destroyed by fire, or if the building is burned to the extent that structural members have dropped on the furniture, then the collapsed springs would not necessarily indicate a cigarette in the furniture.

Indications of a cigarette in furniture or mattress would be:

Heavy charring of the unit and the floor, and immediate surrounding area.

Char pattern on furniture frames, heaviest on inside.

Heavy staining and blackening of mirrors and window glass in this area, indicating a long, slow fire—a burning time of at least 1½ hours and up to 3 or 4 hours.

Collapsing of part or all of the coil spring.

Cigarettes will ignite foam rubber padding to about the same degree as other padding. Lying flat on the surface they will usually char a small hole and burn out. If the cigarette is partially covered at the sides or bottom, a fire usually results in an hour or so. With foam rubber padding, fire will occur a little faster since smoldering in foam rubber reaches its ignition temperature faster and burns with greater intensity. (C. W. Stickney, "Cigarette Fires," in *How to Identify Fire Causes* (National Fire Protection Association, 1960), pp. 7–8. Reprinted by permission.)

Pilot Lights

Furnace and stove pilot lights are open flames common to many households and other occupied buildings. While there are exceptions, in the majority of cases where fire results with these elements as the source of heat, the human element is involved. Generally speaking, the pilot light for any appliance is not in itself hazardous, but when combustibles are allowed to come in contact with the flame through carelessness fires result.

Undoubtedly the greatest danger from pilot lights is their ability to ignite flammable vapors. We hear frequently of fires occurring in household garages, storage rooms or sheds, utility rooms, or similar areas where someone is cleaning a motor or a piece of machinery with gasoline. Ignorance or sheer stupidity contribute to the frequency of these incidents. Many people cannot or will not accept the fact that gasoline in a confined, unventilated area is extremely dangerous and that a pilot light 20 or 30 feet from an open can of gas can ignite the vapors. Unfortunately, many lives have been lost because of the failure to understand that it is the vapors given off by the flammable liquids, not the liquids, which ignite and burn.

While fires of this nature generally are not suspicious, the fact that fatalities often occur makes an investigation necessary. Many times only routine questioning of the survivors is required to determine what happened. Often the physical evidence is equally revealing, the nature of the victims' burns, the open can of cleaner, the item being cleaned, the indications of very rapid, intense heat of short duration. Fire damage may be insignificant, for the vapors are consumed very rapidly, almost as in a low order explosion.

Stoves

Fires resulting from cooking stoves generally involve people participation. Every year thousands of fires occur in the United States and other industrial nations from human carelessness around cooking stoves. A pan of grease left on a burner during a telephone conversation, or while answering the door or refereeing a children's squabble, ignites. The fire is discovered in its early stages, but panic, ignorance, and lack of a fire extinguisher make this early discovery meaningless. Occasionally, the discoverer will throw water in the flaming pan, thus spreading the fire, or remove the hot pan through the kitchen door, resulting in serious burns and a trail of burning grease which ignites the flooring.

Most serious fires result when burners are left on under pans of grease for longer periods of time. In all probability the flames will reach wooden cabinets which are often far too close to the stove. Once these cabinets ignite, the blaze spreads rapidly, quickly involves the entire kitchen area, and in all probability the entire structure.

Questioning of occupants in cases where the cooking stove is the suspected heat source may bring negative results. No one likes to admit responsibility for a fire, particularly where extensive damage results. Loss of insurance coverage is a consideration in the mind of the careless party. The investigator must examine the areas above and around the stove, studying the burn pattern, depth of charring, lines of demarcation, and other physical factors which indicate this as the heat source. Detailed examination of the stove itself in many cases will reveal that a burner or burners were in the On position. This examination may require the assistance of appliance people who deal with the type of stove involved, either gas or electric.

While the majority of households today have either electric or gas stoves, there are many wood-burning stoves still in use, primarily in rural areas. These appliances are relatively safe, but improper installation causes numerous and sometimes tragic fires. Primarily, the fault lies in failure to insulate the pipe leading to a chimney or directly out of the house. Such pipes come in close contact with sections of wood in the structure over a long period of time, creating pyrophoric carbon with a low ignition temperature. Fires which result from these circumstances often occur at night, causing tragic loss of life to sleeping victims.

An even greater danger of this type of heater is the longstanding custom of "bringing up the fire," which consists of putting fresh wood in the fire box, pouring some kerosene, fuel oil, or even motor oil over the wood, and then applying flame. Although the odds against an explosion are great, occasionally there is enough heat or hot ash in the firebox to allow the fuel to come within the explosive range. When ignition occurs, the stove explodes, scattering burning wood particles and burning fuel over anyone or anything in the immediate area. Since the odds against such an incident are extremely high, no amount of cautioning brings any meaningful results. The standard answer goes something like this, "We've been doing this in my family for over a hundred years and nothing ever happened like you say." True, but the next time may be one time too often. Apathy or just plain stubbornness will cause one more needless tragedy.

Heaters

Heating devices come in such a variety of shapes, sizes, and types that a detailed coverage of this topic would be too lengthy to be practical. The investigator who faces electric heaters, gas heaters, electric, oil, coal, or gas furnaces as a possible heat source in a fire often must call for assistance from experts in the appropriate field. Each of the appliances mentioned is a heat source which may become a fire cause for any of three reasons: (1) improper installation, (2) human carelessness, and (3) a mechanical malfunction. Improper installation has become increasingly common as many people have attempted to change heating systems in response to the energy crunch. Lack of technical and mechanical knowledge led to many jack-leg installations with improper venting, insufficient insulation and clearance between heater and combustible materials, and a variety of other flaws too numerous to mention.

Human carelessness relating to heaters consists primarily of allowing combustible materials to accumulate too near the heater. Sometimes heaters are used for drying clothes. Space heaters and floor furnaces concentrate a tremendous amount of heat in a small area and for this reason are particularly capable of igniting combustible materials, especially when the combination utility/furnace/laundry room becomes a catch-all not only for clothes, but also for boxes, and papers that magically accumulate.

Mechanical malfunctions are a rather rare occurrence because of safety factors built into most of today's heaters and furnaces. Nevertheless, oil and gas leaks do develop, and carburetors and controls do fail, causing excess fuel to reach the firebox or escape onto the floor or into the room, often with disastrous results.

A word of caution to the investigator is appropriate when heaters or furnaces are suspected as the heat source. Even the most inexperienced arsonist wants the fire to appear to have a logical accidental cause. What more reasonable accidental cause than a faulty furnace, malfunctioning carburetor, flooded firebox, or even a hole in the firebox? The arsonist may loosen connections in the line, or pour flammable liquids on the floor around the heater/furnace. For this reason it is necessary to examine all fittings, as well as the burn pattern on the floor, with great care.

Miscellaneous Heat Sources

Other open flame sources of heat include welding and blowtorches. Once again fires resulting from this source normally involve the human element. People have the impression that if the flame from the torch does not actually come in contact with the combustible, no fire will result. We know that through the principles of both radiation and conduction burning can result without direct contact. Not only do fires occur as a result of the skilled welder using his equipment carelessly, but householders often cause ignition of combustible materials while thawing out frozen pipes with a torch.

Though such fires are not incendiary, often an extensive investigation is required to establish the blowtorch as the heat source, for in large losses involving buildings under construction or repair, the contractor or subcontractor employing the welder does not want his company to be pecuniarily liable. The householder who causes a fire while thawing out his pipes (or making repairs requiring use of the torch) may conceal the truth from the investigator for fear insurance coverage will be denied because of his careless act.

Another heat source which must be considered in every fire cause determination is hot surfaces. Just a few examples are heaters, soldering and electric clothes irons, steam pipes, and light bulbs. When we consider heaters as hot surfaces we do not refer to the flame or heating element itself. As has been mentioned previously, combustibles placed too near a heater surface for long periods of time may reach ignition temperature. Typical materials are clothes, papers, and cardboard boxes. The prolonged exposure to heater surfaces dries out such materials and thereby lowers their ignition temperature.

The probability of a soldering iron being a heat source in a fire depends almost entirely on the materials exposed to the surface and the length of such exposure. Soldering irons of 100–125 watts produce temperatures of 600–800° F. This appliance has no thermal control and will continue to produce maximum heat as long as it is plugged in. In the initial stages of exposure to a wooden surface only charring will occur, particularly with the small 600° F. iron. As heating continues, smoldering can change to flaming, especially with the 800° F. iron, after approximately three to four hours. While paper and cloth laid flat placed directly under the iron may be consumed without damage to the surrounding area, crumpled paper and cloth coming in contact with the iron's surface will normally ignite within thirty minutes or less.

Opinions vary on the danger of electric clothes irons as a heat source. While it is true that thermostats permit only 450° F. heat surface, these thermostats can malfunction. Tests run under various conditions indicate that normally only charring to the ironing board cover will result when the thermostat functions properly, but the iron may burn completely through the wooden ironing board. Low-ignition-temperature combustibles exposed to the iron under these conditions could be ignited. It is certainly not reasonable to conclude that an iron left on will only char exposed material and never cause a fire. If the fire under investigation originates in the vicinity of an ironing board and/or iron, the investigator must eliminate this as a possible cause for the fire.

In evaluating light bulbs as a heat source there are two prime considerations: (1) the wattage of the bulb and (2) condition of combustibles exposed to heat from the bulb. Heat generated from light bulbs varies with the wattage of the bulb. A 25 watt bulb will generate only 110° F at its surface, while a 300 watt bulb will generate 374° F. Wattage of bulbs between these two sizes will produce degrees of heat in between the two extremes. While the surface of a bulb seldom exceeds 400° F., the temperature of the filament can reach almost 5,000° F. and is capable of igniting almost any combustible material.

The key consideration in establishing a light bulb as the probable fire cause is the condition under which the bulb contacted the combustible. An overturned lamp may permit direct contact between a bulb and paper, cloth, or wooden surface, but, unless the heat from the bulb is confined, it will dissipate and only charring to the exposed surface will result. If, however, a lamp should fall into a trash container of some type and bury itself in paper, the heat cannot dissipate and combustion will occur. Similar results can occur when an overturned lamp falls into an upholstered chair and the bulb is confined in a corner of the chair. No heat dissipation occurs, so ignition takes place, with the time involved influenced by wattage of the bulb and combustibility of the material.

In this chapter we have discussed the procedure for determining origin and cause, which revolves around a basic understanding of fire. Oxygen in sufficient quantity to support combustion is normally present. Likewise fuel in various forms of solids and liquids is ordinarily present. The critical phase of the fire scene examination then becomes locating the heat or ignition source.

In concluding the discussion of fire scene search, one comment seems appropriate. That every fire has a cause is obvious, but it has been written that if the investigator is diligent and persevering he can establish the cause of every fire. This is pure hokum. There will be many fires with total destruction where the investigator cannot locate the area or point of origin or establish the cause. There will be fires where the destruction is far from total in which no conclusion as to origin and cause can be reached.

A fire occurred in the kitchen of a rural home occupied by an elderly couple whose reputation was spotless. On this day at 11:00 A.M. these people had been working in their garden for an hour approximately 50 feet from the kitchen door. Suddenly they noticed smoke coming out of the open kitchen door and, rushing to the house, they discovered an ordinary paper wall calendar on the back of the kitchen door in a full blaze. The fire was extinguished without difficulty, the point of origin was clear, the calendar and only the calendar burned. The entire front of the house was locked, and only the kitchen door, in full view of the owners during the entire time they were in the garden, would permit entrance into the house. The conditions thus eliminated the possibility of an intruder igniting the calendar. An identical calendar was tested for spontaneous ignition possibilities with negative results. In short, the cause of this fire was never determined, much to the frustration of the investigators.

7 Scientific Aids

Material in this chapter is based, for the most part, on field experience, study, and consultation with recognized authorities in arson investigation. It was deemed advisable to utilize the expertise of individuals knowledgeable in the field of scientific aids. As a result, the majority of the material which follows either was prepared upon request or reprinted with the permission of the authors.

Great advancements in the use of computers for arson investigation have been made by David J. Icove, Arson Investigator for the State of Tennessee. The information which follows was submitted by Mr. Icove and Dr. James R. Carter, Department of Geography, University of Tennessee, Knoxville, Tennessee.

Arson Pattern Recognition System (APRS)

In the last several years, in part because of economic conditions, there has been a dramatic rise in incendiary crime losses throughout the United States and Canada. This large increase in arson activity has placed a burden on those responsible for arson prevention. The nation's fire and casualty insurers have encountered large underwriting losses. Fire prevention intelligence analysts, where they are employed, are overburdened with heavy caseloads and are not able to pursue to their satisfaction every suspicious fire. Organized crime activities flourish under these conditions. For these reasons, fire and law enforcement agencies are urgently seeking out new techniques for combating incendiary crime activities.

FIGURE 7-1. The Arson Pattern Recognition System located at the University of Tennessee, Knoxville. (Courtesy Office of the Tennessee State Fire Marshal)

The Arson Pattern Recognition System (Figure 7-1) is a systematic intelligence analysis tool for use by the arson investigator in the detection, prediction, and prevention of incendiary crimes in his jurisdictional area. Pattern recognition is an effective tool for identifying and classifying trends in data. Arson-related data, which frequently contains numerous trends, lends itself to pattern recognition analysis. Using APRS predictions of where and when future incendiary crimes will be most likely to occur, investigators can be sent to these areas for patrol and surveillance activities. The utilization of the APR System in detecting and apprehending arsonists is best illustrated by a diagram (Figure 7-2).

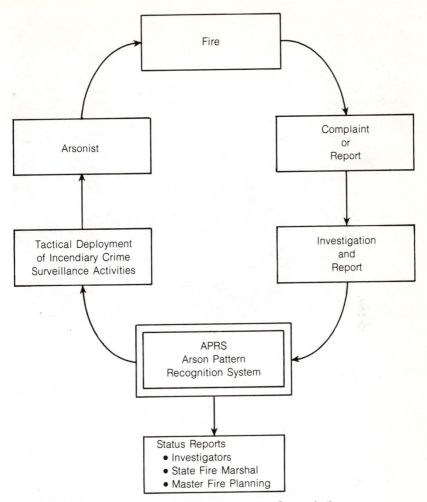

FIGURE 7-2. The role of the Arson Pattern Recognition System in the detection, prediction, and prevention of incendiary crime.

Intelligence analysis calculations done by the APR System could be handled manually. However, computer-assisted analysis can take full advantage of the computer to manipulate, transform, and display the data taken from investigators' reports. Using historical data and logical associations, APRS is programmed to recognize trends in arson cases that form distinctive patterns (Figure 7-3). These patterns may be as simple as time-of-day trends or as elaborate as multidimensional correlations involving hundreds of fires over several years.

FIGURE 7-3. An arson investigator using the APR System for interactive analysis of fire incidents. (Courtesy Office of the Tennessee State Fire Marshal)

Summarized in Table 7-1 are the data elements necessary for using the APR System. The coding scheme used with these data elements is consistent with the National Fire Protection Association No. 901 Standard. This coding standard is used exclusively with almost every regional fire reporting system, including existing statewide systems.

The fire prevention analyst gains most by using the computer-assisted version of APRS for the detection of complex, multidimensional patterns. While APRS generates information that can be used for ongoing arson detection, prediction, and prevention, the system also adds the present fire incident data to the library of past fire data. (Figure 7-4).

Future users of the APR System can rely upon patterns established in the past to verify future incendiary crime activities possessing similar trends. Furthermore, two or more jurisdictional data bases could be linked together with APRS for fighting organized crime on a regional basis. Such linkages might take place on the national, regional, or state levels and could involve the facilities of the National Fire Data System (NFDS) presently maintained by the National Fire Prevention and Control Administration (NFPCA) in Washington, D.C.

TABLE 7-1   DATA ELEMENTS FOR THE APR SYSTEM

Incident Information

— Investigator Number
— Fire Incident Number
— Type of Incident
— Action Taken

Geographic Location

— Map Row or Latitude
— Map Col. or Longitude
— County or Census
  Tract Numbers
— City and Street Address

Temporal Information

— Time of Fire
— Date of Fire

Fire Data

— Area of Fire Origin
— Equipment Involved in
  Fire Ignition
— Form of Heat of Ignition
— Type of Material Ignited
— Form of Material Ignited
— Act or Omission

Property Information

— Type of Property Complex
— Property Classification
— Property Type
— Construction Type

Human Factors

— Socioeconomic Factor
— Motive of Arsonist

FIGURE 7-4. A removable cartridge disk contains the APRS computer programs and data base. Over 15,000 fire incidents can be stored on a disk. (Courtesy Office of the Tennessee State Fire Marshal)

Applications

The APR System has been applied with success at the city and subcounty levels in the Washington, D.C., area. Mr. Icove, a former

Fire Marshal for the City of Hyattsville Fire Department, tested APR System analyses in his jurisdictional area. Based upon APRS predictions, an annual incendiary fire problem involving juveniles was eliminated.

Mr. Icove also provided APRS analyses to surrounding areas. The District of Columbia experienced in 1975 a series of Metro Bus Fires in which one of the fires killed a thirteen-year-old boy who was asleep in a bus. After this incident, an APRS analysis of the four previous fires predicted within four hours the date of the next incendiary fire. The District of Columbia Fire Marshal was provided a two-week advance notice predicting the fire, but unfortunately the arsonist set fire to a bus stored in an Alexandria, Virginia, depot.

This action lead to a one-year APRS analysis of all vehicle fires that had occurred in Alexandria during 1972. The results indicated the existence of a continuous organized crime operation involving stolen vehicles. It was found that vehicles stolen in the Washington, D.C., area were driven south into Alexandria, stripped, and then burned at a predictable time, day of the week, and geographical area.

In the State of Tennessee during 1975 and 1976, the APR System was employed at a regional level for a group of counties that shared a rash of incendiary fires. The investigator using the APR System was able to supply and update surveillance schedules for the Tennessee State Fire Marshal's Office. Previous historical patterns brought by Mr. Icove from the Washington, D.C., area indicated that fire fighters were involved. An intensive investigation by a team of State Fire Marshals resulted in the arrest and conviction of five part-time fire fighters who were paid on an hourly basis and had been setting fires to increase their incomes.

In the earliest applications of the APR System the only geographic identifier used was a map grid cell, based upon a map of the local area with a simple grid superimposed upon it. As the system is being set up for statewide operation, greater care is being given to the design of the geographic identifiers.

Precise geographic coordinates are necessary for techniques such as cluster analysis of fire incident data. Also, geographic coordinates can be collected, combined, and manipulated for any location in the world.

By collecting data within census tracts or counties, it is possible to combine fire data with information concerning social, economic, demographic, and political factors which might provide some influence or insight. As an example, the number of mobile home fires becomes more significant if we can also determine the number of mobile homes in the area.

Recommendations

Based upon the experience gained in the design, development, and implementation of the APR System in both the Washington, D.C., and state of Tennessee areas, several recommendations by these and other authors would help bring the incendiary crime problem under control.

Recognizing that arson should be classified as an FBI Class 1 crime should be a national priority. The inability of law enforcement agencies to perform adequate arson investigations is not a reasonable excuse at this time.

Common geographic coding and uniform fire incident reporting should be encouraged for regional and state levels. Too often, neighboring jurisdictions cannot interface their information systems for effective law enforcement. Federal funding should be made available with the goal of eventual linking of information systems at a national level.

The Combustible Gas Detector (Sniffer)

The material which follows was compiled by R. Hilliard and C. Thomas, Crime Laboratory Scientists, Michigan Department of Public Health, Crime Protection Laboratory.

An instrument being used at many Michigan fire scenes is the J. W. Combustible Gas Detector. This instrument has been purchased by some departments as an aid to the fire investigator and is not intended to replace laboratory analyses. It is a portable instrument and is easily carried and operated in the field. Its purpose, to the fire investigator, is to detect any flammable liquid vapors that may be in the debris at a fire scene. In several instances, the laboratory has shown negative results when there has been a positive reading on the Gas Detector. These discrepancies have encouraged the laboratory to make an evaluation of the instrument.

The J. W. Combustible Gas Detector, commonly known as the Sniffer, detects the vapors given off by a vaporizing liquid by using a thermal conductivity detector. The vapors from the immediate area of the material to be sampled are drawn by a hand pump or electrical pump through a probe and on through the detector. If liquid vapors are present, a reading can be noted on the meter upon the instrument. The meter reading is expressed in two different scales: a parts per million scale (PPM) and a less sensitive explosive scale (expl). The ratio of these two scales differs depending on the vapors tested. Both scales are found on the two models studied. The basic difference between the two models is that the Model SS has a hand-driven pump and the Model SS-P has a motor-driven pump.

The authors tested 23 different materials which could be common to a fire scene. These were ignited in a 12'' × 12'' × 32'' chamber, allowed to burn for 30 seconds, were extinguished, and the smoldering debris was immediately sampled by the two different models of the Sniffer. The burnt residues were then sealed in individual 92-ounce plastic containers and allowed to remain at room temperature for 24 hours. The following day the vapor samples from each cannister were collected for Gas Chromatographic Analysis. A glass syringe was used to withdraw 2 cc of vapor from within the cannister. The vapor was then injected into a Varian 1400 Gas Chromatograph equipped with a 8' × ¼'' aluminum column, packed with 15 percent Apiezon L on Gas Chrom RA (45/60 mesh) at 160 deg C and 60 cc min/N(2) and re-sampled by the Sniffer.

In most cases the readings obtained from the Sniffers corresponded to the presence or absence of flammable liquids in the residue. There were, however, a few notable exceptions.

Ammonia vapors, present in many common household cleaners, give Sniffer readings of greater than 1.0 on the explosive scale. Burnt cotton mattress padding yields Sniffer readings of 600 and 700 parts per million. Number 2 fuel oil, on the other hand, gives surprisingly low readings of 80 and 60 parts per million.

Gas Chromatographic analyses correctly identified all flammable liquids when present and yielded negative results in their absence.

Either of the Sniffers tested, when operated as specified in the instruction manual, seems to be a useful tool for the fire investigator. The investigator must be aware that the Sniffer will indicate the presence of flammable liquids at times when none exist. Samples of debris should be taken whenever the Sniffer indicates a flammable liquid vapor is present. However, no conclusion concerning the presence or absence of flammable liquids should be drawn until specimens of debris submitted to the laboratory have been analyzed and a report received.

A problem of greater concern to the investigator is the lack of sensitivity of the Sniffer to Number 2 fuel oil. The slight needle defection (60–70 ppm) could easily be overlooked by the fire investigator using the Sniffer. He must be aware of this lack of sensitivity to heavier petroleum products. For this reason the investigator who obtains a very low or negative reading with a Sniffer is advised and encouraged to obtain samples of debris from apparent points of origin of suspicious fires and submit those samples to the laboratory for analysis. (Hilliard and Thomas, "Combustible Gas Detector (Sniffer), An Evaluation," *Fire and Arson Investigator* 26 (January–March 1976): 48–50. Reprinted by permission.)

Gas Liquid Chromatography

The following information concerning this process is from an article by
Charles R. Midkiff, Jr., which appeared in the July–September 1971 issue
(volume 22) of the *Fire and Arson Investigator,* the official publication of
the International Association of Arson Investigators.

Gas liquid chromatography (GLC) is a technique for detecting and
separating very small quantities of volatile liquids or gases. The
separated components can then be identified as to type and quantity.

A sample of the material to be examined is placed on a heated
column where it is separated into its various components in a manner
similar to distillation, e.g., distillation of moonshine to separate the
alcohol and water from the other components. The separation effected
by chromatography is extremely efficient in comparison to ordinary
distillation, being equivalent to hundreds of successive distillations
with each distillation resulting in a cleaner separation than the
preceding one. The separated components are detected and recorded
for identification.

GLC is useful for the identification of flammable liquids, such as
gasoline and kerosene, used in arson fires. A sample of burned
material from the scene can be examined for the presence of volatile
liquids either by extraction of the liquid with another material or by
examination of the vapor from the material (if the sample is packaged
in such a manner as to prevent the loss of volatile components). GLC
is also useful for the characterization of liquids (e.g., moonshine) to
determine characteristic or foreign components.

Ultraviolet Light

The material which follows is quoted from an article entitled ''Ultraviolet
Light—Gem or Junk?'' by C. M. Lane.

In recent months those involved in arson investigations have heard the
pros and cons of the value of ultraviolet light (UVL) as a detection
device. This equipment has been used successfully for years in other
criminal investigations. . . .

A brief technical description is in order at this point so that we
might understand what we are discussing. The wavelength of UVL is
in the region from 3,000 to 4,000 angstrom units (shortwave UVL
ranging downward from 3,000 a.). In our investigations both
wavelengths have a place, but the short wave is the best suitable.
When UVL strikes a surface, it is absorbed by some substances and its

energy is transferred and reflected back as radiant visible light. Although UVL is invisible to the human eye, its effects are quite visible in the form of fluorescence. When an object reflects visible light from an invisible light source, it is said to fluoresce. It is this phenomenon which hopefully we will be able to use in arson fire investigations.

First let's understand that UVL is not a magic wand. It does not perform miracles. It is, however, much like your camera—its efficiency depends upon the operator. Imagination and common sense are vital.

When using UVL for the first time, everything appears to be blue. Close your eyes and adjust to the darkness. Use a good hand light in conjunction with the ultraviolet light. When you make a discovery, check the natural state of the material under the white light.

Most people who use ultraviolet light to any extent begin to realize the value of this tool in adverse conditions. Wind does not affect the light as it does the Sniffer. Camouflaging odors do not affect the ultraviolet light. Two things which will affect ultraviolet light are external light and time. The search area should be as dark as possible. If necessary, cover windows with black polyethylene (4 mil visquene). Since in many cases you are looking for a volatile liquid, the fire scene investigation should take place within a reasonable time after the fire. Seven days or less is desirable. UVL should not be abandoned after this time, however. You may detect other fluorescent materials which could indicate plants or trailers. Explosive wrappings are usually fluorescent.

You need not alter your method of fire scene examination when using the UVL. On the contrary, this equipment will enhance your search techniques. Upon discovering the point of origin, check this area thoroughly for fluorescent residue. When checking under carpeting, baseboards, etc., the light can reveal moist floor residue which you may otherwise mistake for water. Another advantage is that you can use available ultraviolet light with a high speed color film to let others see what you have witnessed.

If you have taken samples in jars or cans, heating the container in warm water often will cause some condensation. Check this condensation for odor and then with the UVL. You may be pleasantly surprised at the results.

If you are using UVL or seriously considering using it, by all means experiment. Use scrap building materials, carpeting, and as many types of flammables as possible in a series of backyard evolutions. Make your own observations—you will then be more at ease with the UVL at the fire scene.

While using the light, you may encounter problems with false reflections. This can be controlled by placing a plain sheet of glass between the light and materials being examined. You will increase your knowledge of UVL as you continue to use the tool.

A fire scene examination of a garage apartment revealed no substantial clues as to the actual point of origin. Thermal inversion was evident. No special odors or burn patterns could be revealed due to an almost complete burn-out. While making a last-ditch attempt, it was decided to try the UVL. A strange observation was made which at this point meant very little to investigators: portions of a badly damaged gypsum board wall fluoresced orange rather than the usual pale white or blue. Mentioning this to a college professor yielded an unexpected reward—the fluorescent properties of materials are often changed when subjected to heat, which acts as an activator. In this particular case, this indicated the point of origin near a recently installed air conditioning unit, resulting in the insurance company initiating subrogation against a heating and air conditioning contractor.

There will be scenes where the UVL will be of little or no use to you at all. This is true of most equipment we use.

If it is a fear of the unknown or worry about high-priced equipment that keeps you from trying UVL, stop—the UVL need not be a complicated, elaborate, expensive system.

Basically, you need three things: (1) a source of desired wavelength—the lamp itself (if a tight budget prevents you from buying a dual lamp unit, go with the standard black light, which is a shortwave unit), (2) a source of power—batteries or AC cord, and (3) a suitable carrying case for field use. You can buy a suitable kit from $40 to $250. The smaller kits are not specialty items and can usually be found in local police supply outlets. . . .

Your success with the UVL will depend on your willingness to learn, your natural curiosity, and a desire to conduct a thorough fire scene investigation. (C. M. Lane, "Ultraviolet Light—Gem or Junk?" *Fire and Arson Investigator,* 26 (October–December 1975), 40–42. Reprinted by permission.)

8 Electrical Fires

Since electricity and electrical systems are a principal cause of fires, it is necessary to devote special attention to the general principles of electricity, electrical systems, protective systems, and types of wiring and to examination of the electrical circuitry to establish or eliminate electricity as the cause of fires.

The discovery and development of electricity have actually decreased fire dangers in our modern society by eliminating the candles and oil lamps that were forerunners of our present lighting system. However, this increase in fire safety is contingent on the proper use and installation of electrical systems.

The Panel Board

In the United States the average single-family dwelling is supplied by sixty-cycle alternating current for distribution throughout the building. Initially, the voltages from power stations are transmitted through wires to substations and then to additional wires for distribution to stepdown transformers that are usually located on utility poles.

The power entering a building may be 110 volts or 220 volts. The service connection may be 60, 110, 150, or 200 ampere service, depending upon the requirements of the structure. The usual breakdown for a single-family residential building is 110 volts to 120 volts for appliances, lights, television receivers, etc. 220 or 240 volts may be required for use with heavy appliances, such as window air conditioning units, central air conditioning units, electrical stoves, etc. The breakdown for these units is done at the panel or distribution board.

Our investigation into the electrical system starts at the panel board, where the utility company may locate a meter along with the fuse boxes and circuit breakers. In many new homes and structures, meters are located on the outside of the building or in the basement facing a small window so that the meter can be read from outside. The meter should be checked for the type of service, such as 110 volts or 220 volts, information which can be found on the nomenclature tag. The serial number should be recorded along with power consumed, which is taken from recording dials. After this information is obtained, it is then advisable to examine the panel board and check for related information on the circuit distribution.

Fuses and Fuse Boxes

It is recommended, and in most areas required, that all main circuits leading into a building have a main disconnect, which will include the rated fuse for the service assigned to that structure. A building designed for 100 ampere service will have fuses rated at that value. A line will be distributed from the main disconnect to a second box which will contain fuses of 15 to 20 amperes for the secondary circuits, which supply lights, small appliances, lamps, wall sockets, etc. Any appliances requiring 220 volts will be in a special box with a higher rated fuse—for example, 40 amps for a window air conditioner.

If fuses failed to function properly, what may have caused the failure? If the face of the fuse is black and appears burned, there has been a full or "dead" short in the circuit. However, if the metallic tab or fuse band is only burned through and there is no darkening of the fuse, there has been an overload or partial short in that circuit. The older type of fuse has an indicating window made of isinglass, which reacts faster than the newer heavily constructed glass face fuse. A fuse of either construction rated at 15 amperes will open at approximately 12 to 13 amps; however, the heavier glass face fuse will absorb more heat and take longer to react than the isinglass type. As fuses operate on the principle of heat, it is necessary to establish the type of fuse used to determine the heat applied.

Fuse boxes should be inspected also to determine whether or not the fuses are of the correct value. If there is a fuse larger than 20 amps in the secondary circuit, it may be the cause of an electrical fault. If a penny or other foreign object is found behind the fuse, we can be reasonably sure that the structure has been experiencing overload problems. Along these same lines, the ground strip of the fuse may be cut, placed on the center point of contact on the fuse, and then placed in the holder to complete the circuit. When conditions such as these are noted, one must wonder whether the occupants were unaware of the danger in this type of fusing or whether they were deliberately trying to cause a fire.

Finally, before leaving the fuse panel, connections should be checked for tightness. Have they been recently loosened? Fresh screwdriver marks on the screw top will indicate this. Is there proper grounding of the return line? Is the conduit corroded around the connecting boxes? Has the panel board distribution section been located so as not to touch a wet wall?

Circuit Breakers

Circuit breakers have come into their own in the last fifteen years. The theory is that with this protective device installed, it is not possible to cause a fire or an electrical problem by overfusing a circuit. The circuitry supplying the circuit breaker is the same as for fuse boxes, and, like fuses, they are U.L. approved and authorized under the National Electrical Code #70.

A circuit breaker operates on the principle of heat; it is a form of thermal device. A 15 amp circuit breaker is designed to break or open the circuit at approximately 12 amps to provide adequate circuit protection. Occasionally, time lag is increased in these devices and the rating of the unit is affected.

The exact location of the breaker and the type of atmosphere or location in which it is installed should be noted. A unit located in a damp area or a moisture-laden atmosphere may be affected in its overall operation by corrosion or moisture on the contacts. All electrical circuits must make a positive contact for proper and effective operation. Look for indications of corrosion, loose connections, or foreign objects in the unit that may impede the operation. A routine investigation into one electrically caused fire revealed that the fire originated from an overload and that the protective circuit breaker on the 15 ampere circuit failed to operate. Further investigation revealed that this breaker had been presenting a problem to the owner of the building which he "solved" by jamming a piece of wood from the base of the circuit breaker control box to the base of the loose breaker. The breaker was not in a tight position to make a positive contact; hence it was not technically operating on a 15 ampere basis, and the overload that occurred exceeded the 15 ampere rating, causing the fire.

It was mentioned earlier that circuit breakers operate on the principle of heat—it takes a certain buildup of heat to effectively operate the devices. During the investigation of a suspected electrical fire involving circuit breakers, the location of the unit should be noted. A circuit breaker placed on the outside wall of a building which is exposed to cold weather may be expected to experience a time delay in operating due to the increased time needed for heat buildup sufficient to activate the unit. It is conceivable that in this increased time a fire could be ignited from heat in the defective circuit if it is located near any combustible materials. A recent investigation concerned a fire involving a throw rug and a chair in the recreation room of a dwelling. The fire was reported at 4:00 A.M., when the family was awakened by the crackling of fire and the smell of smoke. It was quickly confined, controlled, and extinguished. Subsequent investigation revealed that the fire originated under a throw rug where a 16 gauge wire supplying a lamp was located. Constant walking on the rug caused the wires to roll back and forth, destroying their insulation and developing heat sufficient to ignite the throw rug. However, the breaker protecting this circuit supplying the lamp and cord never tripped. Two possibilities were theorized: one, that not enough current was drawn through this circuit to activate the protective device; or, two, that the unit's location in the garage on the cold outside wall delayed its activation.

Before leaving the panel board and distribution area where circuit breakers are employed, the name and model number of the unit should be recorded and a diagram of the circuits from the panel box identification chart should be recorded for the report. This diagram is usually found on the door of the circuit breaker box.

Wiring in the Fire Building

During the course of an investigation wiring may be located that is believed to be either the cause of or a contributing factor to a fire. If an electrical fault is pointed to in a court of law as the cause of the fire, that conclusion must be defended with evidence.

Any electrical investigation will reveal various sizes of wire, types of insulation, and conduits. It is important to understand what wire size (gauge) means and how wire should be distributed in a building. Specifically, size 18 gauge wire is designed to handle 5 amperes; size 16, 7 amperes; size 14, 15 amperes; size 12, 20 amperes; size 10, 30 amperes; and size 8, 45 amperes. If this terminology is understood and the distribution of the circuits has been identified, many hours of work can be eliminated in the inspection of the fire scene.

The outer jacket of the wire, or insulation, can be used as a guide in making a determination of the wire size and number of conductors in the cable. On Romex cable, this information is stamped on the outer jacket for identification. A piece of Romex wiring with the identification 12/2 indicates that the conductors are 12 gauge and can therefore handle 20 amperes of current and that there are two conductors in the jacket. In the case of armored cable (BX), this information is obtained by observing the number of wires in the BX and noting on the insulation of the wire the actual gauge. Experience will enable the investigator to determine wire size by observation.

In our investigation we trace the wire from the fuse or circuit breaker panel to the various sections of the building. Is the wiring in the structure done in accordance with the diagram on the panel door? Is the correct size of wire used for the various appliances in the structure? During this investigation of wire size and circuitry determination some difficulty may be experienced in establishing the locations of certain distribution lines and sizes. If possible, check a remaining unburned section of the building and use this as a guideline in establishing the wiring pattern.

Overload or Short Circuit

An overload will occur when a circuit is required to deliver more current than it was designed to handle. In a typical case, a group of appliances are united into one receptacle with a 14 gauge wire designed for 15 amperes, the total wattage on the line exceeds 15 amps, and the fuse holder or circuit breaker is 20 amps. Heating in this circuit may be sufficient to ignite any available combustible materials prior to blowing the fuse or opening the circuit breaker.

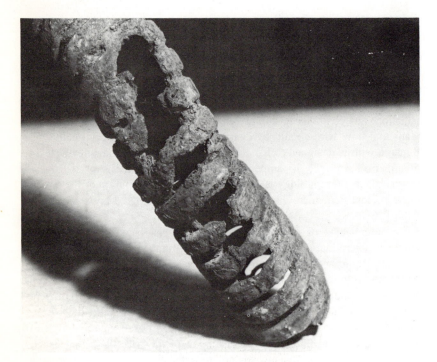

FIGURE 8-1. This 12/2 armored (BX) cable was removed from an electric stove that was mounted on built-in cabinets. The point of origin of the fire was under the cabinet supporting the stove. The cause of the fire was ignition of combustible materials in the area of arcing in the cable. (Courtesy Edison, New Jersey, Fire Department)

A short circuit is the coming together of two uninsulated wires of different potentials; insulated wires may also be involved if the protection on the

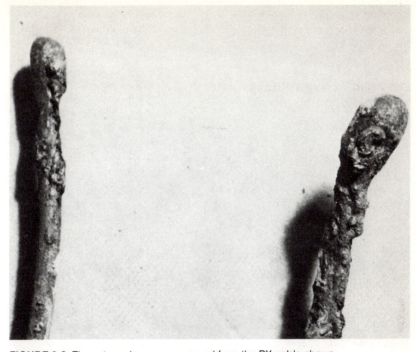

FIGURE 8-2. These two wires were removed from the BX cable shown in Figure 8-1. They were located at the point of the cable arcing. The beading of the 12/2 wire indicates a cause rather than a result of the fire. (Courtesy Edison, New Jersey, Fire Department)

wires has been damaged so as to allow a flow of current from one potential to the other. A short circuit in a suspected electrical fire may involve the shorting of one conductor against the BX or conduit through which the wire was pulled (Figures 8-1 and 8-2). A short at this point may cause arcing which produces great heat, 7000° F or more, and ignition of materials in proximity to the fault may follow (Figure 8-3). Theoretically, the protective device should react to prevent this from occurring. However, if the circuit has been designed and protected with a 100 ampere fuse at 200 volts and arcing occurs in the line at some point, ignition of combustibles may take place prior to fuse or breaker action.

When a direct short occurs in copper wiring the extreme temperature generated by the arcing will cause beading of the wires (Figure 8-2). On the other hand, copper wire will burn through at a temperature of 1900–2000°F, leaving pointed and unbeaded ends. A widely accepted theory is that internal heat burns away the insulation next to the wire, causing the remaining insulation to be loose on the wire. This is commonly referred to as ''sleeving.'' The theory has it that when exterior heat destroys the outer insulation, the inner insulation will adhere to the wire. Our own examination of wiring

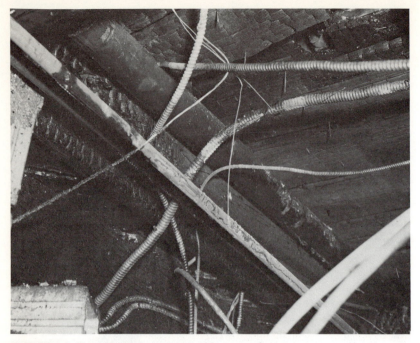

FIGURE 8-3. The 8/3 wire fushed with 100 ampere fuses was removed from a restaurant which sustained heavy fire damage. The fuses protecting the circuit did not function. This cable was located in the deeply burned center section of the building and was lowered for photographic purposes. This was the point of origin, and arcing in the cable was the cause of the fire. (Courtesy Edison, New Jersey, Fire Department)

in burned buildings over many years has shown that both sleeving and adhering occur on wire carrying no current. In summary, drawing conclusions from the appearance of insulation seems rather dangerous.

Aluminum Wire

For decades, copper was the principal metal used as an electrical conductor. As copper costs rose, the demand for aluminum increased, and today nearly half of all electrical cable used in the United States is made of aluminum. Since the mid-sixties, aluminum wiring has been used in significant amounts in single-family dwellings, mobile homes, and multi-family dwellings. The number of homes completely wired with aluminum in 15 and 20 amp circuits had reached 2 million by 1975. This estimate would have been higher if it had included homes partially wired with aluminum.

The primary hazard reported with aluminum wiring has been heat generation at the connection of aluminum conductors to terminal devices. Wall receptacles, wall switches, twist-on wire connectors, outlet boxes, junction boxes, panel boxes (fuse or circuit breaker boxes), etc., may become overheated, resulting in fire if a combustible material is nearby. Overheating at terminal connections has been associated with a number of characteristics of aluminum, including oxidation, a relatively high coefficient of thermal expansion (aluminum expands and contracts approximately 36 percent more than copper), susceptibility to corrosion, and creep (a tendency of metal to relax under stress).

Building codes for electrical wiring vary according to local regulations. Many areas, however, require approval of electrical components by a recognized product evaluation organization. Policy changes regarding the types of terminal devices considered acceptable for aluminum wiring were made between 1966 and 1974. Prior to 1966, aluminum branch circuit wire was recognized for use with any "general use wiring devices" (except for those using screwless push-in terminals). Later, between 1966 and 1971, only devices rated "AL-CU" were recognized. Effective September 1971, duplex receptacles and switches rated "AL-CU" were no longer approved. In July 1972, a new rating, "CO-ALR" (copper aluminum revised), was approved for duplex receptacles and switches. Since January 1974, devices not listed for use with aluminum wire must be provided with a precautionary notice.

In addition, during this period devices with plated steel wire binding screws (usually zinc plated) instead of brass screws were manufactured. A private testing lab later determined these to be incompatible with aluminum wire and potentially hazardous. From 1970 to 1974 specifications for aluminum wiring were revised repeatedly as manufacturers developed new aluminum alloys. Despite these efforts at regulation and the repeated revisions of specifications, some homes were left with potentially unsafe aluminum wiring.

In determining whether aluminum wiring may have been the cause of a fire, we must understand that some circuit conditions are hazardous.

1. The receptacle involved is not in use but is on a circuit in which another receptacle is being used.

2. An appliance is being used on the circuit affected. Appliances using current intermittently are particularly hazardous, as there are alternate periods of heating and cooling of the aluminum wire and wiring devices.

3. The circuit breaker may not trip. Circuit breakers are activated when too much current is going through the circuit. With the aluminum wire, resistance at a connection causes a heat buildup but does not result in excessive current flowing through the circuit.

In making a fire scene examination, keep in mind that electrical malfunction involving aluminum wire occurs with both no. 10 and no. 12 AWG wire for 15 and 20 amp branch circuits, and with the heavier gauge no. 6 and no. 8 wire usually required for larger appliances such as furnaces, ovens, and water heaters. Examples of poor workmanship and code violations may be the cause of malfunctions. These conditions compound the potential hazards surrounding aluminum wire branch circuits, but it should be noted that improper wiring generally is not a factor in the incidents.

Other receptacles in the involved structure must be examined to determine whether the CO-ALR devices previously mentioned were properly installed. Has the insulation been removed from the wires without nicking the wires? Have the wires been wrapped with adequate distance and proper direction around the terminal screws? Have the screws been tightened with the proper torque? Have the wires been positioned within the outlet box correctly to avoid loosening the terminal connections? Has pigtailing been used to improve aluminum wiring connections? Pigtailing involves connecting a short piece of insulated copper wire between the aluminum wire and the switch or receptacle connecting terminals. Although this technique may be an acceptable practice for new installations, the addition of more wires and splices into existing outlet boxes is not generally recommended.

An examination of other receptacles in the structure may reveal burned insulation on aluminum wire and charring and discoloration of receptacles. Obvious deterioration of these electrical components indicates that a defect in the receptacle causing the fire was not an isolated defective condition.

The occupants of the involved building can be a source of valuable information to the investigator. There may be a history of conditions which point to aluminum wiring as the fire cause. Inquire as to whether any of the following trouble signals have been noted:

1. flickering of lights not traceable to appliances or obvious external causes

2. an electrical component inoperative, overheated, smelling of burning, charred or melted

3. strange or distinctive odors or the smell of burning plastic in the vicinity of a receptacle or switch

4. warm switch or receptacle face plates

5. arcing at the terminal

6. smoke or fire

Summary

Investigation of electrically caused fires requires a special approach and knowledge of the subject. The investigator must be able to detect basic problems and faults that exist in the suspected circuitry. The following guidelines should be helpful.

1. Start the investigation at the panel board or distribution area of the fire building. Inspect the fuses or circuit breakers involved in the fire. Record all available information from the nomenclature tag.

2. Pay particular attention to the size of the wire and distribution method used for the branch lines. Trace down the secondary circuits to the fire area if the point of origin has been established.

3. If possible, determine the type of outlets, appliances, etc., that were supplied by the circuits in the fire area.

4. Examine all connections in the circuitry for tightness. Loose connections permit heat buildup that can ignite combustible materials in the area. This is a major cause of fires in electrical circuits.

5. Finally, if a fire involving electrical circuitry is investigated to the full extent of our knowledge without reaching a conclusion, seek assistance of a qualified outside agency to further the investigation.

(The material in this chapter was provided by H. Ray Vliet, Chief of the Edison, New Jersey, Fire Department.)

9 Rural Fires

At one time the term *rural fires* would have been used only in connection with farmhouses, barns, outbuildings, tobacco-curing barns, farm machinery, sheds, and miscellaneous storage structures. Normally, rural dwelling fires were associated with a pile of ashes, one or two standing chimneys, washtubs, bed springs, and other debris which might typify rural living conditions. The burned structure was often isolated, with no neighbors for miles around. Possibly the fire department was not called, either because no one saw the fire, or because no means of communication existed, or perhaps everyone reasoned, "Why call; it'll burn down before they can get here anyway."

This situation has changed drastically, as we now associate rural fires with fine farmhouses, modern equipment, and machinery stored in substantial buildings. The migration to the country from the city has produced expensive housing in rural surroundings, with people commuting forty to fifty miles a day to their places of employment. The development of resort properties in isolated areas and the location of industries in the "country" has necessitated a revision in our concept of rural fires.

The most significant change is in the realm of fire protection, because residents in outlying areas remote from any paid fire department have organized, equipped, and trained their own volunteer fire departments. Not only are volunteer departments more numerous, but improved communication, equipment, and fire-fighting know-how enable them to provide better protection in rural areas. Paid departments now respond to outlying areas under contract agreements, while volunteer departments under mutual aid agreements not only respond promptly, but also with mutually supporting equipment. The lack of an adequate supply of water has been corrected in part by converting old fuel tank trucks into 5,000-gallon water tankers. Additionally, many farms now provide a water supply in the form of ponds created by dams built with local, state, or federal financial assistance. Another source of water supply in suburbia is the backyard swimming pool, either portable or permanent.

As a result of this improved fire protection, fewer structures in rural areas are completely destroyed by fire than was the case several years ago. Obviously, the more of the building left standing, the more we have to investigate.

The suspicious rural fire is perhaps the most challenging of all investigations. In the following pages, we will explore some problems and suggest routine procedures and specific techniques to combat these problems. For purposes of this coverage, we will confine our discussion to three types of fires: (1) revenge or spite fires, (2) fires in a series, and (3) insurance or fraud fires.

Revenge or Spite Fires

Fires set for this motive are normally the easiest type to investigate for four reasons.

1. The property owner or occupant will cooperate by furnishing names of suspects and making accusations, unless he or she is fearful of a repeat fire set. Contrast this with the insurance fraud fire from which the owner may benefit and about which he will tell the investigator as little as possible.

2. Neighbors will furnish information. A friend has been affected by this fire, and these people will be friendly witnesses unless they fear retaliation. Again, contrast this with a fraud fire in which sympathies are with the property owner because they believe the insurance company is attempting to escape paying a just claim.

3. The fire is not planned. In the majority of revenge or spite fires, the act of incendiarism is committed in anger and in haste. As a result, the destruction is probably not great. Of course, there are exceptions where the arsonist carefully carries out a cleverly designed scheme and completely destroys a selected possession or property of the victim.

4. The suspect is probably known to the local officials. At the time the fire victim is making accusations against some person or persons, the local authorities can evaluate the likelihood that the accused is the perpetrator of this act.

Dogs for Tracking

The investigation of a suspected revenge or spite fire includes the use of a well-trained police dog, which is capable of picking up a trail and tracking under most conditions. The procedure normally followed is to take the animal out 100, 200, or 300 feet from the fire scene and make a complete circle. In this way we avoid the massive number of tracks in close proximity to the fire scene, which will only confuse the dog.

Tire Tracks

The terrain and weather conditions will dictate the possibility of finding these. If the road or lane leading up to the burned structure is dirt, there is a strong possibility tire tracks will be found, particularly if there have been recent rains. In looking for tire tracks, consider nearby locations where the fire setter might have parked a vehicle before approaching the target structure. Potential locations include adjoining lanes, lovers' parking areas, logging or fire trails, or the shoulders of hard-surfaced roads. Upon discovery of such tracks routine photographic and casting procedures should be followed.

Footprints

Again the terrain and texture of the soil in the area are critical. Since most revenge or spite fires are set under cover of darkness, the perpetrator has difficulty avoiding leaving tracks. The procedure for searching out footprints is the same as that used with dogs, circling the fire scene out away from the fire itself. In searching for footprints, look particularly for prints going in opposite directions on the same general path. The incendiarist approaching the scene of the fire-setting attempt proceeds cautiously and deliberately to avoid detection. Immediately after he lights the fire and the flame flares up, his only thought is to escape. What more logical route of escape than the same path he used coming in, since he is familiar with this? Two sets of tracks which appear to be the same and go in opposite directions—with one set indicating slow, deliberate short steps and the other indicating pell-mell flight with long strides—are very likely the coming and going tracks of the arsonist.

Search for Physical Evidence

Keep in mind that the fire may have been set by a person in a highly emotional state, who at the time was indifferent to the possibility of apprehension. Typical of this type of fire is kerosene thrown on the porch or against the side of the house. Often residue of such flammable liquid may be found in the soil alongside a structure or under a porch. Cracks in any flooring should be examined carefully for odors of flammables. The area around the fire scene should be searched thoroughly for containers of accelerants which the arsonist may have brought along and discarded in hasty flight. Book-match covers may lead to the eventual identity of the fire setter.

Discussion of Possible Suspects with the Victim

Be careful at this point to develop genuine suspects and to eliminate innocent persons whom the victim may wish to involve. We must determine the validity of any accusations leveled and weigh the probability of an individual's setting a fire to avenge the wrong which the victim cites. We must also keep in mind that what may appear as an insignificant occurrence which would not drive most people to commit a crime may be the catalyst for some individuals.

Locating the Suspect

If the information provided by the victim or other factors justify immediate action, move aggressively. Go to the home of the suspect and check for dust, dirt, leaves, or mud on clothes or shoes. See whether the suspect's clothes are torn from crossing a fence or going through woods and whether they retain traces of the odor of an accelerant or of smoke. Seek anything that may physically place the suspect at the fire scene. There are cases on record where the investigators have caught the arsonist in the act of burning his clothes because a flammable liquid splashed on him when he set the fire.

Questioning the Suspect

If the circumstances justify, interrogate the person as soon as possible, complying with all legal requirements prior to and during the period of questioning. The logical attitude in this instance would be to seem to sympathize with the individual, implying that he or she cannot be blamed. If this person is still angry and not fully aware of or concerned about the seriousness of the crime when questioned, the result may be a rather easily obtained confession.

Continuing the Investigation

If the accusations made by the victim are general and questionable and other factors indicate that no immediate action is justified, there is no option but to continue the investigation over a longer period of time. A reasonable delay will not jeopardize the success of the case under these circumstances and will give the investigator an opportunity to explore fully the accusations made and possibly develop other suspects.

Fires in a Series

Investigative procedure for such fires should also include getting a dog for tracking, looking for tire tracks, and looking for footprints. In addition, follow these procedures:

Searching for Physical Evidence

Often the person or persons responsible for a series of fires acts on the spur of the moment and uses whatever is handy to start the fires. The substance chosen may not burn readily, and a significant residue may be left to examine. Frequently, the chronic fire setter can obtain satisfaction from a small fire accompanied by much smoke. This type of fire can also leave meaningful physical evidence.

Observing the Crowd

The "firebug" will usually remain at the fire scene; after all, the purpose of setting the fire was to observe the burning, to be a part of the excitement. As was previously pointed out, fire fighters should be asked to look for individuals who appear or act unusual and for repeated appearances of the same individual at the fire scene. Investigators also have a responsibility in this area and, because the fire fighters are occupied, probably have the best opportunity to observe the crowd.

Obtaining Photographs of the Crowd

Collect not only pictures made by police or fire personnel but also any photos or films taken by the news media. These may reveal the previously unnoted presence of the same individual at several in a series of fires.

Cruising Around

In the general area of the fire, cruise around to detect individuals leaving the scene by car or on foot. If a person's actions are peculiar, pay particular attention. Any attempt to evade being observed, such as ducking off the road into the bushes, is significant.

Arranging a Conference

A meeting of all fire and police agencies should be arranged. This meeting should not consist merely of a general discussion of the fire situation; it should be a day-long or longer meeting of representatives of all agencies in the area which may have information pertinent to the investigation. Attendance should include state and local fire marshals, state police, sheriffs, constables, federal and state foresters, and key fire department personnel.

Proceedings of this conference should be made a matter of record for intensive study. As much time as is necessary must be allocated to review the following:

1. Persons turning in false alarms. Often the person in the early stages of development as a chronic or compulsive fire setter is content with false alarms and the noise and excitement of sirens and flashing lights.

2. Suspects in minor fires. Fires set in brush, trash cans, garages, small sheds, and the like may point to a firebug who has graduated from false alarms and can no longer get enough "kicks" from them. If there must actually be smoke and flame at this point, this individual is reaching the truly dangerous stage.

3. Persons discovering or reporting several fires. Most people go through their entire lives without discovering or reporting a single fire. Is it not then a phenomenal coincidence when one individual discovers and reports four, five, or six fires in a relatively short period of time? What prompts someone to set a fire and then report it? Often the motive is the desire to be recognized and accepted, to gain the appreciation of the fire fighters and public. The arsonist seeking hero status may want to fight the fire and draw the "ohs" and "ahs" of the crowd as he braves the searing flame and blistering heat with complete disregard for his own life and safety. The crowning achievement is to be carried nearly unconscious from the fire by rescuers, treated and revived in front of a large crowd of worshippers, and then to fight off those who would restrain him from returning to fight the evil archenemy, fire.

4. Familiar faces at fires, past, present, and future. The importance of this must be emphasized with the conferees, particularly as it relates to fires which may occur in the future.

5. "Take charge" individuals at fires.

6. Fire records. Reviewing such records is critical to the success of the conference and requires active participation and full cooperation from everyone. Using a map of the area, every false alarm, every fire, no matter how small, is identified by number and pinpointed as to location. As each incident is identified, anyone having any pertinent knowledge should make this known. Information compiled concerning each incident should include, but not necessarily be limited to, the

type of property involved, discoverer and reporter, weather conditions, time of day, day of week and month, and modus operandi.

The purpose of this exchange of information is to establish a pattern for these fires, some connecting link between the incidents. Could there be some common ownership of property, an individual or corporation against which the fire setter has a grudge? Can the fires be linked to a time when school is just letting out or to an area where a school bus has just discharged a load of students? Are fires set only during the day or early evening, thus indicating a juvenile fire setter? Have the incidents occurred on weekends during the school year, thus pointing to a school-age arsonist?

Perhaps a word of caution is in order. On occasion a definite pattern seems to be developing when suddenly fires occur in another location, at different times of the day, days of the week and month, to entirely different types of property with a new modus operandi. This development does not necessarily mean that the original procedure was faulty or the information obtained incorrect. It probably indicates the presence of one or more chronic setters in other locations. Sometimes the hysteria which envelops a community causes a borderline arsonist to become involved in the fire setting. When, as recently happened, there are three firebugs active in a city of 22,000 people, the difficulties of investigation are multiplied many times over. Additionally, there is the possibility that the fraud fire perpetrator may decide the occasion is right to go into action, under cover of the suspicion that all fires are being set by some pyromaniac. This would be the occasion when the fraud fire profiteer screams the loudest, demanding action and condemning the investigators for their incompetence.

Another investigative hint may be appropriate at this point. Let us assume evidence points to a suspect. In the course of an investigative interview this person receives just a faint impression that he is a suspect in the series of fires. To throw off suspicion, this individual may set fire to his own property. The burning may be minor in nature, and the property involved may be relatively valueless. The suspect reasons that surely no one would suspect him of setting his own property on fire.

Conducting Surveillance or Stakeout

Having developed an apparent pattern, the investigator can keep certain areas of operation of the fire setter under observation at the time the fires have been occurring and ascertain what activities take place in this locality. Is the neighborhood deserted, with few vehicles, no pedestrians, and therefore few witnesses or suspects? Is the area bustling with possible witnesses and suspects? This observation may reveal potential witnesses who routinely are in the area at this time, such as the milkman, paper boy, people coming and going on shift work or other odd hour jobs, and trash collectors. Most important, this investigative procedure may reveal the fire setter himself, coming home from work, leaving a tavern, or just wandering in the neighborhood looking for something to burn.

Checking the Area

During a series of fires, the investigator should make every effort to keep up with changes in the neighborhood, new people moving in and the like, by cruising the area several times a day, closely observing any unusual events. This may deter the firesetter, and it is good public relations, showing the citizens official concern about the pyromaniac.

Obtaining Names of Releases from State Mental and Correctional Institutions

In a few states the law requires that investigative agencies in every locality be advised of the release of an individual from a mental institution or correctional system unit who was committed for setting fires. While all states may not have such laws, a working agreement may be established which will benefit all concerned. The records of an individual committed to a mental hospital for treatment or observation may not arrive until several days later. If local authorities advise the hospital administration at the time of admission that an individual is a dangerous fire setter, it would be appropriate to expect and ask for notification of the subject's release. Thus a mutually beneficial exchange of information can be informally arranged.

Asking Questions

After a long series of fires and a prolonged, intensive investigation, someone often tells an investigator, "I could have told you all the time who was setting these fires, but nobody asked me." While in most cases this is pure bologna, we must realize that the average citizen does not come forward to furnish information or evidence. Even the promise of financial gain seldom produces results. Several years ago a leading newspaper in a city of half a million launched, with good intentions and great fanfare, a project designed to assist law enforcement officers solve crimes. Simply by calling a telephone number and providing information in connection with a crime, the caller would receive a rather substantial reward if an arrest and conviction followed. Through an elaborate system the anonymity of the secret witness was guaranteed, and the reward money reached the informant by a very circuitous route. The results of this effort were negligible, and the project collapsed after less than a year of operation. Even when questioned face to face by a skilled investigator, the average citizen is reluctant to provide significant information. Nevertheless, people must be interviewed during a series of fires, for one cannot anticipate walk-in witnesses.

Obtaining Information on Sex Deviates

Keeping in mind the distinct possibility that the fire setter may be motivated by strong, abnormal sex drives, the investigator can develop suspects from reported incidents of peeping toms, indecent exposure, and other acts indicative of sexual deviation.

The investigator must be resigned to continue searching until the fire setter is apprehended. He will not "wear out," for it is much easier to start fires than to investigate them. Unfortunately, the reward for apprehending the culprit is often negligible: "It's about time they caught somebody, now that the community is about burned down. I could have told them all the time who was setting these fires."

Insurance or Fraud Fires

The rural fraud fire is probably the most difficult to investigate for three reasons. First, the act is committed at the convenience of the owner. Unlike the revenge or compulsive fire setter, the fraud fire perpetrator can select the exact moment when chances of detection are least and chances of a successful fire are greatest. He can make detailed preparations with elaborate incendiary devices, streamers, accelerants, and the like. Members of the family can be sent to visit friends or relatives. The fire can be set during a thunderstorm so lightning seems to be a logical cause, or when the roads are covered with ice and snow so as to prevent or delay response by the fire department and increase the chances of a complete and "successful" fire.

Second, destruction in a rural fraud fire is likely to be complete. Various factors contribute to this, including delay in reporting the fire and the distance from the fire station to the scene. A fire which has been burning fifteen to twenty minutes prior to arrival of fire fighting equipment in most cases has totally involved a structure. Many times the fire department can only direct their efforts to protecting other buildings and exposures.

Third, the start of investigation is often delayed. Investigative agencies may not be able to respond to a request for investigation for days or possibly weeks on account of insufficient manpower and excessive case loads. Normally, investigations are initiated in rotation unless fatalities or other unusual circumstances dictate otherwise. Another factor which may cause delay is that the fire may appear to local fire and police officials to be a legitimate accidental fire. It is not until the insurance adjustor arrives on the scene and discovers excessive insurance coverage or two or more policies on the same property and contents that the origin and cause become questionable. The adjustment may not be initiated for several days after the fire occurred, so there may be an unavoidable delay in the investigation.

Immediate Investigative Procedure

Some investigative steps can be taken immediately at the fire scene at the time of the fire and subsequent to its extinguishment by a person with some training in arson investigation, whether it be a sheriff, constable, local fire marshal, or investigator within the fire department structure.

Interviewing the Person Reporting and Discovering the Fire   If it is not practical to do this during the fire, at least obtain a name and address of this potentially valuable witness for a future interview.

Observing Dress of the Owner or Occupant   It is probable that the local investigator will have a greater opportunity to make observations of the owner or occupant's dress than the fire fighters, who are principally involved with preventing loss of life and property. Refer to Chapter 3 for a fuller discussion of this matter.

Noticing Items Removed from the Structure

Talking to the Fire Department Officer in Charge   Discover the means of fire department entry; color of smoke and flame; unusual reaction of the fire to water; presence of streamers, odors, or other indications of an accelerant; absence of clothing, furniture, and personal effects; and any other observations pertinent to the investigation.

Examining Outbuildings for Furniture, Clothing, and Personal Effects   It is possible that prior to the fire items were packaged and removed to a safe location for concealment. In addition to proving obvious preparation for the fire, the appearance of these items on the insurance claim later may establish fraud.

Preserving Any Physical Evidence   Just what form physical evidence may take is difficult to predict, but look particularly for accelerants and containers of accelerants. Cans of gasoline, kerosene, and motor oil are around most properties, but it is the location of such containers that is significant. Why would such items be in the kitchen or dining room, or in any room in the house, for that matter?

Taking Pictures   Pictures taken as the fire develops may prove quite useful later in studying the spread of the fire. Photographs of the exterior, showing location of furniture, personal effects, clothing, the family auto, and farm trucks and equipment may provide the investigator with questions to which the insured may have interesting answers.

Interviewing the Occupant or Owner   The tone of this conversation should reflect no suspicion that the origin and cause of the fire is questionable; the tone should reflect an attitude of concern over the tragic loss (which it may actually be) suffered by the family. At this point, the head of the household may not have prepared any story of what allegedly took place. Listen closely and at the first opportunity make notes on what is said about who first noticed the fire, where it was located, and how occupants escaped from the burning structure. Probably he or she will have at least two additional opportunities to repeat this, once to the insurance adjustor, and once to the investigators. Note inconsistencies in the retelling of the tale.

Continuous Investigative Procedure

Assume that all investigative activity immediately possible takes place before pursuing the investigation. Time must be allowed for several developments. First, in some states and jurisdictions, the investigator must allow time for the insured to file his insurance claim in connection with the fire. The investigator must determine not only state laws on this matter, but also the policy of the prosecutor having jurisdiction. Some insurance adjustors state that if they accept a proof of loss as a representative for the company, they are obligating the company to pay the assured a mutually agreed upon sum for his loss. The legal and technical requirements connected with filing a claim and submitting a proof of loss must be clearly understood by the investigator, or the chance of conviction may be jeopardized because of some legal technicality.

Second, cooperative contact with the insurance adjustor must be established. After all, who knows more about the property values and insurance, including overinsurance, than the adjustor? In addition, the adjustor can obtain information from many sources without arousing suspicion and putting the assured on guard.

Requesting Information from the Insurance Adjustor   Request the following from the insurance adjustor:

1. General description of property. Find out approximate age and general condition, dimensions, number of floors, number of rooms, types of rooms, exterior and roof material, heating and electric system, and any other information which may be of assistance. Comments concerning the surrounding property and its value should be included.

2. All financial, mortgage, and insurance information. Find out the purchase price of property, interest rate, monthly payments, and

whether payments have been paid promptly. The adjustor can assist greatly by obtaining copies of deeds, payment records, and mortgages. Careful scrutiny of these documents may reveal a strong motive.

3. Any previous fire record of owner, occupant, or families of either. This information can be difficult to obtain because there is no central source from which this information can be sought. Efforts to correct this deficiency are presently being made on a national level.

4. Circumstances of loss. There should be a narrative version of the story of the fire, including results of interviews with appropriate individuals, such as fire department personnel. All information pertinent to the loss and of any potential value to the investigator should be included.

5. Statement of owner or occupant. There should be a detailed statement including (1) movements and actions of the assured owner or occupant for several hours prior to the fire; (2) circumstances surrounding the owner's or occupant's discovery or notification of the fire; (3) actions subsequent to (2) above; (4) some version of the owner's or occupant's financial status relative to loss of or reduction in income, sickness, indebtedness, garnishments, collection pressures, and similar information.

6. List of items allegedly lost in the fire. A list of lost items should include furniture, clothing, and personal effects. The adjustors should ask when this list was prepared. An inventory completed a short time before the fire points to anticipation and preparation.

7. Sketch showing major items destroyed. This diagram, not necessarily to scale, should consist of the general plans of all floors of the structure involved and the location of major pieces of furniture and appliances. Included also are articles of unusual value, such as silver, coins, and items of sentimental value, such as wedding pictures and the family Bible.

8. Present whereabouts of any physical evidence. Occasionally an adjustor will gain possession of some physical evidence which he considers significant. If no procedure for storage and custody is established the evidence may be inadmissible. As a basic rule, evidence must be kept in a locked, secure storage facility to which only the adjustor has access. Information concerning any physical evidence should be provided to the investigator.

9. Statement of basis for request for investigation. There should be a brief summary of the circumstances connected with the loss which justify an investigation. A list of factual information justifying the investigation might serve the same purpose. Items such as two separate

insurance policies far exceeding the value of property, gross overinsurance, financial condition of the assured, circumstances of the loss, or physical evidence of an incendiary fire should be included.

Making a Neighborhood Check   There are several neighborhood check techniques with which the investigator should be familiar. Since the majority of people who live in the area around the fire scene may know the assured, it is probable that they are sympathetic toward him or her; at least they are more in sympathy with the assured than the investigators. For this reason an approach to the neighbors must not indicate suspicion that the assured may be responsible for the fire but only the desire to determine what caused the fire so that this will not happen again to other homes or properties.

After reassuring the potential witnesses that the interview is in the public interest, the investigator can employ the simple technique of stating that before examining the ruins, he would like to have some idea how the rooms were arranged in the house or structure and where furniture and other items were in each room. Oftentimes a male witness cannot give this information, but the average female has a remarkable facility for remembering details after only one trip through a house: room arrangement, furniture location, wallpaper, upholstery patterns, curtains, appliances and their locations. The investigator may attempt a sketch of the floor plan and room arrangement of the dwelling, deliberately making mistakes and exaggerating the problem, and then put a pen or pencil and pad in the neighbor's hand and say, "I'm making a real mess out of this. Could you make this diagram for me?" Usually no further persuasion is necessary and soon she is hard at work, many times with other members of the family assisting. The end result may be crude, but often it will be remarkably accurate as to floor plan, room arrangement, and furniture and appliance location. The investigator may get unexpected bonuses as the group works together on the sketch. As the deep freeze is pinpointed in the kitchen, one of the family may say, "Oh, no, they didn't have that any more because the finance man came and got it." Or, "They took the television over to her sister's house just last week." These are gems of information, showing potential motive and preparation.

There should be close cooperation between investigators representing agencies with varying interests. Sometimes a team of investigators will consist of one local official and one from outside the area. The local official with knowledge of individuals in the community should share this information and comment on the reliability of witnesses before the investigators contact them. When coming face to face with a witness for the first time, it is demoralizing when the local officer says, "Sally, this is Mr. Jones, an investigator for the state, who wants to ask you some questions about the Dinkam fire," and then he turns and walks away, leaving the investigator in the presence of an individual about whom he knows absolutely nothing. It is possible that she is a hostile witness, friendly to or even related to the assured. A cooperative official should convey any knowledge of a witness's reputation for truth and veracity, relationship to the assured, and any previous experience with her, favorable or unfavorable, as a source of information.

Conducting the Fire Scene Examination   Armed with sketches or diagrams of the burned structure, one prepared by the assured and at least one provided by a neighbor, the investigator is not completely unprepared. The insurance adjustor has provided a list of items alleged by the assured to have been lost in the fire, so the investigator can now search with a definite purpose, to ascertain whether these items actually were destroyed. Nobody will be convicted of arson for filing a false claim; however, in a number of states knowingly filing a false and fraudulent claim is punishable.

The real purposes of the thorough search are to determine the origin and cause of the fire and to prepare for the interrogation by establishing that claimed items were not lost. The assured may say, "Why should I want to burn my house? I lost everything I had." The investigator can reply, "Tell me what you lost." When he rattles off two televisions, a stereo, a deep freeze, two refrigerators, a complete living room suite, 120 silver knives, forks, and spoons, 22 suits, and 18 pairs of shoes the investigator can look him squarely in the eye, say, "John, you didn't lose those things in the fire," and point out where the television was supposed to be but wasn't, because he has dug through this debris, sifted every pile of ashes, and can tell exactly what was burned and what wasn't. However, without an inventory, without sketches and diagrams, such an approach is impossible; the investigator who must guess at destroyed contents will fail to bring about a confession, for the assured will see the bluff.

Contacting Sources of Financial Information   There may be occasions when information from the insurance adjustor is incomplete, sketchy, or of questionable accuracy. Probably the most reliable indication of an individual's financial status is his bank account. Examine this with care, noting a diminishing balance, bad checks, "kiting" checks, and any other indicators of financial problems. Promptness in payment of loans, past and present, should be determined. Attempts to obtain additional loans should be discussed with bank officials. Credit reports from various credit agencies provide information which is not always completely accurate; credit investigations are sometimes made hastily and result in a report which is superficial and at best serves the investigator only as a guide to other sources of financial information. Reports concerning businesses may be several years old when a fire occurs, so their significance is questionable. All financial records may have been destroyed in the fire. In spite of these limitations, do not overlook such reports as a source of financial information concerning individuals and businesses. Depending upon whether the property involved is being purchased or rented by the assured, contact either the landlord or mortgagor. If rented, question the landlord concerning timely payments of rent, requests for extensions in rent payment, and any inquiries by the assured regarding the lease, particularly relative to its termination. If the assured is purchasing the burned property, were the monthly payments on time? Had any effort been made to cancel the mortgage? Had there been communication regarding refinancing purchase of the property? It is possible that either a landlord or mortgagor had frequent opportunity to contact the assured and observe firsthand any financial problems.

The purpose of contacting a real estate agent is to establish whether the assured had made efforts to sell the property prior to the fire. If so, what was the asking price and was this within reason? Had the assured paid too much for this property? Had property values in the neighborhood decreased appreciably? Why did the assured wish to dispose of this property? What plans did he or she have for the future? Had the real estate agent been requested to locate property for the assured in another location, less expensive perhaps?

Examining Court Records   Seek information concerning judgments, garnishment proceedings, delinquent taxes, law suits, liens, or claims pending which involve the assured. If these exist they are potential indicators of financial problems and represent motive on the part of the property owner.

Contacting Reliable Sources of Information   Community leaders can usually be counted on to cooperate with the local authorities. The "outside" investigator may do well to let the local officials contact such individuals initially, as they may be reluctant to discuss the case otherwise.

Assembling All Information   At the point in the investigation when the investigator has done everything possible short of interrogating the suspect, he should gather all notes, statements, photographs, documents, and other pertinent information. When several investigators are involved, as is normally the case, review all the evidence together to determine whether further action will be productive. If there are areas which need further exploration or information from various sources which is inconsistent or contradictory, resolve these matters.

Contact the Prosecuting Attorney   Contacting the prosecutor may be appropriate to review the facts of the case and seek guidance prior to interrogating the suspect. The prosecutor may express the opinion that sufficient basis exists only for a general interview with the suspect or advise that no interrogation is necessary and that a warrant for the suspect's arrest should be obtained and executed. Often the investigators must know whether the prosecutor will approve arresting the suspect if arrest is required to take the person into custody. The investigators may face a suspect who says, "If you've got a warrant, arrest me. If you don't, I've got nothing to say to you. Get off my property." Whether they leave or make an arrest will be determined in many cases by the recommendation of the prosecuting attorney.

Planning and Conducting the Interrogation   We will discuss interrogation elsewhere in the text, but it is important to note that the investigator must *plan* the interrogation prior to picking up the suspect. Without this preplanning, the interrogators will be hesitant and unsure of himself or herself, a condition which the person being questioned will immediately observe and which will increase his confidence in his ability to withstand any questioning.

Writing a Complete, Comprehensive Report   Regardless of the outcome of the interrogation and investigation, the officers must complete the sometimes distasteful assignment of writing the report without delay. Additional information may be developed later which enables the prosecution to reopen the case and bring charges. A sketchy, poorly prepared report will prove a severe handicap in such an event.

Goals of the Investigation

It would be less than honest not to admit that the majority of investigations of rural fires will not result in apprehension, arrest, and conviction. Nonetheless, the investigator must not be discouraged from pursuing the following objectives, whatever the degree of success.

Criminal Prosecution

Since they are charged with enforcing the law, the principal goal of investigators will be to bring criminal charges against any perpetrator of the crime of arson.

Deterrent Effect

The great majority of those who violate traffic laws are not apprehended, but think of the slaughter on our highways and streets if there were no efforts to apprehend such offenders. It is a recognized fact that when a thorough, well-planned, complete investigation is made of every suspicious fire in any community, the number of such fires diminishes in frequency. Every individual who contemplates setting a fire, regardless of the motive, must face the stark realization that there will be an intensive investigation. This realization may well be the one factor which will cause would-be arsonists to have second thoughts about carrying out their plans.

Removing the Profit

This objective in fraud fires can be accomplished in several ways. In an unusual case the assured may become alarmed when he realizes the intensity of the investigation and withdraws his claim against the insurance company completely. Second, when the assured becomes aware of the investigation in depth, he knows that any attempt on his part to collect on nonexistent items or a padded claim will be detected, and, as a result, he files a realistic claim rather than the exorbitant one originally contemplated. Third, a thorough investigation may develop sufficient evidence to enable the insurance company to deny liability. In criminal action the guilt of the defendant must be established beyond a reasonable doubt, whereas in civil action there need only be a preponderance of evidence weighing in favor of the defendant, in this instance the insurance carrier.

In summary, regardless of our motivation, as officers charged with the responsibility of enforcing the laws of appropriate jurisdictions, we must accept the challenge of investigating suspicious rural fires and perform our duties to the very best of our ability.

10 Urban Fires

Fires in metropolitan areas of all sizes follow certain patterns. Let us take a look at a typical urban fire, the circumstances surrounding it, and subsequent actions by the investigators.

Ideally, the fire is detected and reported in its early stages, and the fire department responds promptly. The skillful efforts of the professional fire department prevent total destruction. Well-trained fire fighters, alert for indications of arson, are careful not to destroy any evidence; the salvage company protects the contents and evidence. The scene is secured and a guard is instructed to permit no one to enter the area.

A well-trained, efficient arson squad responds with the fire department and observes the entire scene, taking still photos and movies of the fire and the crowd. Potential witnesses are interviewed at the scene, using tape recorders to assure complete accuracy. Members of the fire department are questioned concerning their observations on the fire. As soon as practical, the fire scene is entered and, with the assistance of first arriving company personnel, origin and cause are established. Physical evidence is gathered, with mobile lab equipment assisting in the effort.

As a follow-up, the scene is searched in more detail, with extensive photography. The intelligence file on this neighborhood is reviewed, with particular emphasis on the history of fires in the area. Background information is developed on the property owner or occupant, and insurance information is obtained through the cooperation of the insurance agent and adjustor. If there have been previous fires in the area, suspects in these cases are studied and their whereabouts are determined. If circumstances seem to indicate a revenge or spite fire, the victim is questioned on any problems with groups or individuals.

Members of the arson squad expand the investigation by conducting a thorough neighborhood check and contacting informants. The modus operandi of the fire setter is circulated to other investigative agencies with similar interests. If insurance fraud is a possible motive, extensive background work begins into the personal and financial history of the assured. The real estate agent handling the property, the lessor, banks, suppliers, competitors, and court records are examined in the event the fire involves a mercantile establishment.

A city work crew or fire department personnel under the supervision of arson squad members go to work cleaning up the debris, searching for point of origin and cause of the fire if this has not yet been determined. At all times squad members are on the alert for physical evidence of a set fire. An inventory of contents is carefully maintained, and contents are examined with an eye to locating obsolete or replaced merchandise as well as empty boxes or shelves.

At the conclusion of an uninterrupted investigation of several days or more, all pertinent information is assembled and correlated, the suspect is successfully interrogated, and an admissible confession is obtained. The arson squad member submits a detailed report to the prosecuting attorney and testifies with competence as an expert witness at the trial so that a conviction of the accused results.

We have described an arson investigation in urban areas conducted under ideal conditions. Let us examine now some of the obstacles which make this ideal investigation a rarity.

Personnel Problems

There can be no argument with the fact that the number of arson fires has increased dramatically in the past decade. Incendiary fires in urban areas account for a big percentage of this increase. One major East Coast city reports an 83% increase of arson from 1972 to 1975. Suspicious fires in that city increased by a whopping 104%, with a 35% increase in fires of undetermined origin; property loss in the last year of record exceeded one million dollars. In another major city almost ten million dollars was paid out in one year by insurance companies for fire losses in one small area of the city! In spite of such dramatic figures, increases in personnel assigned the responsibility for arson investigation are unusual. When the city government looks for an area in which to reduce manpower, the investigative agency often becomes the target.

It is apparent that most governing bodies fail completely to realize the immensity of the incendiary fire problem. The long-range effect on the community and the necessary increase in insurance rates don't seem to register. The city cited above which suffered the ten-million-dollar loss in one area had an increase in insurance rates of 35% in two years. While city officials cannot be expected to appreciate and understand the intricacies of fire investigation, the facts should at least convey the message that additional manpower is a high-priority need.

The ideal investigation at the start of this chapter made repeated reference to members of an arson squad, who are involved in many activities which must be conducted simultaneously, such as taking photographs and movies, observing the fire and crowd, and interviewing witnesses. Many follow-up activities are conducted concurrently, including fire scene search, further interviewing, record search, and other necessary investigative procedures.

These tasks cannot be accomplished by a handful of people, however dedicated they may be. Nor can effective arson investigations be conducted by part-time personnel who have other duties and responsibilities. An arson squad which exists on paper only, as names on an organizational chart, is an ineffective unit.

In summary, governing bodies must accept the fact that incendiary fires are a major problem in their community, that the incidence of arson fires is not diminishing, but is increasing at an alarming rate. If this problem is to be dealt with directly and realistically, a significant first step would be to assure that adequate personnel are assigned full time to investigate fully and completely all suspicious fires. An effective arson squad must be on twenty-four-hour call, with a supervisor and investigators available at all times.

Qualified Personnel   There is a tendency in some jurisdictions to load any fire prevention and investigation body with persons who cannot perform other duties. Fire department personnel who, because of physical disabilities, can no longer function as fire fighters or line officers are designated as inspectors, presumably because these duties are less physically demanding. But effective investigation of fires is not for the lame or lazy. Whether the arson squad consists of fire or police personnel, they must be individuals of the highest caliber, physically, mentally, and morally. The arson squad must be considered an elite organization, a prestige unit which commands respect from every quarter. This can only be attained if the rank or grade of squad members and salary for that rank attract qualified people.

Authority

"The Chief of the Fire Prevention Bureau of the Bureau of Fire is vested with the responsibility of investigating the cause, origin, and circumstances of all fires of questionable origin." So reads the code of many cities. However, one important accompaniment to this responsibility is often lacking—authority. Personnel in the Fire Prevention Bureau, acting under the provisions of the code, are held responsible for investigating what may be a major crime without police power. Under these circumstances, the inspector completes his interviews of fire department members, makes his fire scene examination, determines that the fire was not of accidental origin, and then calls in a police detective. The inspector will then go over the fire scene, pointing out all the facts concerning the fire, and give the detective all the information which has been obtained from the fire department personnel and other witnesses.

This procedure has certain built-in disadvantages. First, the detective thrust into the middle of the investigation does not have the opportunity to interview all witnesses, to evaluate their credibility, to ask his own questions. Second, the inspector works under a considerable handicap. What would happen if the subject of an interview told the inspector that he burned the building and wanted to confess? We assume he would be told, "Wait here, I'll be right back. I'm going to get a policeman."

Defenders of this system counter that inspectors have the right to make a citizen's arrest. They either do not know or do not admit that a citizen's arrest is a historical relic, that it has no force in the present age. Inspectors or investigators must not be sent out to investigate a major crime with both hands tied behind their backs. All members of the investigative unit should be granted full police powers by the jurisdiction having authority if the unit is to function effectively.

Training

Excellent instructional material and literature are available in the area of the arson investigation, and many departments have conducted intensive training for a limited number of personnel. Unfortunately, the training is not always made available to the fire fighters, who often have the best opportunity to detect indications of arson. As a result, line personnel fail to give pertinent information to an investigator because they do not realize the importance of their observations. Since fire department members in most urban areas are salaried, a requirement that all personnel attend such training courses is reasonable and feasible. Even in those urban areas where fire protection is provided by a part paid, part volunteer department or on-call personnel, the professional competence of these people should be upgraded by this type of instruction. If fire personnel are not trained and fully involved in arson detection, the best efforts of the arson investigators may be in vain, regardless of their level of competence.

Members of an arson squad usually come from either the fire or police ranks. In either case, there is a requirement for additional training. Dozens of arson investigation seminars are conducted annually in the United States, most of which are excellent and greatly benefit the investigator who attends. However, some courses which do not have the personnel, equipment, or time to provide in-depth instruction give very broad-based instruction that is not related to specific local problems encountered by the investigator. There is little coordination between the various agencies conducting such courses, and as a result an investigator attending three such seminars in a year may hear the same instructor on the same subject three times. The National Fire Academy for the National Fire Prevention and Control Administration is in the process of developing a standard curriculum for fire investigation training which should provide not only a coordinated effort and a standardization of subject matter, but instruction at various levels. These courses will probably be offered nationwide as well as on the main campus of the National Fire Academy. Training sessions will, in all probability, vary in length from as little as 40 hours to as much as 480 hours.

While NFPCA personnel are aware of the immediate need for this training and are attacking the problem vigorously, we cannot rely entirely on this organization for instruction. Members of the arson squad must be constantly involved in an in-service program to keep informed on all the latest investigative techniques and must be provided with a thorough understanding of building construction, chemistry, law, psychology, electronics, and criminology.

A major consideration in training the arson squad is the background of its members. If the investigator's background is fire-oriented, instruction provided will differ from that of the police-oriented individual. The fire department person must receive extensive training in law enforcement procedures—laws of arrest, rules of evidence, search and seizure, judicial systems, collection and preservation of evidence, interviewing and interrogation, report writing and case preparation, courtroom demeanor, and firearms training. In addition, the fire-oriented individual must develop a change in attitude towards those he is dealing with as an investigator. He must be fully aware of the fact that he no longer is an inspector enforcing ordinances or codes, but an investigator enforcing criminal laws. Although an inspector is not always welcome in making his rounds, he is ordinarily in no physical danger, for the owner or occupant of a building is not likely to assault an inspector. A suspect in an arson case, on the other hand, may attack the investigator physically. The ex-inspector must realize that he is now dealing with the criminal element and cannot afford to be the friendly inspector in uniform, totally unarmed and defenseless. He must be alert to the dangers of physical attack. Additionally, he must accept the fact that people are going to lie to him in criminal matters. His past experience is not oriented to this philosophy; he has been exposed to a different element of society under different conditions. The school principal, nursing home operator, apartment or office building owner do not pose a threat to his safety; the criminal element he now encounters does.

Instruction provided for the investigator with a police background is quite different, for this person is already knowledgeable in all areas dealing with police procedures, though additional training in special areas such as fire investigation may be required. It is in the area of fire technology that this individual needs intensive and extensive training—chemistry of fire, fire causes, fire scene search, determining origin and cause, incendiary devices, electricity and building construction. In addition, fire-fighting activities and their effect on burn patterns, debris, and residue must be clearly understood or the police-oriented investigator will be severely handicapped.

Arson Squad Organization

The crime of arson is unique in that it involves two major public services, the fire and police department. This may create problems of two sorts. First, the fire chief may believe that arson is the responsibility of the fire department and that fire personnel should make the investigations, while the police chief considers arson a crime and believes that police personnel should make the investigations. On the other hand, the fire chief may consider arson investigation a police responsibility, while the police chief regards it as a fire department responsibility. The composition, authority, and function of the arson squad must be clearly established by the chiefs of the two departments in conjunction with the urban governing body. Whatever the structure of the arson squad may be, complete cooperation between the two services involved is essential.

Let us assume that arson investigation responsibility is assigned to the fire department. The fire chief may not realize the necessity for an effective arson squad. In most instances he has risen to head of the department through the suppression ranks. His in-the-field experience in areas related to fire investigation is nil, and his knowledge in this area is sketchy, generally gained by reading or listening to a few lectures on the subject. Lacking understanding of the judicial process, he faults the investigator for not solving more arson cases. This individual should take some time to get into the trenches with the investigators and accompany them through an investigation or several investigations, noting the problems they encounter on a day-to-day basis. This process is guaranteed to give him an entirely new attitude towards the activities of the arson squad and develop his awareness of the needs of the squad in terms of manpower, equipment, and time.

Let us assume arson investigation responsibility has been assigned to the police department. The police chief probably did not want this responsibility because of the low percentage of arrests and convictions in arson fires. Since police performance is judged on crime facts and figures, percentages of increase and decrease in crimes, the police chief does not want this toughest of all crimes to influence the statistics on his department's crime-solving record. Many chiefs of police will categorically deny this charge; but there are those who will frankly admit that this is accurate.

If arson investigation is assigned to the police department, the police chief is not likely to realize the necessity for an effective arson squad since his exposure to arson is either nonexistent or very limited. An effective arson squad operation must develop informants in this highly specialized area; be aware of prime suspects whenever a series of fires occurs; be aware of the arrival in the city of a professional torch; and maintain an intelligence file on property owners, real estate agents, insurance agents, and adjustors who have been involved in previous fires. A few days in the trenches with arson squad members is a necessary education for a police chief who has just been assigned arson investigation responsibility.

An arson squad may be composed of representatives of both the fire and police departments, in which case close cooperation and coordination between fire and police members of the squad is essential. Personnel selected for squad membership must be accustomed to working with others as part of a team with a common objective. A squad member who is a loner, withholds information, and doesn't relate well to other squad personnel will destroy the morale, the esprit de corps, of the unit in a very short time.

In summary, whatever the background of squad members and the method of operation, arson squad personnel must be selected carefully to ensure the smooth functioning of the unit. In an investigation unit comprised of both fire and police personnel, the chief of each service must determine periodically whether the group is functioning effectively.

Equipment

In most metropolitan areas necessary equipment is available at a nearby station, but certain special equipment must also be readily available to investigators. Such items as ladders, axes, and lights can usually be brought to the scene within a matter of minutes from the nearest station, but some equipment should be immediately on hand, which means in the investigator's car. Each investigator on duty must have mobility at all times, so although a car may be assigned to each investigator coming on duty, this is not as desirable as having a vehicle at all times, which enables the investigator to respond to emergency conditions even when off duty. For communication, each vehicle must be radio equipped to receive traffic from central dispatch, and the investigator must be provided with a walkie-talkie or pager through which he can be reached when he is out of the car.

The urban investigator should also be equipped to protect himself in dealing with the criminal element. To them the investigator represents enforcement authority and may therefore be a target for physical attack. For this reason, we strongly recommend that all members of the squad, however constituted, be armed and be trained in how and when to use arms. The investigator need not be a walking arsenal, with mace, handcuffs, and other restraining equipment, but it is only logical that people investigating arson be provided the same capability to protect themselves as those investigating other crimes.

Records and Data

Urban blight has contributed sharply to the increase in incendiary fires in metropolitan areas. In most urban areas there has been a consistent decline in the population of the central city. With increased mobility, white-collar and blue-collar workers commute daily from homes in the suburbs to their place of employment in the city. The former living quarters of these emigrants either become vacant, or they are occupied by members of lower-income ethnic groups. Abandoned property, a likely target for vandals and looters, becomes a mere shell in a relatively short period of time, with all plumbing and heating fixtures and anything of value torn out. The owner realizes that even if he restored the property to a condition where it could be occupied, no one will rent it, and it occurs to him that it is insured far in excess of the present value. A building completely unmarketable for any purpose at any price may be covered by $60,000–$70,000 fire insurance policy. Under the Fair Access to Insurance Requirements which exist in many localities, the insurance coverage on such high-risk properties is assigned to various insurance companies on a rotating basis, and even where the FAIR plan does not exist, many such properties are covered by agents whose primary concern is collecting the premium. In most areas insurance coverage is based on replacement cost, and replacing a three- or four-story tenement house might cost this much even though market value of the present structure is much less. What more does the owner need in the way of a motive than the prospect of collecting such a sum on property which, for all intents and purposes, is completely valueless? If there is a fire, he can collect a tidy sum and rid himself of a white elephant at the same time.

Unscrupulous individuals have entered the "buy and burn" business on a massive scale, purchasing such properties for a pittance from owners glad to get this much and rid themselves of a headache at the same time. The purchasers intend to insure the property and burn it for profit. Lending agencies showed no suspicion of this intent, for instances where mortgage money was refused are practically nonexistent. In all probability the lending agencies made no effort whatsoever to examine the property or determine its condition, for a loan of $5,000–$6,000 on a three-story apartment house with twenty-two rooms and six separate apartments would on the surface appear to be a solid investment. The insurance agent who wrote the coverage in all probability never saw the property involved, as the requests come in by telephone in many cases, and $60,000–$70,000 coverage sounds reasonable for a three-story apartment house with twenty-two rooms and six separate apartments. In the unlikely event the agent inspects the property after he has written the policy and realizes what he has insured, there is still a waiting period of thirty days between notice of cancellation and actual cessation of coverage. If the company finds the risk unacceptable, the same thirty-day period of coverage still exists. There are documented cases of conspiracy involving the lending agency, the insurance agent, a real estate agent, and the buy-and-burn business entrepreneur in which the role of the real estate agent was to locate properties on the market at a giveaway price and advise his coconspirators of the "business opportunity."

The federal government's entry into the housing business has been a major factor contributing to urban blight. In an effort to provide low-cost housing to limited-income families the Department of Housing and Urban Development entered into agreements with contractors to build large numbers of low-cost housing units. In Detroit, over 14,000 empty and dilapidated houses are currently owned by HUD. How did this situation develop? In the case of Detroit and other major cities, investigations have revealed that massive frauds have been perpetrated, with unscrupulous builders, real estate agents, and local officials involved. The basic problem is that the houses are of such substandard construction that the owners soon abandon them, enabling the mortgage holder to collect insurance guaranteed by the federal government when the owner ceases to make payments on the property.

The estimated 65,000 vacant dwellings across the country initially become the targets of vandalism and looting accompanied by fire setting. More significantly, in its frantic effort to rid itself of these properties, the government will sell these dwellings for a pittance, reportedly $1 in some areas! What a bonanza for the unscrupulous! Purchase property for practically nothing, insure it for replacement value, and either burn it or have it burned. The return might be $10,000 on a $1 investment.

What of those properties in urban areas which are partially occupied, normally by low-income families? The absentee landlord who wants the few remaining tenants out of the building prior to having a major destructive fire sets or pays somebody to set a series of minor fires. As a result, the apartments become vacant one by one until eventually the entire building is vacant and can then be totally destroyed by fire.

Outsiders may set fires in order to loot the building when tenants evacuate. Tenants may also set fires in frustration and in protest of poor services, particularly lack of heat. In some cities there are benefits to be gained from being burned out, especially for those families on welfare. If a welfare family is burned out, they automatically receive a two-thousand-dollar payment and are put at the top of the list for city housing.

There are, therefore, several motives for fires in these areas of urban blight: the landlord, for profit and to escape the squeeze of rent ceilings and increased maintenance and tax costs; the outsider, to attain a personal goal—looting; the occupant, in frustration or protest and for financial gains.

Record keeping or data compilation to predict and prevent arson are becoming increasingly sophisticated and important. While computers are the ultimate weapons in developing patterns and trends, the lack of a computer system does not mean a locality cannot develop an effective record-keeping system. A manual system can enable investigators to predict the occurrence of arson in certain areas at certain times. To develop such a system, information compiled on each fire must include the name of the property owner, insurance involved (name of company, amount claimed, and amount paid), names of witnesses and others involved, and pertinent information about the fire, such as date, time, location, and general description. In a more comprehensive arson prevention effort, other non-fire related information should be included, as suggested by the discussion of urban blight: transfer of property, the new and old owner, the real estate agent, the lending institution, tax status of property, inspections made and violations noted.

Adequate records and data represent one positive step toward arson prevention. The individuals involved in setting urban fires for profit are real pros, with a definite plan for carrying out their scheme, and methods employed over the years are not slowing down the incidence of arson. Therefore, although investigation after the fire will be successful at times, every other possible avenue must be explored. Prediction and prevention may well be the answer.

Developing Public Awareness

In the first place, the fire and police departments are part of the public who must be made fully aware of the frequency of arson and its impact on their service so that positive steps may be taken to combat the problem. Training and education of both fire and police personnel at all levels is needed: fire fighters, as well as line officers, must be trained to look for and recognize indications of arson; investigators must be trained on a higher level, which should not be confined to attending regional arson seminars on a sporadic basis. Their training must be continuous—a planned, coordinated course of instruction as well as in-service training with refresher courses on the basics and an emphasis on exchange of information between investigators. Most important, the chiefs of these departments must recognize the seriousness of the arson problem and lend their full support to efforts to overcome this situation.

Second, under the term *public,* we refer to those who have broad supervision over the activities of the fire and police departments—mayors, city managers, city councils, boards of supervisors, and other governmental officials. Without an understanding of the impact of incendiary fires on the economy and overall well-being of the community, these people will not authorize the necessary financial and administrative support to combat the problem.

Third, the public includes mortgage or lending organizations, real estate agents, and insurance agents and adjustors who may be unwitting parties to buy-and-burn schemes. When the names of certain individuals come across the desks of these people, a red flag of danger should be raised immediately. Their cooperation with the investigating agencies by alerting them to any transactions involving people who have suffered numerous previous fires may enable the investigator to prevent still another fire. If, on the other hand, the buy-and-burn gangs continue to get easy mortgage money, insurance without inspection, and payment for questionable claims, their schemes will continue to profit and flourish.

Fourth, an essential ingredient in the success of the arson suppression effort is coordination with the prosecutor's office in the area having jurisdiction. Investigators report that on occasion coordination with the prosecutor in presenting their case is accomplished at the courtroom door or on the elevator trip to the courtroom. The investigator should keep the prosecutor informed of the status of the case from its inception, for many prosecutors want to assist in any way possible during the actual investigation and will do so if given the opportunity. Prosecutors state that they need the active assistance of the investigator in case preparation because, since arson prosecutions are rare, the average prosecutor has little experience in this field. The investigator, who deals with this subject on a day-to-day basis, is in a position to point out certain pitfalls which must be avoided in the courtroom. Case load and time, however, are major obstacles in accomplishing this very desirable working relationship. The fact, for instance, that the investigator cannot or is not willing to qualify as an expert witness must not come as a surprise to the prosecutor from the witness stand. Until better liaison between investigators and prosecutors is established, the arson situation will not improve substantially.

Fifth, judges are part of the public who must become more aware of the serious nature of arson. Some 195 years ago, Noah Webster said, "A law without penalty is mere advice," and too often our courts are inclined to dole out lenient penalties to convicted arsonists. In a recent case, the subject pleaded guilty to setting fire to an occupied church with resultant damage of almost $600,000. The judge, in sentencing the subject to five years' probation, cited as major considerations in his decision the man's lack of any serious prior criminal record and the fact that he was a family man supporting five children. Prior to being apprehended in the church fire, the subject was suspected by arson investigators of complicity in over a dozen fires, and after his sentence, he put investigators on notice that he was out to get them and "better not ever catch them with their backs turned!" If a single factor could be pinpointed as the major cause of today's arson epidemic, it would have to be the inexplicable leniency extended to convicted arsonists by our courts. No effort, however strong, in the areas of detection, investigation, and prosecution will be effective unless the individuals convicted are dealt with realistically in our judicial chambers.

Sixth, by *public* we mean the citizenry in general. The emphasis and publicity which incendiary fires have received in the last few years has alerted most citizens to the arson problem, but most do not know what they can do about it or think somebody else is taking care of the matter.

How can public involvement help? An example may illustrate one instance where public interest brought results. In this case the clergymen of an area struck by incendiary fires realized the effect arson was having on their community and approached the city fathers with the question, What can be done about this problem and how can we help? Within a short time, meetings were held with the district attorney, police and fire commissioner, housing authorities, welfare department personnel, and representatives of the insurance industry. As a result, an arson task force was organized and additional fire and police personnel were assigned to arson investigation. The district attorney assigned several assistants to the sole task of prosecuting those arrested and charged with unlawful burning; the housing authority discontinued the practice of moving people who suffered a fire to the top of the housing list; the welfare department ended the $2,000 automatic payment to welfare recipients who were burned out; the insurance crime prevention bureau ruled that insurance payments in the case of a fire were no longer to be based on replacement value, but the tax value of the property.

The success of this effort cannot be determined at this early date, but logic would indicate that positive results will be forthcoming. Perhaps the most effective action the arson task force took was going into the affected area and explaining the problems of the arson fire, how it affects the community, and what the ordinary citizen can do to help apprehend the arsonist. Residents were advised to notify the fire and police departments of any unusual incidents in their community, and pamphlets were distributed in several languages but conveying the same message: these fires are hurting your community and we urgently need your help.

Another procedure adopted in several cities is to send members of the arson squad into the troubled areas on a sort of roving patrol. The question of whether to use marked or unmarked cars for this purpose is not resolved. One chief insists that the presence of a car with Arson Squad marked on the side in big, bold letters serves as a deterrent to the would-be arsonist and lets the public know that the squad is on the job. Another chief declares emphatically that he would never send a marked unit into certain areas, for the big, bold lettering on the car door would make too good a target.

One city fire chief launched an unusual campaign to inform the public of the arson problem. An individual, posing as a businessman in financial straits, let the word out that he wanted some help in burning his place of business. Several days later, he was contacted by a professional torch, several meetings were held, and arrangements, including pay, were made. But the entire transaction, including telephone conversations was recorded, videotaped, and run on a TV news program in several segments. The public became sufficiently interested to call the TV station and fire department trying to get advance information on what would happen on the next episode. In criticizing this activity, another chief suggested that this would just show the public how to get an arson job done. Once again, only long-range evaluation of results will determine the effectiveness of such a program.

11 Automobile Fires

"Sunday after lunch I decided to drive over and see my brother-in-law to show him my new gun. I was driving down the road when my car spit a time or two. Then all of a sudden a big ball of fire rolled out from under the dash. I pulled over and jumped out as fast as I could, but my hair got singed and my eyebrows were burned. Just as I stopped, some fellows I didn't know came by and pulled up. We didn't have no fire extinguisher but we throwed some dirt on the motor. The whole inside was burning by this time so there wasn't nothing we could do but back off because I was afraid she would explode. I sure hated to lose that car 'cause she was the best car I ever had. I had her in perfect shape, new tires, new seat covers, just the perfect car. My rifle got burned up in the car; it was on the back seat and I couldn't get to it before I had to bail out. I had about three hundred dollars in tens and twenties in the glove compartment and this got burned up too."

So goes the familiar saga told to so many insurance adjustors by so many car burners. The similarity of these statements and of the circumstances surrounding the incendiary automobile fire is striking. The owner/driver is usually alone, going nowhere in particular for no specific purpose. The burning spot is normally isolated from traffic, is not close to any houses, is shielded from view by natural barriers or woods, and is in an area familiar to the car owner.

In this chapter we will examine some facts and perhaps explode some myths in connection with auto fires. Investigative procedures and techniques which have proved successful and resulted in convictions of car burners will be covered.

Police and fire officials in some jurisdictions indicate that incendiary automobile fires are practically nonexistent in their area of responsibility. Is this actually true, or is there simply a failure to recognize arson where it exists? The National Fire Protection Association Annual Report of Estimated United States Fires indicates that there were 574,000 motor vehicle fires in 1973, with a monetary loss of $135,300,000. There are no statistics on how many of these were total losses, but it is probably safe to assume that at least ten percent were, thus giving us a round figure of 60,000. We must believe that many of these fires were deliberately set for a variety of reasons. Too many public officials in too many localities believe that a motor vehicle can catch on fire accidentally, become totally involved in a matter of minutes, and eventually end up a burned-out shell with everything that can possibly burn completely consumed, including all four tires.

The records of the National Automobile Theft Bureau, a nationwide organization dedicated to the investigation of automobile fires and thefts, show that the South, particularly the southeastern states, has the greatest problem of incendiary auto fires. We cannot help wondering whether the training given to law enforcement and fire officials in this region does not have an impact on these facts and figures, for it is difficult to believe that there is an invisible line running east and west across the country above which no autos are deliberately burned. Until police and fire officials become convinced that total automobile fires should be viewed with suspicion, we will have many undetected incendiary fires in many jurisdictions.

There are certain other facts which must be considered when evaluating the frequency of incendiary motor vehicle fires. Fact #1: Statistics show that women do *one-third* of all driving annually in our country, yet *less than 1 percent* of all reported total fires occur while women are driving. Fact #2: Ninety percent of all total car fires involve a financed automobile. Fact #3: Uninsured cars rarely burn. Fact #4: Fleet-owned cars, such as taxicabs, rental cars, or company-operated vehicles, are driven millions of miles annually, yet they seldom burn. Fact #5: Police and emergency vehicles, in spite of constant use and special equipment, catch fire infrequently.

Under certain conditions there may be total consumption of a vehicle by fire without criminal wrongdoing. Complete burning often results when a car is involved in an accident or is in a burned building. In the case of a single-vehicle accident which results in a car burning, the question arises whether it was an accidental or deliberate accident. When a vehicle is destroyed in a small one-car garage, the investigator should ask whether the building involved was insured as well as the car. The point we wish to establish is that even though a motor vehicle can be completely destroyed under some conditions, the investigator must not accept this as a clear indication that the fire was accidental.

In summary, the origin and cause of any total automobile fire should be viewed with suspicion, and a thorough investigation must be conducted concerning the circumstances of the incident.

Motives for Motor Vehicle Fires

While cars are burned on occasion by individuals other than the owner, this is the exception rather than the rule. In cases where the vehicle is set on fire by other persons, the motives parallel those connected with structural fires: revenge, domestic quarrels, protest against law enforcement activities, furthering a cause.

Since most car fires are set by the owner/assured, we will concentrate our discussion in this area. Generally speaking there are three principal motives for an individual to burn his own car: (1) financial difficulties, (2) mechanical problems, and (3) dissatisfaction with the vehicle. Often a combination of factors convinces the owner that the only escape from his predicament is to "sell his car to the insurance company."

By way of explanation, let us examine a typical case. An hourly wage earner of limited means may trade in his five-year-old car on a three-year-old model. A certain amount of pressure by the salesman accompanies the sale, and there are vague oral references to "guarantees" and "standing behind every car we sell." The vehicle is always in "mint condition" and won't stay on the lot very long because "another fellow" is interested. Eventually, the victim gives in and the deal is completed.

Upon arriving home, the proud owner receives a violent tonguelashing from his wife. How could he do this when she has to have a new washing machine and the kids need shoes? Several hours later a friend adds to his discomfort by telling him that he knows a fellow who bought the same model car in much better condition for $700 less.

Several days later the sale papers arrive in the mail and for the first time the full extent of the buyer's financial commitment registers. Further, he realizes that he owes far more on the car than it is actually worth. His wife informs him that she is pregnant and will have to stop working and that their ten-year-old needs braces on his teeth which will cost $1,600, payable in advance.

His trauma is compounded a few days later on the occasion of his first visit to a service station. Only 184 miles since purchase, but his pride and joy requires three quarts of oil and 23 gallons of gasoline. To add to his woes, he has noticed the transmission slipping, particularly on any grade. Ah, but he will return to his port of refuge, the friendly salesman. After all, the car is guaranteed.

On arriving at the used car lot and coming face to face with this "consultant on his transportation needs," he is disappointed that the red carpet of welcome is absent, along with the friendly smile of recognition. Actually, the fellow hardly remembers him at all, and remembers any guarantee even less. However, he agrees to do a ring job for him for just the cost of labor, which is $225. He departs in a state of shock.

As he starts back home, he realizes that he is losing speed. The motor is running wide open, knocking and clattering, but he finally comes to a complete stop—the transmission is slipping. He gets out and raises the hood, revealing a steaming hot motor with various knocking noises. Why, he suddenly realizes, this car is almost hot enough to catch on fire and he does have fire insurance. The seed is sown; he has a built-in explanation. He can hear himself telling people, "She began to run hot, so I stopped and raised the hood. When I lifted the hood a big ball of fire jumped out at me."

In this case, a combination of all three motives exists: financial woes, mechanical problems, and dissatisfaction with the car. Now that the owner has decided to solve his problem by burning it, let us examine some typical methods he may employ to carry out his intentions.

Methods of Car Burning

One procedure used by car burners which creates an additional problem for investigators is the false theft. The owner, usually with assistance from a friend or relative, takes his car out to an isolated location and burns it. He then proceeds to notify law enforcement authorities that his car was stolen while he was at the movies. A problem in investigating this type of suspected arson is that the owner cannot be placed at the scene at the time of the burning. The possibility must be considered that this was a legitimate theft and that thieves actually stripped the car and burned it to eliminate any evidence, particularly fingerprints, which might connect them with the crime. If it was an owner arson, however, there very likely will be accomplices who, when properly questioned, may admit that the theft report was a fabrication and that they and/or the owner burned the car. After all, what does the accomplice stand to gain?—the owner will get the insurance money. What does this person have to lose?—a great deal, perhaps a few years of his life behind bars.

There are other methods of disposing of unwanted cars which do not involve fires, and the law enforcement officer should be alert for indications of fraud in these cases. Included in this category are driving the vehicle into deep water in a quarry or other body of water, or leaving the car on the tracks at an isolated rail crossing. Another technique employed is the deliberate accident, usually staged in hilly or mountainous country. The owner rolls his car off the road over a steep slope down into an inaccessible ravine, reasoning that the car will be totally destroyed and the insurance company will pay him off. What often happens in these cases is that the car hangs up on a stump or tree and very little damage results. The only recourse for the owner under these circumstances is to set the car on fire to assure complete destruction. How many times have we heard this version of such an event: "When I came around the curve, I got over on the loose gravel and couldn't keep her in the road. I rode her down through the woods and finally got her stopped. Just then I noticed smoke coming from under the hood. I got out and scrambled up the bank. When I got up to the road I looked back and she was burning all over—just a mass of flame. There wasn't nothing I could do, so I just walked on home. Best little old car I ever had, etc., etc.''

It usually comes as a shock to the average car burner that his automobile is much harder to burn than he thought. Having witnessed on television many spectacular scenes depicting cars exploding into a mass of flames from some slight impact or minor accident, he believes his car is a highly combustible machine; all he has to do is get a fire started and the rest will take care of itself. His first effort to burn may be under the hood. Much to his amazement, a fire started with some gasoline burns itself out with very little damage. After three unsuccessful attempts on the motor, he decides to try the tires, because he *knows* they will burn. Once again he is disappointed—just a few minutes of burning with insignificant damage. At this point he realizes that he has only one recourse, he *knows* the seat will burn. This is an old standby—gas poured on the seat on the driver's side, then a match tossed in. The result is rapid combustion and eventually a total fire with the interior completely gutted.

Now the arsonist's concern is to concoct a story that will prevent his getting caught. At the same time, police and fire officials must be alert to the possibility that a crime has been committed. Let us now follow from their inception actions taken by fire and police personnel and representatives of the insurance industry to assure that justice prevails.

Immediate Investigative Procedure

It is almost impossible to establish a standard procedure which can be applied by fire and police officials at the scene of an auto fire. There are some cases where the fire is obviously set and others which appear obviously accidental. The cases which fall between these extremes do create problems. Common sense and sound judgment must be used in deciding just what course of action to take and how far to pursue this on-the-scene investigation.

As in the case of dwelling fires, the less damage done to the auto in extinguishing the fire, the greater the possibility of finding significant evidence of incendiarism. When a high-pressure straight stream is used, particularly on the interior, valuable evidence may be washed out the door. There are cases on record in which flammable liquids have been found in the residue weeks after a fire, but if the car is flushed out down to the metal floorboard, all such evidence normally is gone.

Experience and case reports indicate that the explosion of a gas tank is an extremely rare occurrence. Nevertheless, in some instances the gas tank has been punctured by fire and police personnel to prevent this anticipated explosion. When ten or fifteen gallons of gas are allowed to run out under the car, the results are disastrous, particularly if the car is on a slope and the gas runs under the car. In one case, a local gendarme arrived on the scene when smoke was coming from under the hood of a high-priced imported automobile. The fire department was prepared to extinguish without difficulty a minor electrical fire, but the lawman ordered all to stand back so he could shoot holes in the gas tank to prevent an explosion. In spite of all efforts to convince him that this was not necessary, he proceeded to carry out his intentions. As a result, approximately twenty gallons of gasoline were released, flowed under the car, and were ignited by a piece of insulation falling from the burning wiring. A conflagration of immense proportions followed, completely consuming car and contents. The occupants of the car watched their $12,000 car, clothes, personal belongings, golf clubs, cameras, and other vacation paraphernalia completely destroyed. Thus, because of an act of stupidity, what was originally a $200 incident became a $20,000 disaster for the occupants and the insurance company as well.

In most jurisdictions, burning a car is not per se a criminal offense, unless the owner/assured files a claim against the insurance company. It follows that the assured must be given an opportunity to enter such a claim against the carrier. In some localities, simply advising the insurance company by phone or in person that the fire occurred and that the assured wants to be paid is sufficient. An actual proof of loss must be submitted in some instances before the charge of burning to defraud the insurance company can be brought. If it is thought the fire was set to collect insurance, the owner should not be accused or in any way led to believe that the officer at the scene is suspicious until the claim for the insurance has been filed in some form. In one case on record a law enforcement officer arrived at a fiercely burning car and proceeded to question the owner/occupant/assured. After a brief interrogation, a confession that he had burned the car was elicited, the motive being anger because the car was giving him so much trouble he wanted to get rid of it. The owner was arrested and jailed, the charge being "burning to defraud the insurance company." An attorney obtained by the family visited the cell and asked the owner whether he had filed a claim against the company. Upon being told that no claim had been filed, the attorney advised both the carrier and the lienholder that the owner had no intention of collecting any monies from the insurance company and would pay the lienholder the entire amount owed on the car. He further advised that the owner had burned the car in a fit of temper and was very sorry for what he had done. As a result, the car burner was released forthwith and an overeager officer was officially reprimanded for what might otherwise have been commendable investigative action.

Now for some specific recommendations to the officer arriving at the scene of a burning automobile. These actions will vary from situation to situation and no one standard procedure can be followed.

Note Time

The time at which the incident occurred can become quite important as the investigation continues, for the owner may attempt to establish an alibi relative to his whereabouts prior to the fire. Additionally, the extent of burning may be illogical in view of the short period of time elapsed since the claimed inception of the fire, if this can be established.

Contact with the Owner/Operator at the Scene

It is extremely important that contact with the owner be conducted as a routine matter so as not to alert the subject to the fact that the origin and cause of the fire is suspect. Handle this person easily, encouraging him to talk. Much of the information sought can be obtained during a routine conversation, and unless it becomes necessary, don't ask pointed questions about facts which would be directly incriminating. Properly framed questions will usually get the desired information without putting the owner on the defensive:

1. Get name, residence, and business address; how he can be contacted at home and at work.

2. Where was he going and for what purpose?

3. Where was he coming from?

4. Who, if anyone, was in the car with him, either at the time of the fire or shortly before?

5. What happened?
   (a) Exactly where did he first observe the smoke or fire? Insist that he be specific without putting him on the defensive.
   (b) What action did he take?
   (c) How did the fire spread?
   (d) About how long had the fire been burning when the officer arrived on the scene?

6. Who was the first person to arrive on the scene?

7. Was the fire department called? By whom? If not called, why not?

8. Obtain insurance information:
   (a) Name of company
   (b) Policy number
   (c) Agent

9. If practical, inquire as to the contents of vehicle (clothes, tools, etc.).

10. What was the general condition of the vehicle, if that information can be obtained without direct questioning.

Observations at the Fire Scene

It is essential that the officer on the scene take notice of certain conditions at that time and place, because these conditions probably will be changed within a relatively short period of time. In other words, the chance to make certain key observations is a one-time opportunity which will not continue in the hours, days, or weeks following the fire.

General Terrain   What is the nature of the immediate area? Woods? Protected by hills or trees from observation? Is the soil rocky, sandy? Would an accelerant penetrate to any depth? Would it be possible to throw dirt on the burning vehicle? Is the underside of the car in close proximity to leaves, stubble, grass, or other combustible material?

Proximity to combustibles has become increasingly significant with the introduction of catalytic converters on the 1975 model cars. Prior to this time there was only the unlikely possibility that combustibles might be ignited by the muffler or other components of the exhaust system. Catalytic converters are new and a new and serious problem. The U.S. Army has conducted extensive field tests on the converters and, as a result of these tests, banned the use of converter-equipped vehicles within 50 feet of any aircraft, fuel spills, explosive area, or other potentially hazardous area. A memorandum warning industries and consumers of the danger has caused at least one industry to issue instructions that automobiles equipped with converters must be parked on clear land, safely away from combustible materials.

Most catalytic converters normally operate at temperatures between 800° and 1800° F., depending on the type and make of vehicle. Certain conditions, such as a poorly tuned motor, can cause the temperatures to increase noticeably. Service representatives of major auto dealers indicate that each malfunctioning sparkplug can raise converter temperatures 100 to 200 degrees above normal. As these cars accrue additional age and mileage, poorly performing engines will serve to increase converter temperatures—and the hazard.

Tests at a major oil refinery indicate that when a 1975 vehicle runs out of fuel, temperatures just before fuel exhaustion increase enough to destroy the catalyst. Apparently misfiring associated with low fuel supply allows unburned fuel to enter the converter, causing higher temperatures.

Catalytic converters remain hot long after the rest of the exhaust system has cooled. Mechanics often refuse to perform under-car maintenance until the converter cools because of the possibility of serious burns. Converters have literally melted because of extreme high temperatures, estimated as high as 2000° F.

What hazards do these extreme temperatures create? Tests show that dry grass and leaves can be ignited by heat from catalytic converters. Excessively high converter operating temperatures are also capable of igniting the asphalt-base undercoating compounds used on motor vehicles. Areas near the catalytic converter cannot be undercoated. Car dealers report that vinyl tops of cars shipped from the factory are frequently blistered and damaged by latent heat in catalytic converters on cars loaded on upper decks during transport. Floor mats and carpeting of 1975 automobiles have been scorched or burned by heat from the catalytic converter. Recently, according to the Army, a 1975 automobile traveling on an interstate highway was damaged when the catalytic converter ruptured—with enough force to shear the mounting straps of the fuel tank—causing the tank to fall off the body of the car. The fuel tank did not rupture.

All of these incidents serve to emphasize the need for close observation of conditions under the car at the fire scene.

Weather Conditions   Is it rainy or cold? Would it be logical for the windows to be down? What is the wind direction? Would the fire have spread through the car as a result of the wind? In a case on record the owner/operator alleged that the fire originated in the trunk and that when he raised the trunk lid, a strong wind blowing from east to west spread the fire through the car almost instantly. However, fire department personnel responding from the east advised that they encountered heavy black smoke at ground level half a mile before reaching the scene, thus refuting his story.

Nature and Location of Burning   How intense was the burning? What color was the flame? The smoke? In exactly what part of the vehicle was the fire? Had other portions of the vehicle already been involved or did the fire spread to these after the investigator's arrival? Was there anything unusual about the way the car burned?

Location of Vehicle   Was it on or off the road surface? On an uphill or downhill slope? Would an accelerant have run under the car or to the right or left of it? Is the location of the vehicle consistent with the owner/operator's version of the fire?

Conduct of the Owner/Operator   Does his reaction to the fire appear normal? Is he excited or unusually calm? Does he appear to be putting on a big act over the loss of the "best car he ever had"?

Physical Appearance of the Owner   Is he intoxicated or under the influence of drugs? Does he display burns on his hands and arms, or singed hair and eyebrows? Often the operator will relate his heroic efforts to extinguish the fire, such as jerking out wires and removing burning upholstery material. In this case any burn injury should be confined to the palms of his hands, with some singing to the hair and eyebrows. However, if hair is burned off the back of his hands, it probably means that this occurred when he tossed a match or other torch material into the interior previously saturated with gasoline. A delay between actually pouring the accelerant and igniting it allows vapors to accumulate which explode with force. In this situation the arsonist may be seriously burned and may have to try to explain his condition.

Vehicle Tire Tracks   If there are tracks other than those of the burned vehicle, were there indications of a high-speed takeoff? Many times another vehicle is used to transport the perpetrator from the fire scene, particularly in cases where the car is reported stolen. Are there tracks which indicate the vehicle was pushed or pulled to the scene? This is incriminating if the owner states that he was driving the car, and it is probable that later detailed examination of this vehicle will indicate it was inoperable prior to the fire.

Footprints   Are there prints visible? If so, are they those of the owner? Again, this information is particularly significant if the car was reported stolen. Location of the owner's footprints at the fire scene would be most difficult to explain and would prove valuable physical evidence in court.

Containers   Are there cans in the immediate area? Many times the gasoline or kerosene to be used as an accelerant is purchased in advance by the perpetrator and carried to the burning site. In his excitement the car burner may dispose of the container in the nearest cover or throw it over into a nearby woods or field (Figure 11-1). A search of the immediate area may locate such a container, which may have a small amount of gasoline or kerosene, or perhaps the owner's latent prints. The investigator can later check nearby service stations in an effort to establish the fact that the car burner did purchase gas in that container.

   Other articles the officer should be searching for are a wheel cover and siphon hose. Often the burning of the car is a spur-of-the-moment act for which the owner has made no preparation. Some mechanical failure may cause him to decide to burn the car right then and there. However, he has no accelerant other than what is in the gas tank, so he may siphon some gas out of the gas tank with a section of garden hose which is in the trunk. What can he siphon it into? Better than nothing is a wheel cover, which will hold a small amount of gas. Once again, in his excitement, he may simply throw these things into some nearby area.

Evidence of Accelerants on the Ground   Are there any unusual odors during the fire or after the vehicle is moved? On occasion the car burner will spill some gasoline or kerosene on the ground around the car or some liquid will drip through the floorboard. Check the ground around the vehicle and

FIGURE 11-1. Accelerant container located near the scene of a car fire. The remains of similar cans were found in the trunk of the burned vehicle. (Courtesy Commonwealth of Virginia Arson Investigation Division)

under it after removal. Dig down a few inches, particularly in porous, sandy soil, to find any residue of a flammable liquid. This dirt must be placed in an air-tight container and properly labeled for laboratory examination and potential use in the courtroom. On occasion, a scorched area near the car will be noticeable.

Oil Slick, Skid Marks, Wheel Rim Tracks　　　Are there marks visible in the road over which the vehicle would have traveled prior to reaching the burning site? Often the vehicle involved will suffer some drastic mechanical failure just prior to stopping completely, such as a thrown rod, particles of which penetrate the motor block and/or oil pan. Oil from the motor drains out immediately and leaves a trail between the point of mechanical failure and the burning spot. Sometimes pieces of metal from the motor will be dropped along this same trail.

　　Skid marks indicate a sudden and complete locking up or freezing of the differential, which causes either one or both back wheels to stop turning instantly. This turn of events may necessitate setting fire to the car in the exact spot where it stopped, because it simply cannot be moved. In one such case, the owner/operator, backing up his car to pick up a hitchhiker, ran the rear end up on a concrete bridge abutment, puncturing the differential. From the point of impact, a trail of grease led to a spot in the road where the skid marks appeared. After surveying the mechanical condition of the car and finding it impossible to move, the owner and the hitchhiker burned the vehicle at the exact location where it stopped.

Wheel rim tracks are indicative of several possible circumstances preceding the burning. Sometimes the owner will remove one or two good tires which he wants to save and drive a short distance to the burning site on the rims. Particular attention should be given to the shoulder of the road, for driving is somewhat easier if one rim is off the road. The path of the wheel rims will be uniform and uninterrupted if the wheel had no tire at all.

An intermittent rim path indicates that the tire on that wheel was flat. Searching up the road from the burning site on the route of travel will often reveal portions of tire material back to the point where the tire blew out or went flat.

In one case, four intoxicated men were out for a joy ride in a very dilapidated vehicle. Within a distance of 125 feet both rear tires blew out. From that point the car was driven four miles until it ran out of gas. By this time the beading from the tires had wrapped around the wheel cylinders and rear axle, which were white hot. The combination of the excessive heat and the proper mixture in the gas tank caused the tank to rupture at the seam, sending a blast of burning gas vapors 70 feet from the tank and igniting the woods. Observers at the scene (no injuries resulted) described the jet of burning vapors as resembling that from a military flamethrower. This was one of only two gas tank explosions we have found in the course of reviewing over 2,000 automobile fire investigation reports. The less gasoline in the tank, the more danger of rupture or explosion of the tank. Fire fighters should ascertain from the owner as soon as possible the estimated gas content of the tank.

Collision Damage   Immediate collision damage may have caused the vehicle to become inoperable and been the catalyst for arson. If the car is subjected to damage which the owner believes justifies replacement of the vehicle and the insurance company indicates they will repair the damage, the owner may become angry and reason that if the car is burned, they won't be able to repair that. Sometimes the owner may be dissatisfied with body work and burn the car to ensure its replacement. Occasionally, sensitive owners are convinced that a car is never the same after being in an accident, and will burn the vehicle to obtain a replacement.

Tires and Wheels Switched   Are all the wheels the same color? The same size? Are all the wheel lug nuts in place? It is common practice for the car burner to exchange tires prior to the fire. Replacing tires which may be in reasonably good condition with some completely worn out, he may switch complete wheels with a friend and therefore have wheels of different colors and sizes. It is possible the lugs will not fit properly and only a few nuts will be partially tightened. When this tire and/or wheel switching is done, the owner and an accomplice in their haste may leave off one or more of the lug nuts. Many times the owner will claim that he had brand new tires on the car, believing that the fire will completely consume and destroy his worn out tires, but when a tire burns, at some point during the burning, it goes flat, and the portion of the tire between the rim and the ground will never be destroyed by the fire. Through examination of this remaining portion of the tire, it is possible to ascertain the condition of the tire, the type of tread, and sometimes whether it is a recap.

Often when the vehicle is lifted or moved by the wrecker, this unburned tire pad will separate from the wheel. The officer must note which portion of tire came from which wheel. Some writing in chalk on the interior of the remains will not destroy its evidentiary value.

Are the wheel covers on the car? If not, why not? Is the area where they would normally fit clean in comparison to the remainder of the wheel? This would indicate the car had been run only a short time without the wheel cover, thus increasing the probability that the tires were switched just prior to the fire. If the wheel covers are in place, are there clean places or indications of hand and finger marks on them? This again indicates that they had been removed shortly before the fire, and the reason for this removal should be fully explored.

It is necessary to check the wheels closely at the crime scene because the wrecker driver may be required to replace the wheels in order to tow the car to the wrecking yard.

Indications of the Vehicle Being Stolen   Are there any visible signs of the glass being broken out, particularly the vent glass? Is the key in the ignition switch? Is there any indication that the vehicle was "wired around"? Are both license plates in place and normally installed, or are they loosely wired on? Do both tags bear the same number? Is this the number tag which is assigned to this vehicle? These checks may serve to eliminate or establish the possibility that the vehicle was stolen.

Gas Cap On or Off   If the cap is missing, examine the flanges of the filler tube neck to see if they are damaged. If the cap was blown off as a result of an explosion within the gas tank, these flanges will be bent outward. When the flanges are found to be damaged, examine the gas tank itself to corroborate an internal explosion. In the unlikely event an explosion did occur within the tank, it should be misshapen with the ends and sides bulged outward. A gas tank explosion is a rarity, for the mixture of air and gasoline vapors in the tank normally is far too rich to ignite. However, the gasoline vapors escaping from the filler tube neck may ignite and add to the intensity of the fire. If this occurs, the gasket material on the inside of the gas cap will be consumed and the inside of the cap itself will be noticeably discolored, with heavy soot deposits. Normally, detailed scrutiny of the gas tank, filler neck, and cap is accomplished later during an extensive salvage examination.

In many cases the gas cap is removed by the arsonist to siphon gas out of the tank for the purpose of burning the vehicle, especially if the fire is set in disgust over an immediate mechanical failure and is not preplanned. In his haste, the arsonist may forget to replace the cap and simply drop it on the ground at that point or rid himself of it by tossing it into the interior of the vehicle, a nearby ditch, woods, or field. Regardless of where or if it is found, the absence of the gas cap from its normal position is significant and must be noticed at the fire scene to be considered admissible evidence.

Drain Plug   Does the gas tank have a drain plug? In most of today's cars the gas tank is a solid unit made by joining two original units at a seam running horizontally. In the unlikely event a tank with a drain plug is encountered, examine the area around the plug carefully. If it is missing, is the collar surrounding the plug also missing? This indicates that the solder holding the entire unit (plug and collar) melted and allowed the unit to fall out. A substantial degree of heat on the underside of the vehicle is required to accomplish this, so substantial burning will be evident. If the collar is intact and the drain plug is missing, it had to be removed by someone. The drain plug at one time was the most accessible source of gasoline for the car burner. It must be determined whether the burned vehicle was so equipped. If the drain plug is intact, examine the area of the tank around the plug to see whether it is clean or covered with dust and road film. Note any fresh tool marks on the plug itself or other indications of efforts to remove the plug. Test the plug to see if it is only in finger tight, which might indicate it had been removed for gas to drain out on the ground or into a container, and then replaced without being tightened by pliers or wrench.

Obvious Mechanical Defects   Although a thorough check of the mechanical condition of the car will be made later, it is advisable to examine the vehicle at the fire scene for obvious mechanical faults which would make the car inoperable. In the motor area look for holes in the motor block or holes in the oil pan which indicate major problems such as a thrown rod. Examine the transmission and differential for holes, defects, or damage. The drive shaft may be broken or separated at the universal joint, in which case one end of the shaft will be free and resting on the ground. Making these observations at the fire scene refutes any claim by the owner that such damage was done while the vehicle was being moved to the wrecking yard.

Absence of Parts Essential to the Operation of the Vehicle   Are the radiator, battery, distributor, voltage regulator, generator or alternator, carburetor, and fuel pump all in place? Are there any tool marks on the fittings which indicate efforts to make repairs prior to the fire? In one case the owner claimed he was operating the vehicle in a normal manner, but the steering wheel was missing! It is necessary that these observations be made at the fire scene because parts may be sold off the vehicle subsequent to its impoundment in the wrecking yard.

While examining the motor compartment for mechanical defects and absence of parts essential to the operation of the vehicle, the officer should look closely for residue of matches which often will survive a major fire under the hood. Check closely in the cracks and sunken areas, particularly on top of the motor.

Contents of the Vehicle   Many times the owner will claim various items were destroyed in the fire in order to gain a larger insurance settlement—clothing, guns, fishing equipment, tools, and toolboxes. The interior of the vehicle must remain undisturbed for future detailed examination, but the officer at the fire scene can note the general contents. Was the car full of vacation paraphernalia which was destroyed in the flames? This would normally indicate an accidental fire. Check the trunk of the car, for spare tire and wheel, jack, lug wrench, and normal equipment found there.

Absence of Accessories   Without disturbing the vehicle, particularly the interior, note whether radio antenna, outside rear view mirrors, radio, and tape deck are missing.

Examination of the Area   It is probable that the officer will return to the fire scene at least once to expand the search. This search should include walking over the route taken by the burned vehicle prior to the fire, looking for anything significant, including portions of tires, metal particles from the vehicle, or any item or condition which might be connected with the burning. In the case cited where the car backed up on the bridge abutment, damage to the concrete was apparent and small particles of metal from the differential were found embedded in this cement.

Expand the search into the surrounding woods, fields, and ditches. Such items as a container, siphon hose, gas tank cap, and a wheel cover with the odor of gasoline may reward this search. In one case a cache of clothes, tools, and accessories, removed from the vehicle by the owner prior to the fire, was found hidden in the bushes where he intended to retrieve them later.

Interviewing Witnesses   If the officer does not have an opportunity to interview fire fighters and other witnesses at the scene, he must obtain names and addresses for future use. In the event the witness is transient the interview must be conducted at this time. The neighborhood should be canvassed for any information of value. While we do not anticipate uncovering an eyewitness, information of value relative to events prior to the fire may be obtained.

In summary, follow normal investigative procedures. Photographs should be taken of the area, the car itself, and any evidence prior to its removal. Distances should be measured in miles, yards, or feet as appropriate. Sketches should be made of the scene and pertinent information entered thereon. Accurate notes should be made throughout this preliminary investigation and statements taken if circumstances dictate. Evidence must be properly labeled and sealed in containers which will preserve its integrity. The officer's every move must be predicated on the assumption that every action taken by him at the fire scene will be subject to rigid cross-examination on the witness stand.

Keeping in mind that the assured must be given an opportunity to file proof of loss, the investigator cannot let the owner know that the origin of the fire is suspect. No one should be charged with burning the car at this time unless the car has been burned by someone other than the owner. Impound the car and advise the wrecking yard that the vehicle is to remain intact. Unfortunately, many times this request goes unheeded, and parts are removed and sold prior to a detailed salvage examination. Nevertheless, the effort must be made to secure the car as far as possible.

At this time there are two options available to the officer: (1) He can contact the insurance carrier direct and advise that the vehicle burned, that he was at the scene during or shortly after the fire, that he has information relative to the fire which he believes significant, and that he will cooperate in any way possible. (2) He can contact the state agency responsible for investigation of suspected arson fires and provide the same basic information as that given the insurance adjustor.

Role of the Insurance Adjustor

Whether the adjustor is a company employee or an independent representing the company, he can arrange for the storage and security of the burned automobile. Once the owner has notified the company of the loss, in most jurisdictions the vehicle becomes the property of the insurance carrier.

Ascertaining the mechanical condition of the burned car may require extensive services of a qualified mechanic, and arrangements and payment for this examination should be accomplished through the adjustor. Sometimes the age and condition of the car indicate that such an expenditure is not justified; the investigating officer must convince the company representative that the examination is needed, nonetheless, for the sake of solving a crime.

The adjustor need not provide information on car fires as detailed as that needed for structural losses, but he should obtain background and financial data on the owner/assured. Much of this can be obtained in a statement taken from the assured, but this information must be verified.

The most important function of the insurance adjustor is to obtain a detailed statement of the owner/operator of the vehicle. Many adjustors, in the interest of time, use a tape recorder for this purpose, but a written statement properly initialed and signed is preferable. If a recorder is used, all requirements for admissibility must be met.

No outline or statement format will be suitable for all situations; however, the outline of unknown origin which follows has been widely used by insurance companies for a number of years. There is no requirement that these specific questions be asked or, if used, that they follow this sequence. The object of the interview is to obtain a complete, detailed statement from the assured; and this outline is intended only as a general guide to assist in the undertaking, with modification as necessary for alleged theft prior to the burning.

The purpose of the following statement is to file my claim with (name of insurance company) for (fire or theft) to my (make, model, and motor # of car) occurring on (date and time) and covered under policy number _____ . My car caught on fire/was stolen at (exact location).

1. My name is

2. Age.

3. I live at (full address—city or county).

4. I (do/do not) own my home.

5. I pay rent (amount) to

6. I have lived there for (years).

7. Before that I lived at (where).

8. I lived there for (how long).

9. I am (single/married—wife's name).

10. I have (number) dependents (names and ages).

11. I work at (where—department—supervisor).

12. I have worked there for (how long).

13. My salary is (how much).

14. I (do/do not) have other income.

15. I do credit business with (where).

16. I owe the following (bills).

17. I bought my car (make and model) at

18. The cash price was

19. I traded in and was allowed (dollars).

20. I paid (dollars) cash.

21. The balance was financed with

22. My payments are (dollars) monthly.

23. I owe a balance of

24. I (do/do not) owe anything else on my car. (If so, name of person or company and specify item, tires, battery, motor, etc.)

25. My car had (miles) when burned/stolen.

26. My car ran (well—poorly—details).

27. I have spent (dollars) for repairs (itemize—where).

28. Itemize condition of engine, transmission, rear end, battery, tires and upholstery (good—fair—poor).

29. I feel my car was worth (dollars).

30. I use my car mainly for

31. I have my car serviced at

32. I bought gas and oil last at

33. I have oil changed every (miles).

34. My car (did/did not) burn oil (amount).

35. Go back 24 hours prior to the time of the fire and itemize every action of the insured. Include dates, times, and full names and addresses of any individuals concerned.

36. I drove my car to (where).

37. I talked to (whom).

38. (Names and address) was with me.

39. From there I went to

40. My car ran (well—poorly).

41. If car running poorly, get details.

42. Was car being driven when fire started?

43. (Name and age) has permission to drive my car.

44. I first noticed (fire—smoke) coming from (part of car).

45. I (smelled/saw) smoke or fire first.

46. It was a (flash—slow burning) fire.

47. I stopped and (raised/did not raise) hood.

48. I saw (explain in detail).

49. (Names and address) were with me.

50. (Names and address) came up soon after fire started.

51. I (did/did not) try to put fire out.

52. The smoke was (color).

53. The fire was spreading (how fast).

54. The wind was blowing from the (direction) (strong/mild).

55. The windows were (up/down).

56. The blaze was (how big).

57. The fire was (how hot—extreme/normal).

58. The first witnesses were (names and addresses).

59. Car burned for (how long).

60. I left to get help (how long gone).

61. Called (Fire Dept./Police) from (name).

62. (Name and address) took me back home or to town.

63. I had car towed to

64. My car had the following equipment: (radio, heater, auto. trans. power brakes, steering).

65. I had the following personal effects in my car: (list).

66. I would like my insurance company to (replace my car/settle for cash).

67. I (did/did not) know I had fire and theft insurance coverage.

68. I (have/have not) had any previous fire losses.

69. I (would/would not) want my car repaired if repairable.

70. I (do/do not) have substitute transportation.

_____

(Signed)

If this is a written document, the person giving the statement should place his initials by each correction and at the bottom of each page. In addition, the person or persons present during the statement should sign as witnesses. The person giving the statement should be required to sign where indicated.

When the insurance adjustor has completed his phase of participation in the investigation, the entire file should be turned over to the proper investigative agency. From this point on, the insurance company should not be involved in the investigation in any manner. By steering clear of this portion of the case, any allegations that the authorities are acting in behalf of the insurance carrier can be negated. It is common practice for defense attorneys to attempt to arouse the sympathy of the jury by implying that there is a close tie between the enforcement agencies and the insurance company.

Investigator's Salvage Examination

Armed with the files supplied by the adjustor, the people charged with the investigation of suspicious auto fires go into action. The team of investigators may consist of representatives of a local law enforcement agency, of the state agency with arson investigation responsibility, and of the National Automobile Theft Bureau.

Their first activity is a systematic inspection of the corpus delicti, the burned automobile. The salvage examination, which must be thorough, will of necessity take from three to six hours. Some investigators can conduct a fire scene examination of a burned structure in less than an hour but take several hours to complete an auto salvage examination. The explanation seems to be that a definite procedure has been developed for car salvage whereas no definite system exists for structural fire scene search.

The requirements for the step-by-step inspection of the involved vehicle which follows are not eliminated by any previous general observations at the fire scene by the investigating officers.

The Fuel System

Examine the gas tank to ascertain whether there is gas in the tank. Check the tank to see if a section of siphon hose may have slipped down into the tank. Is the gas cap in place on the filler tube neck? If not, why? Examine the flanges of the filler tube neck for evidence of an explosion. Examine the tank for rupture or loss of shape. Check the drain plug in the bottom of the tank if the car is so equipped. Conclusions to be reached from various conditions in this area were previously covered under fire scene activities.

Examine the fuel line and fitting where it connects to the tank. Is it intact? If disconnected, why? If intact, check the fitting for fresh tool marks and looseness. If this line enters the tank below the fuel level of the gasoline, it is possible that the arsonist disconnected the line and allowed gas to flow from the tank on to the ground under the car. When ignited, the result is severe damage to the underside of the vehicle, particularly in the rear section. Additionally, this line may have been disconnected to allow gas to drain into a container for the purpose of pouring gasoline in the interior or on the motor of the vehicle. Trace the fuel line from the gas tank to the fuel pump, looking for tool marks, indications of disconnection, breaks, or other damage. In one case this line had been mashed against the frame prior to the fire by contact with some object on the ground. The result was that the flow of gasoline from tank to motor was almost nil. The owner was not aware of the damaged fuel supply line. He only knew that the car would not operate properly and therefore decided to burn the vehicle.

Trace the line from the fuel pump to the carburetor. It is common practice to disconnect this line and obtain gas from this source by running the starter. Check the fittings for tool marks, finger tightness, and other indications of disconnection.

Examine the fuel pump and carburetor for missing elements which would make the car inoperable. Look for tool marks on either unit or line connections that would indicate recent efforts to repair the vehicle. In spite of the fact that the fuel pump and carburetor are constructed of white metal which has a low melting point, these parts will not normally melt as the result of an accidental fire. The presence of an air filter on top of the carburetor should be established, particularly in cases where the car's operator claims the fire occurred as the result of a backfire. The air filter acts as a flame arrester, preventing gas from being "blown" over the motor in the event of backfire.

In recent years the combustion system has been vastly complicated by various antipollution devices, some of which were developed in extreme haste under pressure from environmental groups and federal antipollution regulations. As a result, some systems caused accidental engine compartment fires. We must keep in mind, however, that this type of fire involves less than a cup of gasoline on most cars, and this will not create enough fire to spread through the fire wall and totally consume the entire vehicle.

The Electrical System

A malfunction in the electrical system is the most common cause of accidental auto fires and is the cause most often advanced by the arsonist. That fires do originate as a result of breakdowns in the electrical system is undeniable. The important point is that the extent of burning which may result from a short or failure is negligible, and fires which start from this cause do not completely consume the involved vehicle. Nevertheless, the burden is on the investigator to eliminate this as a source of an accidental fire.

There is a logical procedure for eliminating a short in the electrical wiring as the cause of an auto fire. Start with the battery and establish whether it was actually in the vehicle at the time of the fire. Without this source of power, an electrical fire is absolutely impossible. Heat damage to the battery well, especially the bottom, indicates the battery was not in place during the fire. Also, debris from insulation falling from the hood into the well proves the battery was not present during the burning.

If the battery was in place, check to see whether it is still "hot." Using normal care, contact the positive and negative posts of the battery with a section of conducting metal or make contact between the positive post and a metal surface of the car. Using either method, if there is sparking, the battery is still charged. When a short of sufficient intensity occurs to ignite the wiring, the battery will usually be exhausted. Do not, however, assume that because the battery is exhausted the fire started from a short. When the burning is premeditated a worn out battery may be substituted for a good one. Additionally, if several weeks pass between the burning and the salvage examination, the battery may be discharged during this time for lack of use.

In examining the wiring in the electrical system, keep in mind that a short will cause the wires to separate, leaving near the ends of the wires small beads or bubbles of melted metal. Wires burned in two by flames normally will be pointed at the ends. In recent years, several conducting materials have been substituted for metal in the wiring system. When the insulating surrounding some of these substances burns, the substance simply loses shape and dissipates. While this type of wiring creates some problems during the salvage examination, it is unlikely to cause a fire on account of its composition and tendency to disintegrate. Regardless of the type of wiring, remember that the small blaze which originates from a short must be close enough to some flammable material to cause ignition of the material.

If a fire starts from a short while the motor is running, the distributor points should be stuck or fused. If the fire originates as the result of a short while the vehicle is not running, the points in the voltage regulators should be stuck or fused.

We must keep in mind that the burden of proof is on the investigator to establish that the fire did not originate from a short. This can be accomplished only by a thorough, detailed examination of the entire electrical system.

The Motor Compartment

There is not much material under the hood which will burn significantly, except in the area around the fuel pump and carburetor. Extensive damage under the hood indicates that an accelerant was poured on the motor. An accidental fire on the motor may cause some damage to the fan belts and upper radiator hoses; however, if the lower hoses and belts are severely burned or destroyed, the cause can only be an extremely intense fire which is not of accidental origin.

All hoses and belts under the hood should be examined carefully for burn patterns caused by an accelerant being poured on the motor. These parts, normally of rubber, will partially absorb a liquid so that when it ignites and burns, a pattern may be left which could only be caused by direct application or splashes from an accelerant thrown on the motor.

The front motor mounts should be examined carefully. These are in a low and protected area in the motor compartment, so extensive damage indicates an intense fire of other than accidental nature. The condition of the radiator often can convey valuable information concerning the degree of heat present. When fins on the radiator core crumble on touch, this shows extreme heat not associated with accidental fires, particularly if this crumbling condition exists in the lower portion of the radiator core.

FIGURE 11-2. Motor fire not connected with interior fire. (Courtesy Commonwealth of Virginia Arson Investigation Division)

Examine the motor itself, particularly the valve cover plate, either top or side. An accelerant poured or thrown on the engine and ignited will cause burn patterns which are easily recognizable (Figure 11-2). The areas which the accelerant reaches will be burned clean, whereas the surrounding surface will still be covered with grease and road scum. Also, look for this giveaway pattern on the portion of the fender adjacent to the motor, for the arsonist may have spilled or splashed some flammable liquid on these surfaces. These areas may appear as spots where the paint has burned off or as rust spots if the burned vehicle has been exposed to the elements for some time, particularly in a humid climate. A careful search must be made for matches used to ignite an accelerant thrown on the motor, concentrating in creases and sunken areas on the motor itself.

Determine whether there is any dirt on components under the hood. It is not difficult to establish whether dirt was thrown on the motor during or after the fire, for burned soil is usually light in color and of a fine, powdery consistency.

While examining the motor, look for obvious signs of major mechanical failure, such as a cracked block, hole in the side of the block, and holes in the oil pan—obvious signs of thrown connecting rods, broken pistons, or other major problems. If no examination of the vehicle is to be made by a qualified mechanic to determine the mechanical condition of the vehicle, drop the oil pan and look for particles of metal from the connecting rods and pistons. Prior to dropping the pan, do a dipstick test on the oil. If the oil contains water, the block may be cracked from the inside.

Check carefully under the hood for missing parts and accessories, such as radiator, battery, distributor, voltage regulator, generator or alternator, carburetor, fuel pump, components of the air conditioner, power steering, and power brakes unit. Every effort must be made to establish the fact that these parts, if missing at the time of the examination, were not removed after the vehicle reached the wrecking yard. This is sometimes easier said than done because the wrecking yard owner is not willing to admit that he neglected the instructions of the insurance adjustor or investigator not to disturb the vehicle after its impoundment.

Interior of the Vehicle

Determine whether the doors were open or closed during the fire, for this may have a significant effect on the pattern of burning. If a door is closed while the fire is in progress, the burning is complete and uniform, including the door edges. Comparison between burn patterns and extent of damage on open and closed doors usually clearly indicates their position. Wind direction and velocity must be considered when making this determination.

Establish whether the windows were up or down at the time of the fire, for this has a pronounced effect on the degree of damage and rapidity of fire spread. Upholstery can smolder for hours in a tightly closed vehicle with no significant burning (Figures 11-3 and 11-4). Incendiarists have admitted returning to a car whose interior they had set on fire to find the fire had gone out for lack of oxygen. They then accomplished complete destruction of the car by using a similar method, but with the windows lowered to provide

FIGURE 11-3. All windows and doors were closed at the time of the fire, and the lack of oxygen permitted only smoldering. (Courtesy Commonwealth of Virginia Arson Investigation Division)

FIGURE 11-4. A definite pattern of a flammable liquid is evident on the rear of the front seat. The lack of oxygen permitted only smoldering, which caused superficial damage. (Courtesy Edison, New Jersey, Fire Department)

FIGURE 11-5. Complete consumption of upholstery and padding indicate the presence of an accelerant, as fire damage to the remainder of the vehicle's interior is not consistent with such a concentration of burning. (Courtesy Commonwealth of Virginia Arson Investigation Division)

oxygen (Figure 11-5). If all windows were down at the time of the fire in spite of near-zero temperature, there is reason for suspicion. Determine whether the glasses were up or down by examining the glass channels in the doors. If they are at their lowest point in the door, the glass was all the way down; if they are at the highest point, the glass was completely closed. Location of the glass channel between these two points indicates a window was partially open.

The interior must be examined for indications of excessive heat. Are all upholstery, floor mats, and door materials completely consumed? Are all glasses, white metal, and plastic materials melted? The sagging of the dash panel is indicative of intense heat which could result only from use of an accelerant. The temper of the seat springs can no longer be considered a reliable method of establishing degree of heat, especially in inexpensive cars, in which the material used in the springs is readily affected by low temperatures.

Digging into the debris on the floor of the vehicle is a tedious task. Often a mesh screen is used to assure that nothing is missed, regardless of how small it may be. Search for many things simultaneously and do not overlook any of these items:

1. Containers. A metal container will be obvious, but residue of a glass container is most difficult to locate and identify. It would usually melt into a blob, and any other source of such a blob, such as an inside rear view mirror, must be eliminated.

2. Radio, Heater, Tape Deck. While these items will be damaged in varying degrees, they will not burn out of sight but will remain identifiable. Absence of these items indicates preplanning for the fire.

3. Contents. Many times the assured, in order to make his version of an accidental fire more believable or to gain a larger insurance settlement, will claim extensive content loss—fishing gear, guns, tools, cameras, sums of money, and clothing. Careful sifting of the debris will reveal evidence of the remains of these items. In the case of clothing, search for remains of buttons, zippers, snaps, and the like. If the clothes were alleged to be on hangers, the task is much simpler and more conclusive. If sums of money are allegedly lost, it is usually claimed that bills and coins were in the glove compartment of the vehicle. Extreme care in searching in this area will reveal the presence of money if it was actually in the car at the time of the fire.

4. Accelerant. Every handful of debris should be carefully checked for the odor of gasoline, kerosene, or other flammable liquids. The use of a Sniffer is very time-consuming, and our own built-in sniffer, the nose, may produce adequate results. Upholstery and floor matting should be examined, particularly in low places or floor wells where an accelerant might settle. Water applied by the fire department and the normal cover of debris may preserve small quantities of a liquid for long periods of time. They will evaporate rapidly once exposed and must be placed in an airtight container immediately.

5. Glass. Windshield, rear window, and door glasses will either shatter or melt, normally falling into the interior of the vehicle during the burning. Debris serves to protect this glass. Examination should be made, and if the soot deposit on protected surfaces is oily, this may indicate the presence of an accelerant. This test is not irrefutable evidence, however, since various plastics and foam rubber padding may leave an oily residue.

6. Keys. The significance of locating or not locating the keys during the debris search depends primarily on the owner/assured's version of the fire. If the car was reported stolen, the presence of the ignition key on the floor under the keyway would require an explanation. Not

locating the key may be important if the owner/operator has stated that he barely got out of the car alive before being enveloped by masses of flame, for he would not have time to remove the keys prior to making such a hurried escape.

Search of the interior must be done with meticulous care and according to a careful plan. If two people are making the examination, section off the vehicle and don't permit random picking around in the debris by both individuals. Organize the search and allow plenty of time to do the job, for a poorly planned and hasty interior search is a complete waste.

Examination of the trunk area may indicate forced entry into the trunk. If so, establish whether this was done by the fire department while extinguishing the blaze. When the trunk appears to have been forced prior to the burning, this might substantiate that the car was stolen and that the thief or thieves, not having keys, pried the trunk lid up.

Determine whether the jack and lug wrench were in the trunk at the time of the fire. Their absence is extremely unusual and indicates preparation for the fire. Likewise, a missing spare wheel and tire is a suspicious circumstance. Even though the trunk area is severely burned and the tire completely consumed, metal beading will remain on the wheel. Were there other items in the trunk or did it appear to have been cleaned out prior to the fire?

Exterior

Careful examination must be made of the underside of the vehicle. The exhaust system, including manifold, muffler, and tail pipe must be checked for leaks or breaks, for the investigator may be questioned on cross-examination as to whether these accessories, if defective, could have been the source of ignition.

The rear springs should be examined. If these are sagged so that the rear of the car is down on the wheels, intense and unusual heat is indicated whose source must be determined.

Tires and wheels should be examined for indications of switching.

The vehicle should be checked for missing accessories, such as radio antenna and outside mirror. The base of the antenna is constructed of white metal with a low melting point. If it melts, it may appear that the antenna was removed. The extent of damage to the hole in the fender indicates whether the antenna was removed prior to the fire. Likewise, the appearance of the area at the base of the outside mirror is the key in determining whether it was removed prior to the fire or melted off during the fire. In both cases, the burn pattern will be uniform with the surrounding area if the accessory was removed prior to the fire; lesser damage and a pattern consistent with the shape of the base of the accessory indicates melting out during the burning.

Survey the burn pattern on the entire exterior of the vehicle, including the hood, which will be burned more severely if it was down during the fire. Sometimes hood position is difficult to establish; it may have been up in the early stages of the blaze and lowered as a result of heat damage to the suspension springs. Hood position is important in corroborating or contradicting the assured's version of the fire. The burn patterns on roof, hood, fenders, doors, and trunk lid should indicate the areas of most intense burning, taking into consideration wind direction and combustible materials in that section of the vehicle.

Prior to leaving the salvage, the investigators should evaluate their findings and assure that their conclusions and observations are congruent. After generally reexamining the burned vehicle once, repeat the operation to guarantee that no aspect of the salvage examination procedure has been overlooked.

At this point, the investigators must pull the whole case together and develop a projected course of action. The first activity is to review, study, and analyze all information available. This would include the insurance adjustor's file containing information statements from the assured and key witnesses, all insurance and financial information about the assured, the results of the examination of the vehicle by a qualified mechanic, and any other pertinent facts. Any information provided by fire department personnel and other local officials at the fire scene should be reviewed. The investigators must decide whether it is necessary to verify information provided by the adjustor or whether such action may blow the whole case. For example, if the investigators confirm financial data previously furnished by the adjustors, the source of such information may advise the assured that the burning of his car is under investigation by law enforcement officials. Likewise, a witness contacted for a second time may tip off the owner. Every effort must be made to preserve the element of surprise so that the assured does not have an opportunity to shore up his defenses.

The investigators should visit the fire scene and conduct a thorough search in accordance with a procedure previously outlined. It is advisable that the fire department officer in charge and other local officials at the scene accompany the investigator to the burning site to convey any observations as well as specific location of items found by them. The neighborhood may be recanvassed if the investigators believe this will produce information not previously obtained. Recanvassing is not a reflection on the ability of the local officials who made the initial canvass, but a recognition of the fact that at the time of the first interview much information now available had not been developed.

At this point in the investigation, timing and coordination become critical. Once the interviewing of witnesses and the questioning of passengers in the vehicle at the time of the fire begins, the action must be continuous. If there is a time lag, the witnesses will contact each other and the assured, and the element of surprise will be lost. This phase of the investigation may last ten, twelve, or fourteen hours without significant interruption, and ideally, when the assured is picked up for questioning he is not even aware of the fact that the loss is under investigation.

In many auto cases the interrogation approach is factual, that is, based on facts obtained as a result of a thorough investigation. The assured may be told that motive has been established (financial problems, mechanical failure), that there were evident preparations for the fire (switched wheels and/or tires, removed radio, heater, etc.), that the car could not have burned as alleged, and that evidence of accelerants has been found in the salvage. Confessions are obtained far more frequently in incendiary car fires than in structural losses. Of the many factors which contribute to this success, probably the most important is that the investigators are thoroughly prepared with all the facts at hand which enable them to refute the assured's version of an accidental fire.

After a successful interrogation, normal investigative procedures are followed. Contact is made with the local prosecutor and an arrest warrant is obtained which may be served by the investigators or by local authorized agents. Security of physical evidence must be assured, and a comprehensive investigation report must be completed promptly. From this point on we follow guidelines furnished in Chapter 16.

Auto arsonists can be apprehended and convicted, but no investigative procedure, no matter how diligently followed, will guarantee a conviction. Even when no arrest or conviction follows the investigation, the fact that a thorough investigation was made definitely serves as a deterrent to other would-be car burners. Probably the most effective way of curtailing auto arson is to convince every fire and police official that any total vehicle fire should be viewed with suspicion and investigated.

12 Explosions

Explosion may be defined as the sudden release of energy accompanied by noise, a great change in volume, and a going away of material from the source. This definition involves four simultaneous occurrences, all of which must be present: (1) sudden release of energy, (2) noise, (3) increase in volume, and (4) ejection of materials.

Definitions

It is essential to define certain common terms relative to explosions and explosives.

1. Detonation: The rapid molecular splitting-up of an explosive substance under the influence of a shock or blast of a suitable initiator; an extremely rapid and violent explosion, with instantaneous release of chemical energy.

2. Deflagration: An explosion which occurs in a relatively slow manner and may be described as instant, intense burning.

3. High order: Detonation of chemical mixtures or combustible vapors at their optimum rate.

4. Low order: Deflagration of chemical mixtures or combustible vapors at less than their optimum rate.

5. Brisance: The shattering effect or capacity of an explosive to do damage.

6. Power: Destructive influences varying with the type of explosion; excluding nuclear, the most powerful potential is chemical, followed by mechanical, dust, and gas, in that order.

7. Force: Force depends on the rate of release of energy over a period of time more than it does on the amount of energy. The force created is dependent on the type of explosion. If a building filled with explosive gas is ignited, the force is more or less uniformly distributed, and damage will generally be uniform throughout. On the other hand, if the blast cause or source is chemical, the damage will be greater near the source and gradually diminish as the distance increases. The energy of a chemical explosion, being more concentrated at the source, may expand into the earth or floor, causing a depression. A dust or gaseous explosion will not ordinarily cause this indentation. Force can be determined by locating fragments and measuring the distance from the source.

8. Sensitivity: The ease with which an explosive may be detonated; the resistance to shock, heat, and friction.

9. Hygroscopic: An explosive is described as hygroscopic if it tends to absorb moisture from the atmosphere unless covered by a protective coating.

Types of Explosion

Explosions are generally divided into five categories: (1) mechanical, (2) gaseous, (3) chemical, (4) dust, and (5) nuclear. Since an investigator is seldom if ever involved with nuclear blasts, this topic will not be covered.

Mechanical

Mechanical explosions often involve materials, substances, or components which are not hazardous under normal conditions. For example, water and air are not generally considered probable causes of an explosion. However, under certain conditions, they can be the direct cause of an explosion and the resulting fire which may occur.

For example, water in its natural state in a steam boiler is not dangerous. However, if there is a mechanical malfunction in the boiler control system, the internal pressure of the steam rises to a level which the boiler walls cannot tolerate. A blowout or rupture results which may be of high or low order. In a low order explosion the boiler walls split, thus immediately releasing the steam and allowing the pressure in the boiler to dissipate at once. The burst occurs at the moment of maximum pressure, and the pressure drops to that of the atmosphere immediately. On the other hand, in a high order explosion the pressure within the tank may build to the extreme point of boiler wall tolerance and be released by overall bursting of the boiler. The result is an explosion of great power and force which may produce extensive damage.

If the water level in a steam boiler tank is dangerously low or there is no water at all in the tank because of some mechanical problem, air pressure within the boiler will increase to intolerable levels, producing results similar to excessive steam pressure. Both of these conditions can occur during the course of a fire and should be a major concern to fire fighters during the suppression of a blaze of any intensity in the area near the boiler.

A liquid which under normal conditions would not be considered hazardous is the oil in electrical transformers. In the case of a malfunction, this liquid may be heated to the point at which it must seek release, and a low order explosion will occur, usually producing only minor damage and heavy smoke.

In determining source and cause, the investigator must be alert to the existence of inert, nonhazardous liquids which under pressure may create explosive conditions. Buildings under construction which contain concrete columns are an area of concern, particularly when the concrete is not completely dry. Steam pressure can build within the column and cause a high order explosion of devastating power.

Gaseous

Gaseous explosions generally involve natural, LP, sewer, and other flammable gases, including ignitable vapors released from flammable liquids such as gasoline.

Natural Gas   This possesses certain characteristics and built-in safeguards which under normal conditions make its use completely safe. These same characteristics along with a breakdown in the safeguard systems make it hazardous.

First, this agent is very difficult to contain. A flaw or breakdown in the cross-country transmission lines or local distribution pipes can produce disaster.

Second, this fuel is lighter than air. This would appear to be a favorable characteristic, as the vapors tend to rise and dissipate into the atmosphere. However, when escape is blocked by concrete road surface or hard ground, the gas will travel great distances underground, leaking into basements and sewers. When seeking a route of escape, natural gas will follow the course of least resistance.

In one case, a sewer and gas line ran side by side in a ditch. Repairs were required which made it necessary to dig up both lines. After the necessary repairs and replacements were made, both lines were covered with a layer of loose gravel topped by dirt with a high clay content, which was then tamped down. In the course of making these repairs, a hole had been knocked in the sewer pipe leading into a nearby residence. The occupant reported smelling gas in her house, and extensive efforts were made to locate the source of the problem without success. After several weeks, a violent explosion occurred within the dwelling, severely injuring its only occupant. Subsequent investigation revealed that there was a leak in the line at a point over 100 feet from the hole in the sewer line leading into the house. The vapors, unable to escape through the heavy clay, followed the path of least resistance through the loose gravel around the gas and sewer line, into the hole in the sewer line, and on into the house.

The characteristic ability of natural gas to travel substantial distances underground can create problems for the investigator. When seeking the source of gas, he may locate a leak at distances up to 200 feet from the point of ignition or location of the explosion.

Gases lighter than air tend to rise to the ceiling so that when ignition occurs the walls are forced out at ceiling level. The exterior of the structure takes on a bulging appearance at points of accumulation of vapors. The interior may show the same bulging effects where the walls separate from the ceiling at ceiling height.

Third, this fuel is odorless, so codes require that odorants be added to warn of escaping gas. However, when the gas has passed through any substance capable of filtering the odor, especially loose soil, this warning smell is no longer noticeable.

Fourth, the flammable limits of this agent are 4%–5% to 14%–15%, a rather narrow range; but any concentration either above or below the flammable limits can be changed without warning. Thus an entire vapor-filled area can ignite from a spark if the concentration comes within the flammable limits. When the gas at the time of ignition is near the lower limits of the flammable range the explosion will be severe and the fire hazard minimal. At the optimum midway point in the flammable range, force and power will be maximized and the fire hazard increased. At the upper limits of the range, the force and power diminish, but because of the quantity of gas present, the fire hazard is greater, for the amount of heat and fire released at the upper limit is greater, and the gases released by an explosion under upper limit conditions are subject to ignition, thus creating secondary fires.

Fifth, natural gas ignition can have effects on a structure which defy explanation. One wall may be completely blown out while window glass on the opposite wall remains intact. In many cases the interior partitions and doors remain relatively undamaged because of equal pressure from both sides. The effect of a natural gas explosion is one of pushing rather than shattering, and damage to the plumbing, wiring, and contents of a structure is often due to falling walls and ceilings, and possibly the collapse of the structure.

LP Gas   LP gas is generally either propane or butane, manufactured gases similar to natural gas, with one extremely important exception: LP gas is heavier than air.

When LP vapor escapes into the atmosphere in the open, it will settle into pockets or low lying areas, just waiting for a source of ignition. This creates a massive problem when a truck transporting liquified petroleum turns over and leakage occurs. A huge gaseous cloud may cling to the highway, and the first spark from any vehicle entering the cloud will cause ignition and holocaust.

A leaking LP tank of small capacity suitable for residential or small structures can cause significant problems. If not dissipated by air movements, these vapors will cling to the ground and perhaps make their way into the structure to a source of ignition. At ignition, the entire structure may be involved almost instantaneously. The resulting explosion and fire present immediate problems to the fire department and subsequently to the investigator, particularly when the tank is damaged by the blast or fire, because locating a leak around a heavily damaged tank installation can be most difficult.

When LP gas ignition occurs within a structure, the result is different from a natural gas explosion. Since bottled or tank gases are heavier than air and normally settle to floor level, when ignition takes place, pressure is exerted on the lower section of the walls. In a two-story structure the first floor wall may be blown out and the second floor wall will simply slide down into the space vacated by the lower wall.

Other Gases   It is impossible to discuss all the hazardous gases in this chapter. In making an analysis of a scene where gas is the possible cause of explosion, the characteristics of suspected agents can be compared with natural and LP gas. Some factors involved are (1) weight in comparison with air, (2) odor, (3) flammable limits, and (4) normal effect of ignition. Compiling this comparative information may eliminate many gases and help establish others as possibilities.

Vapors from flammable liquids may cause an explosion. If at the time of ignition the vapors are confined, an explosion of substantial power may occur. If the vapor is "free" at ignition, the result is rapid burning.

Chemical

The ignition of certain explosives and blasting agents of the commercial variety, bombs and incendiary devices, and unstable or explosive chemicals are included in the category of chemical explosions.

An explosive is a gaseous, liquid, or solid substance or mixture of substances which, when subjected to heat, friction, percussion, or other suitable initial impulse, undergoes a very rapid chemical transformation.

This forms other substances, mainly or entirely gaseous, which at the time of their formation occupy a volume much greater than that of the original substance.

Explosives are classified as either low or high. A low explosive is one in which the reaction to ignition is that of rapid burning or combustion. The substance involved changes from a solid to a gaseous state slowly, and the effect is a pushing or shoving rather than a rending or tearing. A high explosive is one in which the reaction to ignition is a rapid molecular disintegration or decomposition which takes place throughout the entire body. The change from a solid to a gaseous state is almost instantaneous. Such sudden generation of gases and extremely rapid expansion produce a shattering effect which can overcome great resistance.

Some common explosives and their characteristics are discussed in the following paragraphs. These are readily available to the average person through commercial sources and for this reason are most often encountered by the investigator.

Black Powder   Black powder varies from a black, very fine powder to dense pellets which may be black or greyish-black. It is composed of 75% potassium nitrate, 15% charcoal, and 10% sulphur and can be made from charcoal, sulphur, and saltpeter, items readily obtainable at most hardware and/or drugstores. Even though it is a low explosive, black powder is considered the most dangerous and treacherous of all explosives.

Since this material has an extremely slow rate of detonation and is relatively insensitive to shock, why is it such a problem? A major consideration is the extremely low ignition temperature; even a spark of static electricity will ignite black powder. Once ignited, it burns furiously at temperatures up to 3000° F. When it burns in open areas, there is only burning; however, when confined in any degree, the substance will explode with almost high explosive force.

Black powder has an extreme tendency to absorb moisture, which causes deterioration affecting its strength and sensitivity to detonation. Another factor which makes the substance treacherous is that the components used to produce it can be mixed in varying proportions that will produce varying reactions.

The hazards of black powder may be illustrated by a case history. During the course of a fire in a small town drugstore a tremendous blast occurred in the center of the building. All possible normal causes were eliminated, including various liquids in the prescription department. After several weeks, a senior citizen came forward with information which solved the mystery: the site of the burned out drugstore was formerly occupied by a hardware store which kept black powder in a hole in the ground accessible through a trap door. The black powder which exploded during the fire had been in the hole for over 50 years!

In considering black powder as a possible cause of explosion, the investigator must take several factors into consideration: the composition of the batch, its age, conditions under which it was stored, and whether or not it was confined at the time of ignition.

Dynamite   Dynamite is composed of nitroglycerine combined with a porous filler as a desensitizer. Although it comes in various sizes, the most common stick is a cylindrical cartridge 1 to 1½ inches in diameter and 8 inches in length, encased in a heavy waterproof paper. Dynamite is a high explosive whose shattering effect is over four times greater than that of black powder. A blasting cap is ordinarily required to detonate dynamite, but the substance is easily ignited and can explode while burning, particularly when burned in quantity.

Dynamite can become extremely dangerous if not stored so that the cartridges are horizontal, for nitroglycerine may exude if the cartridges are stored on end. Sawdust should be kept under the dynamite to absorb any nitroglycerine which does exude; this sawdust must be replaced frequently. The storage site must be dry, well ventilated, and free from extremes in temperature. Some experts recommend that if dynamite is in storage for a long period of time each stick should be rotated frequently. An oily substance on the casings of the cartridges or stains on the packing cases indicate the nitroglycerine has separated from the porous base. Dynamite in this condition is extremely sensitive and should be destroyed immediately.

When dynamite is suspected as the cause of an explosion, the investigator must make several determinations: the age of the dynamite, how long it had been in its present location at the time of detonation, whether it was stored under proper conditions, any indications that the nitroglycerine and porous base were separating, and what was used as an initiator.

Ordinarily dynamite is detonated by a blasting cap, either electric or nonelectric. Such a device requires the use of wiring, tape, and possibly a timing device. In spite of a high order blast, remains of this initiator may be discovered in a careful search of the scene.

When dynamite is detonated, particularly in a confined area, the appearance of the affected exposures is quite different from that of a gaseous or black powder explosion. In contrast to the pushing and shoving effect of exploding gases, dynamite produces a shattering effect. The devastation is much more extensive than with black powder. More important, the point of detonation can usually be determined, as damage at that immediate point will be much greater than in the surrounding area. Determining the source of ignition or detonation then becomes the investigator's immediate concern.

Other Explosives   It is impossible to study all explosives in depth; however, the investigator should be thoroughly familiar with all the characteristics of nitroglycerine, TNT, and ammonium nitrate.

Unstable Materials   The list of unstable materials subject to explosion is almost endless. The investigator is concerned with arson, not chemical explosions which occur mainly as the result of accidents. While the hazards of organic peroxides—which are unstable, sensitive to shock, easily ignited, and productive of large fires which are most often accompanied by detonation—may not directly concern the investigator, he should have some knowledge of them.

Dust   Flour, coal, and grain are not the only hazardous dusts. Dust from almost any material is subject to burning and exploding when mixed in proper proportions with air.

The investigator must determine the potential for a dust explosion, particularly when operations in a structure involve agricultural products, metals, soaps, paper, food products, and wood. The results of dust explosions from these products depend on several factors, the most important being confinement of the combustible powder or dust. If ignition occurs when the product is confined, like grain dust in a storage silo, the resulting blowout will be tremendously powerful. On the other hand, if burning is initiated in an unconfined atmosphere, the result can be better described as rapid burning.

There is a mistaken notion that if dust is not actually floating in the air within a structure no hazard exists. In any situation where dust accumulates on exposed surfaces such as beams, rafters, and floors, the danger is present. While ignition of dust under such conditions is more difficult, once a fire occurs these dust deposits will burn very rapidly, and an explosion may well occur. The investigator must take this into consideration when he attempts to account for total involvement of a structure in a very short period of time. Inquiry must be made relative to general housekeeping and procedures designed to prevent dust accumulation throughout the building.

Investigation

In the preceding pages, we have given the subject of explosives and explosions a very general coverage. Extensive literature is available to the investigator on specific explosive materials through the Institute of Makers of Explosives, 420 Lexington Avenue, New York, New York 10017, and through the Manufacturing Chemists Association, 1825 Connecticut Avenue, N.W., Washington, D.C. 20009. Since he cannot be knowledgeable about all explosives, the investigator must on occasion call on individuals possessing particular expertise in this technical field.

The investigator must determine whether there actually was an explosion, a building collapse, or a back draft during a fire. When a back draft introduces air into an atmosphere of superheated gas and smoke, what happens may have all the earmarks of a low order explosion.

Fire fighters responding to an alarm in a large warehouse found the building locked, closed, and tightly sealed. Looking through a window, they observed several minor fires burning in some cloth packing material. To gain access to the fire, they raised an overhead loading door and returned to their truck 30 feet from the building to begin fire-fighting operations. Within a matter of seconds there occurred what was described as an explosion. Flames shot out through the open doorway, enveloping the men and truck, injuring several seriously, and setting fire to the truck.

What happened? No one had been in the building for approximately three hours prior to the fire, and from all indications the fire had been smoldering and burning for two hours or more. Due to the tight seal of this building, heat, gases, and smoke had accumulated. When oxygen was introduced without vertical ventilation to relieve the critical condition, an "explosion" took place. The direction of the blowout was through the open door, the most readily accessible escape route.

General Examination of the Scene

A general examination of the scene should be accomplished as soon as possible. The investigator should be accompanied by the fire and/or police officer in charge at the scene. If the site has not already been sealed off and secured, this must be done immediately for the integrity of the investigation as well as for safety. There may be explosives in the area which did not detonate, or, if gas was involved, it may re-accumulate and cause further ignition and fires.

This general examination and the fire or police officer's explanation of what happened may provide the investigator sufficient information to make some preliminary conclusions. For example, if there is a crater, gas can normally be eliminated as a cause or source. If the walls are shoved or pushed out, very likely gas or dust is involved. The size of a crater may indicate the quantity of explosives and whether they were high or low order explosives.

Interviewing Witnesses

The physical, mental, and emotional condition of the witnesses is an important consideration. Witnesses near the scene are often seriously injured or in shock. Witnessing a blast is a traumatic experience, and for this reason information supplied by different people who have seen the same thing may be completely contradictory.

In fairness to the witness, conditions accompanying an explosion can be confusing. For example, a witness or witnesses may state that there were two explosions, with the second immediately following the first. What may have happened is that the witness saw the light or flash of the detonation and then heard the sound. Remember that light travels 186,000 miles per second, while sound travels 1,000 feet per second. What was a single explosion may have been perceived as two separate and distinct explosions.

On the other hand, there may very well have been two detonations, one triggering the other, for one explosion may have caused the sympathetic detonation of other sensitive substances. Examination of the scene in such cases may corroborate the testimony of witnesses.

In a recent case, a steam boiler exploded in the basement of a large office building, rupturing a major natural gas supply line. Damage from the first blast was minimal, but ignition of the gas which followed devastated the building.

Witnesses should be questioned concerning conditions prior to, at the instant of, and after the blast. Complete destruction may make it impossible to reconstruct the scene physically, so the investigator's only recourse is to re-create conditions from information supplied by witnesses or people familiar with the area or structure involved. Employees, particularly maintenance people or those working in the immediate area, may be helpful. The building contractor or architect may furnish plans or blueprints. Public utility engineers may help to locate electric, gas, and other utility lines both within the structure and in the area. Newspaper files may contain photographs of the building taken prior to the incident. If the fire department has done preplanning on the building, this can be a very valuable source of information.

Information obtained from witnesses on preblast conditions may concern potential causes. The smell of leaking gas may have been detected, as well as other unusual or unnatural odors. Reports of such odors going back several days or weeks may have been reported. Efforts by the gas company to detect the sources of any such odor are recorded. If a manufacturing plant is involved, processes and chemical operations must be studied, a list of all hazardous materials present must be compiled, and their characteristics must be reviewed in detail. Information concerning storage and safety precautions for these substances must be determined. In many cases involving such material, investigators must obtain extensive references or seek technical assistance.

Weather conditions immediately prior to the occurrence must be established, for wind velocity or lack thereof could be a significant factor in a suspected gas explosion. Certain hazardous materials become unstable under conditions of extreme heat or cold.

When witnesses are questioned about observations at the instant of detonation, it is probable that there will be conflicting information. Interview all witnesses, including fire fighters, police, news media personnel, and all people who observed the event. Ask questions about the color of the explosion and accompanying smoke, for certain hazardous materials can be identified by the color at the time of detonation or deflagration and by the color of smoke which follows ignition. How far were the witnesses from the explosion, were they knocked down or protected by a wall or other solid material, did their ears ring, and did missiles fly by them through the air? Were there unusual odors, such as a sweet smell which might identify dynamite, or an acrid odor associated with most explosives, including military explosives?

After-the-fact questions may consist of general inquiries on the conditions observed by the witness. Were there other blasts following the main detonation or deflagration by either seconds or minutes? If a fire followed the blast, what was the color of any smoke or flame? Did the structure collapse immediately or some time after the initial explosion?

Searching the Scene

Once the type of explosion has been determined, the detailed search of the scene begins. If the center of the blast indicates explosives were involved, work from this point outward. Prior to this time photographs, including aerials, should be made of the entire area. A map or diagram to scale of the entire scene must be made. Distances from the blast center to the points where damage occurs and points at which any article possibly connected with the blowout are found can be entered on the diagram. Examine the blast center in detail, not overlooking any article, regardless of how small. Fragments of explosives or blasting caps and pieces of containers, such as pipes or cans, rope, wire, burned fuse, or batteries, may be found. Buried in the debris may be residue of the explosive itself, which must be collected if in soil, or gathered from walls, bricks, cinder blocks, wooden surfaces, or any surface which might have been exposed to the blast. This residue material, which may be removed from solid surfaces with a vacuum cleaner, should then be transported to a laboratory for microscopic examination. Location of each item collected must be noted on the diagram. The evidence must be carefully sealed in separate containers and properly labeled.

After completely examining the debris at the center for any clues, expand the search in an organized manner from this point outward. Again, objects believed connected with the occurrence should be photographed, tagged, labeled, and properly preserved in preparation for laboratory analysis.

When gas is suspected as the possible cause, gas samplings must be taken with appropriate instruments at what appears to be the center of the explosion. From this point on, the investigation should concentrate on finding the source of the gas, which may involve examination of gas appliances and lines within the structure. If no determination can be made here, the search for the source must be expanded to entry lines. It may be necessary to investigate the gas main system for the entire area. If there is a loss that cannot be accounted for, leakage throughout the system may have caused the explosion.

LP gas and natural gas are seldom used by arsonists, but frequently an investigator will be called on to investigate such a gas explosion from which fatalities resulted.

Expanding the Investigation

Once the type of explosive device used has been identified, the investigator's assignment is to apprehend the culprit if a criminal act is suspected. A very important aspect of this phase of the investigation, as with fires, is establishing motive. The victims must be interviewed to identify any individual or group with whom they have had problems. As with fires, an insignificant event may be the catalyst causing some unstable person to seek revenge.

Recently an ex-convict, upon being released from prison, sought revenge against the prosecutor in the case by placing a metal can full of explosives on top of the attorney's car. When the victim raised the can, a mechanism triggered a blast which blew off both of the prosecutor's hands and caused other serious injuries, including eye damage.

Another motive behind many bombings is furtherance of a cause or protest. Action groups, whether for political, geopolitical or religious reasons, plant bombs in public buildings, banks, department stores, airports, or other places of assembly. The truly tragic aspect of this activity is that many times innocent people are killed and maimed. It appears that the only means of preventing such tragedies is by increased and tighter security measures, which may involve some loss of personal liberty, invasion of privacy, or violation of other rights in the cause of securing citizens' right to live in safety.

An investigative procedure which often brings favorable results is tracing the explosives to their source. Any reports of missing explosives should be checked out. Inventories of caps as well as supplies of safety fuse and other items which might have been used in the setup should be carefully checked. Many states require that detailed records be kept of shipment, use, and storage of explosives. Purchases of electrician's tape, wiring, batteries, and rope or string should be investigated. These are very time-consuming activities, but, when the pieces of the puzzle are fitted together, they may lead to the perpetrator.

13 The Juvenile Fire Problem

It has been estimated that as many as 50% of all incendiary/suspicious fires are attributable to juveniles, but this figure may be nothing more than "guestimate" for several reasons. First of all, can we consider a fire set by a four-year-old incapable of malice to be incendiary? Second, is the blaze started by a six-year-old playing with matches in a closet incendiary? Regardless of the questionable accuracy of such figures, however, we must recognize that fires set by juveniles are a major problem. Unfortunately, there is no indication that the problem is resolving itself; indeed, the number of fires falling into this category continues to spiral upward along with all other incendiary/suspicious blazes.

Generally, efforts to solve the juvenile problem take two directions. On the one hand, there is the profound analysis of why juveniles set fires, replete with highly technical terms and verbiage which means absolutely nothing to the average investigator. On the other, there is the analytical study of the ages at which boys and girls set fires and for what reasons, which may be of psychological interest to the person who did the study but is of little value to the investigator. Our efforts in the following pages will be directed toward a common-sense approach and study of the juvenile problem.

Childhood Development

There are three problem areas beyond control of the child which may lead to deviant behavior, including fire setting: inherent problems, environmental problems, and enculturation problems.

Inherent problems such as minimal brain dysfunction, motor neural complications, and genetic deficiencies occur at the earliest stages of a child's life, and in no way can they be construed as being his fault. They are no one's fault, yet in reality, they exist and their subsequent impact on the child and society can be devastating, as the annals of crime show. At the same time, many children suffering from the same inherent problems succeed and live life to its fullest. Why?

Environmental problems such as malnutrition, cultural deprivation and unstable family relationships are the lot of millions of children throughout the country. Again, no one person is at fault; rather, the social forces that result in these problems defy the control of anyone. However, as above, many children suffering from the same environmental problems succeed and live life to its fullest. Why?

The third problem area is that of enculturation. Enculturation means nothing more than teaching a child how to play the "game" of life. Children come into this world a blank. Somebody has to teach them—either directly or by example—how to get along with people, how to satisfy their basic life needs and how to perceive themselves. The child has little control over the quality of this training; he is just a recipient. At the same time, he will be a product of this training. Again, children that share the same background turn out differently—one a success, the other a thief. Why?

The foregoing three problem areas—inherent, environmental, and enculturation— do not, in and of themselves, lead to deviant behavior. If a child starts life without any problems in the above areas, he will probably develop into a healthy individual. However, the more problems a child has in the above areas, the more susceptible he will be to the negative factors around him as he grows up. Now let's look at four aspects of a child's surroundings that will aggravate these problem areas.

Social factors such as the family status, the existence of prejudice and even the availability of outside assistance to the family unit, all impinge on the child's development. These factors are beyond his control and, in fact, exert their influence long before he is even aware of it.

Demographic factors, such as the quality of a child's peer group and the quality of the adults, tend to play a significant role in his social growth. A study . . . showed a significant clustering between the residences of juvenile delinquents and adult felons throughout a series of school districts in Western Michigan. Here again, the child has no control over the selection of the adults surrounding him. Yet, in an almost instinctive manner, he will tend to model himself after them.

Economic factors also play an important part in determining the surroundings of a child. Unemployment is a reality that hangs on the swing of the economy, as is so evident today. Biting sarcasm is flung in the face of the child who appears on the playground in ragged clothes or shoddy shoes. The child does not understand terms like unemployment or layoffs, yet he feels their results just the same.

The final factor is the educational system. One has to travel through but a few schools to see the wide range in structure, quality, and the variety of services offered. To the average child, this difference may have little meaning; however, to a child suffering from a learning disability, the impact may be traumatic. The absence of a special education teacher may mean the difference between academic success or failure. Today, the link between academic failure and subsequent delinquency is obvious.

All four of the preceding factors impinge on the child—to negate or enhance his potential for deviant behavior. Remember, we are still speaking of an eight- or nine-year-old child, a child who is still in elementary school, and yet, one whose future life-style has already been determined—determined to a large degree by factors over which he has absolutely no control.

First we looked at the development of a potential for deviant behavior within a child. This potential originates from the occurrence of inherent problems (genetic deficiencies, motor neural complications), environmental problems (malnutrition, unstable family), and enculturation problems (immature adult models). What we have at this point is a small child who is going to be very vulnerable to the future and what it holds in store. The situation is very similar to the weakened hospital patient who must avoid exposure to any respiratory virus, yet has little control over the situation.

Next, we looked at four aspects of a child's environment—social, demographic, economic, and educational—that impinge on his potential for deviant behavior just as pneumonia attacks the hospital patient. (Philip Hogan, "The Adolescent Mind in Arson," *Fire and Arson Investigator* 26 (July–September 1975): 7–8. Reprinted by permission.)

Juvenile Age Groups

For purposes of discussing motives, "trademarks," and special problems we will loosely classify juveniles into three age groups: infancy—birth through age six; preadolescence—seven through twelve; adolescence—thirteen through seventeen. It must be recognized that the highly intelligent or precocious youngster can and will think and act at a level beyond his age group; by the same token, the less intelligent child who develops slower will perform in an age category below his actual years. The emotional maturity of the individual must also be taken into consideration. In dealing with the juvenile, the investigator must not categorically accept the age as the level of development.

The Infant

Until the child reaches about four years of age he or she does not set fires with any deliberate intent. Standing in the rain, squishing mud through his fingers or toes, encountering firsthand the physical world around him enthrall the youngster at this point. He must experience and experiment with each new discovery. The child's learning process at this age involves experimentation which may take many forms: playing with or poking into open or fireplace flames, igniting paper and sticks, striking matches. This experimental curiosity exhibited by the very young is perfectly normal. At this stage of development they are coming face to face with a fascinating phenomenon of nature—fire.

On reaching the developmental age of four years, the child may begin to set fires with deliberate intent and with motive. Legally and morally he is incapable of malice, but this has little material effect on the damage which may result. Motive can often be established by the location of the fire. Blazes in bassinets, baby cribs, nurseries, toy boxes, and closets or drawers in which baby clothes are kept are an indication that sibling rivalry, competition with brothers and sisters, may be a motive. The offending child sees a younger brother or sister competing for the love and attention of the parents. An extremely serious situation has developed, which must be dealt with by the parents before serious injury or death to a helpless baby results. Usually there are some forewarnings of this in the form of antagonistic acts by the older child—striking the baby, throwing objects in the crib where the infant is asleep, or taking toys or playthings away apparently to cause the infant to cry.

A small child will often set fire to a bed for reasons other than experimentation and mischief. He may have seen his mother and father engaging in intercourse and, believing his mother was being abused, destroys the bed to prevent this from happening again. Perhaps the child was sleeping with the parents prior to the arrival of a new brother or sister who has replaced him or her in the parents' bed. Has a loved one recently died or been ill in the bed in which the fire occurred? The child may think the bed responsible and be striking at a hated object.

Trademarks   Most fires started by this age group occur in the home or in the home of a near relative, because the very young child lacks mobility. Fires set in easily accessible but isolated places, such as basements and closets, point to the small child, as do the remains of match boxes, books of matches, or struck matches. Usually a very simple method is used to start the blaze. Often the things burned are most unusual, such as the rubber tips on door stops, rolls of toilet paper, and similar objects. The fire setter shows little knowledge of what will burn; igniting and dropping paper into toilet bowls and bathtubs is typical.

Special Problems Parents may be the major barrier to successful cause determination of fires set by this age group. The blazes may be written off as caused by careless smoking or of undetermined origin because the parents refuse to accept the fact that little Junior is the guilty party. Even though all evidence indicates this, the parents often become defensive and belligerent when it is implied that one of their children is responsible, for to them such fire setting may imply that the child is "sick," emotionally disturbed, or mentally deficient, conditions which no mother and father like to admit. Establishing and maintaining a positive, problem-solving relationship with the family will require tact and understanding on the part of the investigator.

The Preadolescent

Fire setting is a more critical problem with the preadolescent, who has progressed beyond the stage of learning and experimenting. Gone is the constant supervision of the home. The child now has limited mobility, going to school and the playground by foot or bicycle. He is subject to the influence of peers as well as television and comic books.

Fires set by youngsters in this age bracket are often the result of group activity with frivolous motives. Frequently it is done on a dare or a challenge. A girl may set a fire in order to be accepted by the group, to gain status. If a member of the crowd says, "Let's burn something," no one wants to "chicken out." Setting a fire may be a means of creating excitement, of fighting boredom, of causing some action. There may have been a spectacular conflagration in the neighborhood which was very exciting, and the children may feel, "If we start a little fire nobody will get hurt and we can get the fire department back."

In contrast to the group with its shallow motives, the loner child may be driven to set fires by a deep emotional disturbance. He may attack his own home for a variety of reasons. The denial of a request or stern punishment may be the catalyst which triggers him into action. He may release deep-seated hatred for parents by burning down the home which is a source of pride to them. He may take sides with one parent against the other in a domestic dispute, like a twelve-year-old boy who ignited his bedroom and rigged the evidence so that it pointed to his father, in the hope that it would enable his mother to get a divorce. The neglected child may feel that setting fires is the only means of getting the attention he craves. The loner often strikes out at school or teacher for imagined wrongs in the form of discipline or poor grades.

Although the motive of the loner is often obvious and easily determined, some motives are deep-seated and can be found only after analysis and treatment by professionals. The preadolescent who engages in fire setting usually has deep underlying problems which must be analyzed and corrected by persons skilled in child behavior.

Trademarks   The preadolescent probably leaves more leads that point to him and/or his group than any other age group. While he has less supervision than the infant age group, he is still under some restraint and does not have access to an automobile, so fire setting will be limited to a relatively small geographic area near the home.

Many times the activities of a group or a loner follow a pattern of progression. Initially, turning in false alarms may be enough. In many cases first fires initially involve grass or trash in vacant lots; garbage cans and garages are next on the escalator. If not apprehended, they may graduate to abandoned buildings, then churches and schools. In order to trace the activities and progression of juveniles a situation map must be maintained by officials, pinpointing each fire by location, time of day, day of week, and modus operandi. All interested agencies must be involved, for only through cooperation and coordination can these youngsters be apprehended.

Frequently these fire-setting activities are accompanied by vandalism and destruction, with schools and churches, in particular, targets of these senseless acts (Figure 13-1). Items of food are strewn about; liquids are poured out on the floor; eggs are thrown against the wall; books, papers, and teachers' desks are ruined by ink or other available liquids. Defecating on the floor in the principal's office or on the teacher's desk expresses their contempt or hatred. If obscenities are written on blackboards or walls, careful examination may show tell-tale handwriting characteristics which the teacher recognizes. In churches, acts of sacrilege may be performed, such as tearing pages from the Bible or defecating on the altar or in the collection plate.

Items removed from the scene often serve to identify this age group as the perpetrators. Preadolescents are not likely to remove heavy objects or attempt to open a safe, and things stolen often indicate complete ignorance as to what is really of material value. Athletic equipment such as bats, balls, gloves, uniforms, shoes are favorite targets, which the youngsters may proudly display in the school grounds within a few days, thus giving themselves away. Small sums of cash may be removed from the principal's office, teacher's desk, or vending machines. The teacher's desk may be entered and items previously confiscated from a pupil may be stolen, pointing directly to the owner of the objects.

The manner in which a fire is started also identifies this age group (Figure 13-2). The preadolescent will normally use whatever is available at the scene and will rarely take anything with him in preparation. Contents of trash containers, loose papers, rags, and convenient flammable liquids usually supply the necessary fuel. Flammable liquids with which the youngsters are

FIGURE 13-1. A trademark of the juvenile fire setter is the ransacked desk. This desk was located in the principal's office. (Courtesy Commonwealth of Virginia Arson Investigation Division)

familiar, such as gasoline, kerosene, or lighter fluid, may be used. Elaborate trails, plants, or incendiary devices are almost never employed. In general, the fire set indicates a lack of planning, preparation, or maturity, particularly when this is a group action.

Items found in or near the scene can often lead to identification of members of the group. Youngsters are often so careless in this regard that articles of clothing, such as caps, coats, sweaters, and gloves, are frequently left behind. These items may have laundry marks or, even better, name tags of the culprits. Other identifiable personal items, such as toys, pocket knives, bicycles, skates, and school books, may also be located at the scene.

Occasionally a group will be accompanied by a "tag-along," either a dog or a little sister. While witnesses may be able to give only a sketchy description of the youngsters, they can often describe a dog in enough detail so that investigators may trace the animal to its owner. Little sister may be an unwanted and unwilling participant in the action who doesn't know the importance of keeping quiet.

The fact that he has been in many scrapes does not prove that a youngster has set a fire or fires. However, experience has proven that a fire setter often engages in other antisocial behavior, so the boy who is known to be a bully, to mistreat or take advantage of other children, or to torture animals is a likely suspect who should be closely watched.

a

d

FIGURE 13-2. Typical juvenile fires have little chance of burning extensively. Of the six separate fires set in this school building, only one of the five pictured (Figure 13-2e) required extinguishment by the fire department. (Courtesy Commonwealth of Virginia Arson Investigation Division)

b

c

e

The loner may have an apparent interest in fires. Has he been observed at numerous blazes or leaving the scene? Does he exhibit unusual curiosity about fire department operations or frequent the fire house? Allowing a preadolescent to hang around the station is courting trouble. By its very nature fire fighting is exciting and glamorous. If things are too dull the preadolescent may seek to liven them up.

A series of blazes near a public school, playground, or park where children assemble is indicative of juvenile activity. This is particularly true if the incidents occur when children are on their way to and from school along certain alleys, walkways, or thoroughfares which offer good cover and concealment. If school is in session when the fires occur, a check with school officials will reveal the absentees. When the events occur only on Saturdays, Sundays, or holidays, group activity by preadolescents should be suspected.

Special Problems   As is the case with the infant, the parents of the preadolescent fire setter pose a problem. The mother and father may resolutely refuse to admit that their youngster is guilty. In all cases involving juveniles, if there is no cooperation by the parents, correcting the problem is almost impossible. The attitude and approach of the investigator should be understanding and sympathetic, not vindictive or accusatory; but, in the event the parents refuse to cooperate, the investigator can change tactics and, if proof is conclusive, so inform the parents.

In the case of juvenile group activity, it is often possible to identify and apprehend one or two members of the number involved, but this does not mean that the names of all the participants will be easily obtained. The youngster's devotion and dedication to the group will prevent his "squealing" on his accomplices. He may admit his own guilt in almost anything, but to squeal on other group members is an unpardonable sin for which there is no forgiveness.

Identifying and apprehending the loner is a particular problem, for he may operate in the same general pattern as a group but no one else knows that he is responsible. Further, his home situation may provide little or no supervision and therefore allows him the complete freedom of movement to set fires at times and in places not normally associated with the preadolescent. This makes the task of establishing a pattern consistent with juveniles especially difficult and can lead to the assumption that these acts are the work of an adult. A case history will illustrate this.

Fire was discovered at an elementary school located in a deteriorating neighborhood at 10 P.M. on a Thursday night. Fire fighters found an open window whose ledge was about six feet above ground. All other windows were secured and all outside doors were locked. Fire department members entered the open window, located and extinguished the fire. Point of origin was determined to be a wastepaper can in a corner of the room remote from the window, from which point the blaze had extended up the wall to the ceiling and done several hundred dollars in damage. The lunchroom had been broken into, several dozen eggs had been broken in the hall, and coffee was scattered in the eggs. Numerous appliances, such as audiovisual equipment, radios, TV sets, and tape recorders, had not been disturbed. A vulgarism was printed on the blackboard in the fourth grade classroom. Further inspection the following morning revealed that the fourth grade teacher's desk had been opened and that a small rubber ball, a toy kaleidoscope, several jackstones, and a small plastic horse had been taken, all objects which the teacher had taken from Joe, one of her students, to keep him from playing with them in class. A goldfish bowl containing six fish had also been removed from the classroom. Joe, incidentally, did not attend school on Friday, the day after the fire.

The following Saturday at 2 P.M. a fire was reported in an apartment building six blocks from the school. Entrance had been gained through a partially open casement window. Curtains in one apartment bedroom were on fire, a burning pillowcase was found in the hall, and all burners on the kitchen gas range were on. The apartment had been ransacked. Although the usual appliances were present and a pistol was in plain view, nothing had been taken except a piggy bank containing several dollars in change. Feces were noted in the commode.

Joe returned to school on Monday, was questioned by the teacher, and convinced her that he knew nothing about the fire.

Within a few days, a small grocery store in the immediate area was entered and several cans of dog food were removed. A few nights after that the front glass of a large supermarket was shattered by a chunk of concrete; however, nothing was reported missing. During this period several bicycles were stolen in the neighborhood and a small pet dog disappeared.

On the following Saturday at 9 A.M. fire was reported in a dwelling adjacent to the apartment that had been ransacked the previous week. Fire fighters found that the back door had been forced. Curtains in the kitchen were on fire and a burned apron was on the floor. Again, the house had been ransacked but nothing taken except a child's piggy bank. Feces were noted in the commode.

On the following Saturday at 10 A.M. fire was reported in a dwelling three blocks from the previous fires. Fire department personnel found curtains in the bathroom on fire and remains of burned newspapers in the corridor outside the bathroom. Additionally, all burners on the electric stove were on high. Once again, the house had been ransacked, but nothing was missing except a piggy bank. Feces were noted on the toilet seat.

On Monday, seven-year-old Billy, summoned to the school principal's office for an infraction of rules, told the principal that he knew who set the school on fire. He had been playing with his brother, Sam, and Joe on the night of the school fire when Joe suggested that they break into the school.

They went to the school where Billy stood on Sam's shoulders and tested windows until they found one that was unlocked. Billy entered the building, went to the front door, pushed the panic bar, and the other two joined him. They went first to the kitchen, obtained eggs and coffee, poured these items in the main hall, and slid for a while. Joe told them that there were some of his toys in his teacher's desk which he wanted back, so they went to the room and got the toys. Joe suggested that they steal the goldfish because the teacher was very fond of them, and then he said that they should set the school on fire so that they would not have to go to school. Sam and Billy observed Joe strike several matches and toss them into the wastepaper can. When the fire blazed up, they ran out the front door and closed it behind them. In a little while they heard the fire trucks but did not go back to the fire.

Sam, interviewed in the presence of his father, corroborated Billy's statement and volunteered the information that the three of them had broken into several places, but he insisted that they had never been with Joe when he started fires except for the one in the school. He further agreed to show investigators where Joe had stashed the stolen items. Everything was recovered, including the pet dog, which was alive and healthy. Included in the cache was a hammer, a railroad spike, and two screwdrivers, tools which had been used to break into several places.

When Joe's mother was interviewed, she stated that the boy was born out of wedlock and she was not sure who his father was. He was often out at night, sometimes all night long. She was not particularly interested in where he went or what he did as long as he "stayed out of her hair," but she had no objection to investigators talking with Joe. Joe, interviewed in the presence of his teacher, admitted everything Sam and Billy had related. He had taken money to buy food because his mother would not feed him. When he broke the window at the supermarket, he entered the store and stole only a package of weiners and a sack of potato chips, so nothing was noted as missing. The fires were started in the hope that the break-ins would not be discovered. When it was brought out that there was always evidence of bowel movement at the fire scene, he blurted out "I didn't s--- on the floor." He had stolen the puppy because he wanted something to play with. Joe agreed to go with investigators and point out the places that he had broken into and/or set on fire, a tour resulting in the clearing of a number of cases of breaking and entering, petty theft, and several fires that had not been suspected as incendiary. As an interesting sidelight, investigators, doubting that he could use the tools found, thought it was possible that he was acting with older persons, but when several doors of various types were locked, he opened them easily.

When his confession was repeated in the presence of his mother, she expressed no interest in the matter and no concern about Joe. Asked what he thought should be done with him, Joe replied with tears streaming down his cheeks, "I don't care what you do with me, 'cause nobody loves me or cares anything about me."

All three boys were referred to Juvenile Court, where Sam and Billy, as first offenders, were remanded to the custody of their father. Joe was placed in a foster home and has not been in trouble for five years. This case history is recited as typical, illustrating some hows and whys of the preadolescent fire setter.

The Adolescent

More serious arson problems are encountered with the adolescent than with the infant or preadolescent. No class of property is exempt from their attacks. Many fires are started in the nighttime in occupied buildings where people are sleeping, and respect for property and human safety is rarely a consideration. Since adolescents have access to transportation, they can strike in a much broader area. This mobility increases the problems of the investigators immensely, because the probability of developing a pattern diminishes.

While this age group is subject to the same motivating forces as both preadolescents and adults, another motive seems to exert a powerful influence on their activities—pure vandalism. Hooliganism is perhaps a more fitting term for this wanton, vicious, senseless destruction for destruction's sake. Today's young hoodlum may ice pick or slash all four tires on a car, throw paint on a dwelling, or heave a rock through the window of a living room. Chances are the victims never did him any harm whatsoever and he doesn't even know them.

What factors cause these persons to behave in such an antisocial manner?

Independence   Our society, and in particular our schools, allows and encourages the young to be independent, to think for themselves, rather than stressing the bounds of accepted behavior. When their independence is challenged by rules, regulations, laws, discipline, or threats of punishment they resent and resist such restraint vigorously, often directing hatred toward the source of the restraint, which may be fire and police personnel. In the case of groups, such hatred can be fanned into mob action, resulting in injury to public safety personnel.

Influence of the Entertainment Media   All forms of violence are fed into movies and television. Although the media claim that this has no effect on youths, when a recent movie portrayed a gang of youths pouring gasoline on a person and burning her alive, this same act was carried out within a few weeks in several areas where the film had appeared. Included among the victims was a woman motorist whose car had stalled in a strange neighborhood. She was dragged from the car, taken to a vacant lot, stripped, doused with gasoline, and set afire. Obviously, there are some indications that media programming affects the behavior of the audience.

Narcotics and Alcohol   Narcotics and alcohol are easily obtained by adolescents, although they are expensive. Adolescents may break into places, steal whatever they can to obtain money to satisfy a hard drug habit, and then set fires to cover the crime. Under the influence of alcohol or drugs, inhibitions against antisocial behavior may be subjugated and antisocial emotions may take over.

The Group Influence   The adolescent, like the preadolescent, strongly desires to be an accepted member of a group and dares not be different in dress, style, mannerisms, and conduct. If antisocial behavior is a trademark of the group, every member goes along with the gang or else he is out. Some very militant groups have infiltrated both junior and senior high schools. Youngsters have been indoctrinated into hate programs against the establishment, which includes parents, school, church, government, authority, public officials. In many cases detailed instruction in fire setting and creating incendiary devices accompanies the hate training.

Lenient Attitudes of Courts and Society   Stern disciplinary action taken against the youthful fire setter results in a dramatic decrease in set fires. Discipline does not necessarily mean punishment or penalties. Except for the incorrigible, the solution to the juvenile problem is education and training.

Contact with the Juvenile Fire Setter

Great care must be exercised in dealing with the juvenile fire setter, for the United States Supreme Court has ruled that the juvenile has all the rights of any citizen, and that these rights must be scrupulously respected. Following are some guidelines for dealing with juvenile arson suspects.

1. The warning of rights must be given. It is legally inconsistent to say that the juvenile cannot waive his rights because he doesn't understand all the legal jargon. The investigator must make a conscientious effort to explain a juvenile's rights so that he can understand them. Without this effort, a confession may be ruled inadmissible.

2. Parents must be present. While this is not required in all jurisdictions, in many areas any questioning of juveniles without the presence of one or both parents is specifically prohibited. It is doubtful also that a school official can legally permit the questioning of a child suspect without the approval of parents and out of their presence.

3. A third party should be present. It is advisable to have a disinterested third party present at interviews with juveniles, for youngsters may allege that they were threatened or abused and later deny all that they said previously to the interviewer. Female juveniles may allege undue familiarity or worse. Children tell very convincing stories which can be a source of embarrassment to the investigator.

4. Make no promises. The investigator may be inclined to tell a cute little boy or girl, "Would you like an ice cream cone or some candy? Tell me about the fire and I'll give you a treat." Such promises and inducements must be avoided.

5. Don't lead the juvenile. After rapport has been established between the interviewer and a small child, great care must be exercised to ensure that the youngster does not make statements, accusations, and confessions to accommodate the investigator. The subject may tell what he thinks the questioner wants to hear, not what is true. In every instance it is necessary to corroborate information given with physical evidence, verification of others, or observation.

In conclusion the most important ingredient in coping with the juvenile fire setter is the investigator. He must understand youngsters in order to communicate with them, and without communication he can learn nothing. An investigator's success with juveniles should not be judged on the number of convictions or the number of kids sent to reform schools, but on the number of young lives salvaged.

14 Interviews, Notes, Statements, and Reports

Interviewing may be the most neglected phase of investigation. Investigators tend to concentrate on fire causes, point of origin, examination of debris, preservation of physical evidence, and other technical matters. At arson seminars, interviewing is often combined with the subject of interrogation, and several minutes are spent on this topic while several hours are spent on interrogation. This neglect is difficult to understand, for the success of an investigation may very well depend on obtaining information from witnesses through effective interviewing.

At the same time very little instruction or information is available on the purposes, mechanics, and suggested procedures to be followed in taking notes, another vital phase of the investigation.

Taking statements is another area to which little attention has been directed. Without direction or instruction, each individual is inclined to develop his own format. The result is improperly taken statements which are of no value to the prosecutor in preparing his case or in actual courtroom situations.

It is essential that a complete, comprehensive, clear, and concise report be written, but no guidelines concerning format, content, and rhetoric of the report are ordinarily provided the investigator.

In the pages which follow, we will address ourselves to interviewing, notetaking, taking statements, and report writing in an effort to provide information and instruction which may prove valuable to the investigator.

Interviews

Definition

For purposes of our discussion, we can define an interview as a seeking after information by questioning witnesses or potential witnesses.

Types of Witnesses

Witnesses may be divided into three classes: (1) the hostile witness, who may have no respect for law or law enforcement officers or may be friendly to the suspect and will not cooperate freely; (2) the friendly witness, who respects the law and law enforcement officers, is not friendly to any law violator, and will cooperate freely; and (3) the average witness, who probably has mixed emotions about the law and law enforcement officers, may not know the suspect or have any feeling towards him pro or con, and will cooperate unless there is fear of retaliation against his family or himself, losing time from work, embarrassment on the witness stand during trial, or becoming involved.

Specific Witnesses and Purposes of Interviews

Certain classes of people are sure to be interviewed in the course of the majority of arson investigations.

Fire Department Personnel   Information sought from officers and fire fighters has already been covered. However, we must consider which of the three types of witnesses these individuals may be. The same factors that make the average witness reluctant to cooperate apply to fire department personnel in many instances.

Discoverer of the Fire   The discoverer of the fire may be a friendly, unfriendly, or hostile witness. Information obtained from the discoverer is of vital importance to the investigator and should include the following:

1. Circumstances under which he or she discovered the fire. In the event of a series of fires, the person discovering the fire may well become a suspect.

2. Time of discovery. Who gave the alarm? How was the alarm given? Was there any delay?

3. Location. In what part of the building was the fire?

4. General appearance. What was the color of smoke, of flames? Was the burning normal? Did the fire spread rapidly? Were there any

explosions? If more than one building involved, were both burning at the same time or did fire spread from one to another? In which building did it start?

5. Condition of windows and doors. Did the discoverer approach the building to try doors? If so, were they locked, closed, or open? If he entered the structure, what did he observe? Were windows closed or open? Were they covered with blankets or other material to prevent observation from outside?

6. People at the scene. If the building was occupied, did he observe the occupant? How was he or she dressed? Did he or she act normally? If the discoverer had any conversation with the occupant, what was said? Did he notice anyone leaving the building or the area? If so, can he describe this person?

7. Weather. What were the general conditions—humidity, temperature, wind direction, clear, cloudy, rain, or stormy?

8. General observations. Was there anything that struck the discoverer as unusual? Is there anything he might want to add that has not been asked?

Neighbors   Information obtained from neighbors is not acquired by chance, but as the result of a carefully planned and coordinated effort. In urban areas, this is a very time-consuming but essential activity, involving many man-hours of block-by-block knocking on doors, asking questions, and seeking information. Many doors will not be opened, even though it is obvious that someone is at home; others, once opened, will be slammed in the investigator's face. Garbage may even be thrown on him. In rural areas, neighbors may be scarce and scattered over a wide area, and the investigator may travel many miles, encounter many deadends, watch many farmers continue their plowing until they are ready to talk. He may be threatened, pursued, and eventually attacked by a fierce farm dog.

The investigator is seeking information which includes the following: Where was the neighbor when he first knew about the fire? Did he go to the scene? If the answer is yes, ask basically the same questions posed to the discoverer of the fire, omitting those which are not pertinent. If the witness states that he or she was not home on the night of the fire and did not know of it until later, a different line of questioning is followed.

If this was a dwelling fire, did he or she know the occupants? How long have they lived here? If recent arrivals, where did they come from? Where are they employed? Was the neighbor in their home occasionally or frequently? Would he or she help with a diagram of the floor plan? Could he or she locate on this diagram the major appliances and items of furniture?

During the course of the neighborhood check, the investigator always hopes to discover a busybody, who may be a pain in the neck to the neighbors but is the greatest friend an investigator can have. Valuable information concerning the personal and financial problems, morals, and habits of the occupants of the burned dwelling can be gotten from such a source.

If the investigator feels, after contact with several neighbors, that some information is established, he need not pose all these questions to every witness.

If the fire involved a business or mercantile firm, how long had it operated under present management? What were the hours of the store or business? Did business appear successful? Did the neighbor shop there? When was he or she last in the store? Was it well stocked? Were premises neat and attractive? Was merchandise obsolete? How many employees were there? Were sales mostly cash or credit? Had a competitor taken much of the business? Had there been any damage done to the store by hoodlums? Were there recent burglaries or armed robberies? Was the store closed for several days or longer without explanation? Did the owner mention retiring, going out of business, selling out, or moving? Had there been any special sales recently, such as "going out of business," "selling out to the walls," and the like?

The investigator will encounter hostile, friendly, and average witnesses from all levels of society in checking the neighborhood. His ability as an interviewer will be fully tested during this important phase of the investigation.

Insurance Agent   The following questions should be asked of the insurance agent:

1. Circumstances of policy writing. When was the insurance placed? Did the insured apply, or was the policy "sold" to him? Did the insured ask for a definite amount? Was any reason given for taking out insurance?

2. Changes in policy. Had any changes been made in coverage? Was insurance increased? If changes were made, what reasons were given?

3. Premiums. How much are premiums? Were payments up to date? How were payments made—in lump sum or time payments?

4. Personal and financial information. How well did the agent know the insured? What was the insured's financial condition? Was the property involved overinsured? Had he talked to the insured since the fire? If so, what was the nature of this conversation?
   Caution should be exercised in contacting the insurance agent; he may well be a reluctant, if not hostile, witness for several reasons.

Since he handled this insurance policy for the insured, the agent may be a close friend with a desire to protect the insured. Details of the investigator's interview may be relayed to the insured immediately.

The agent, particularly the independent, will be concerned about the reputation he establishes for prompt settlement of claims. A delay caused by an investigation in which he cooperated can damage his business. Rumors may spread in the community that he won't pay, tries to get out of paying, or calls in the police. Contact with the insurance agent should be handled through the adjustor to eliminate problems created by direct contact between the agent and the investigator. Pertinent information can be obtained just as effectively in this manner without alerting either the agent or the insured that an investigation is being conducted.

5. Insurance adjustor. Different types of adjustors have varying objectives. The public adjustor is employed by the insured to protect his interest, so contact with this individual should be avoided if possible. The independent adjustor and the company adjustor have similar and yet slightly different interests. The independent is anxious to please the company to acquire future business. He would like to be in a position to advise the company that the fire is under investigation by the authorities. In order to accomplish this, he may exaggerate the suspicious aspects of the fire to secure the participation of various investigative agencies. The company adjustor is anxious to settle a claim promptly with as little difficulty as possible. Lengthy adjustments are time-consuming and expensive, and many times they do not eventually benefit the company. Overinvolvement or participation in the inquiry/investigation can result in damage suits against the company for defaming the character and reputation of the insured. Additionally, in recent years the interest of the insurance companies in incendiary fires has noticeably decreased. This is attested to by the discontinuation of the fire investigation bureau of the American Insurance Association, apparently because of the withdrawal of financial support by a number of companies. We can only assume that this action was precipitated by a lack of interest concerning suspicious fires.

Other Sources of Information

Some information may be obtained principally by examination of written documents or records, access to which must be gained by personal contact with the individuals who have custody of them. The degree of interviewing skill displayed by the investigator will often determine the degree of cooperation accorded him by these custodians. Such information sources include credit agencies, banks, landlords, mortgagees, suppliers, employees, creditors, real estate agents, and court records.

Investigator Etiquette

The initial impression made on a potential witness by an investigator will often determine the degree of cooperation and amount of information obtained. Therefore, the abrupt, blunt, tactless manner of some investigators, who display a tough front, perhaps to intimidate the witness into cooperation, seems quite inappropriate. Let us examine some desirable traits and characteristics of a good interviewer.

Adaptable   The good interviewer must be flexible in manner, approach, and technique. He must be capable of functioning effectively while talking to witnesses in the filthy tenement, the tumbledown shack, or the plush home or office. He must be prepared for unexpected responses by witnesses which open up new avenues of inquiry.

Courteous   The investigator may believe that courtesy is unnecessary, particularly in dealing with certain elements of our society, but it will pay off, particularly in dealing with women. Investigators develop an ability to control the situation during interrogation, and frequently, to maintain this control, they may interrupt the subject of an interrogation who is going off on a tangent. A tendency to interrupt during an interview must be overcome, for the witness may become hostile if he or she is never allowed to complete a sentence.

Personable   Since initial impressions are so important, the individual who is well groomed, neat, and has a pleasing personal appearance has a distinct advantage over the seedy-looking investigator.

Poised   The interviewer must maintain poise regardless of what transpires during an interview.

Persistent   The investigator may feel his efforts are in vain after several interviews have produced no information of value or if business establishments, financial institutions, and governmental agencies are reluctant to make available records, reports, and other documents. Unfortunately, sometimes persistence may not be enough, and he must resort to the threat of a subpoena duces tecum to secure the ''cooperation'' of some cautious individual.

Positive   The investigator must be confident of success as he approaches each witness. When the investigator enters a business establishment or financial institution, his entire manner must convey the impression that the purpose of his visit is to obtain certain information and that he *will* obtain that information.

A Good Listener   The interviewer must concentrate on listening to what the witness is saying rather than just hearing but not understanding, comprehending, or absorbing the information being conveyed.

Unbiased   The witness should not be led into saying what the investigator wants to hear. Any preconceived impressions about what the witness should have seen may subconsciously guide his responses in this direction. Questions must be framed so that they do not cause the witness to give information which he does not actually possess. For example, when attempting to establish identity of a vehicle, there is a vast difference between "What color was the car?" and "The car was light green, wasn't it?"

Concern   While the investigator does not have the time to become acquainted with every witness, he should keep in mind that people respond to those who show some interest in their interests. A few minutes spent with a farmer talking about his crops, with a mother about her children, with a service station manager about his neat station, may produce dividends far beyond expectations. People do not normally communicate with strangers, so every effort must be made to overcome identification as a stranger.

Discerning   The investigator must be able to evaluate the reliability of the witness and make some judgment as to his or her veracity. Are there indications of prejudice, either favorable or unfavorable, toward anyone who may be connected with the fire? Would the witness profit in any way, personally or otherwise, by casting suspicion on someone? In general, does this person appear truthful?

Knowledgeable   The witness in many instances may observe early in the interview that the person asking the questions does not know his business. If the fire fighter, while describing suppression operations, detects an obvious lack of knowledge on the part of the interviewer, he will lose interest and terminate the conversation as soon as possible. Any witness who notes that the investigator does not know the facts of the case will react to the questioning very negatively.

In interviewing, the biblical maxim, "As ye sow, so shall ye reap" is applicable. The investigator who displays the characteristics discussed above in dealing with the public can gain the respect and confidence of witnesses which will induce them to convey pertinent information. The conscientious investigator must constantly strive to improve his interviewing techniques.

Notes

The investigator who remembers that the dullest pencil is better than the sharpest mind will avoid agonizing moments trying to remember which witness said what, when, where, and under what circumstances. Any notes in any form written on anything are superior to none at all.

Definition

For our purposes, note taking may be defined as the hand recording of facts or information obtained.

Purposes

At various stages of inquiry into a fire loss it is useful to analyze progress by reviewing notes, not only to keep the investigation on a logical course, but also to reveal other possible motives, witnesses, or suspects.

Notes are needed to write the final investigation report. While the original notes must be rearranged and reorganized prior to being used for this purpose, clear, concise notes can be of immeasurable assistance.

Notes will assist the investigator in testifying. A study of his original notes prior to going on the witness stand will refresh the investigator's memory and fix facts in his mind. Under certain conditions, these original notes can even be used on the witness stand.

Mechanics

Investigators disagree on the type of notebook that should be used. Some say the notebook should be inconspicuous and compact enough to fit in the coat pocket, but this creates a problem in diagramming a scene, making voluminous notes, or taking a lengthy statement. Others suggest a looseleaf notebook of a convenient size, but then there is the possibility of losing some sheets or being accused on the witness stand of deliberately removing pages. The type of notebook that an investigator uses is a matter of personal preference. Whatever the design or style, as long as it enables him to function effectively from start to finish of the investigation, this is the type he should use.

How should the investigator use the notebook? When interviewing a witness, when does the investigator bring out the notebook? Normally, as soon as a person observes that an interview is being written down as a matter of record, he tends to freeze up. There are several possible procedures for overcoming this problem.

The investigator may bring out the notebook at the outset of the interview and begin to write the name and address of the witness. The witness will become accustomed to seeing him write and not be apprehensive when giving pertinent information concerning the case.

The investigator may bring out the notebook at an appropriate time during the course of the interview—when the witness is furnishing information on dates or times, or citing figures of some kind. He can at this point advise the witness that in order to avoid any mistakes, he will take notes. Once the concern of the witness is overcome, there will probably be no further problem and the investigator can continue with his note taking.

After the witness has given what seems to be a true version of his knowledge of the case, the investigator may then bring out the notebook and review the entire matter, making notes as he does so. The witness, who has already committed himself, normally does not object to the information being written down at this point.

Suggestions

First, make notes promptly rather than delaying until a more convenient time. Delay may produce disastrous results, such as failing to recall which witness gave what information. More important, for notes to be admissible, it must be established that they were made within a reasonable period of time after the information noted was obtained. What constitutes "a reasonable period of time" is a decision made by the court having jurisdiction over the case at hand.

Second, write legibly. Any authorized person should be able to read the notes without difficulty. Too many investigators have found reading their own writing an almost impossible task after the notes have "cooled."

Third, keep notes organized. Jotting down notes on the back of envelopes, scraps of paper, matchbook covers, or whatever is handy is risking their loss. Whatever type of notebook is used, keep it readily available.

Fourth, keep notes separated. Only those notes dealing with a specific case should be in the case notebook. Defense counsel, under certain conditions, has access to the investigator's notes and, with the consent of the judge, can show them to the jury. Information concerning other cases or personal matters might prove embarrassing to the officer and others.

Lastly, be accurate and complete. Spelling should be reasonably correct, at least enough so that the words are recognizable without difficulty. If possible, avoid abbreviations; if abbreviations are used, make certain they are standard, commonly known, and accepted.

Statements

Statements of witnesses are vital to an investigation report, for the prosecuting attorney often builds his case on such evidence. Therefore, the investigator must be capable of taking statements which provide the prosecutor with the necessary information.

Definition

For our purposes, a statement may be defined as a written record of what is said by a witness. Included under this definition is the taking of confessions.

The results of an interview included in an investigation report, which relate only generally what an individual said, are not a statement. Normally, under the WITNESSES part of a report, this information would be conveyed in the third person. For example, an excerpt from this portion of a report might read as follows:

> Henry Clark Kribbens, WM, DOB 9-18-1919, 2270 Cedarcrest Lane, Ebright, Virginia, stated that he returned home from the Gutterball Bowling Alley, 1102 Through Street, Ebright, at about 11:10 P.M. on the night of the fire. He is sure of the time as the bowling alley closes at 11:00 P.M., and it takes him about ten minutes to walk to his house. When he passed the Tillery Warehouse at 1202 Main Street, he saw no lights and observed nothing unusual.

On the other hand a statement is a concise report of what a witness said in the first person and is, as far as possible, a direct quote, for example:

> March 5, 1977
> Ebright, Virginia
>
> I, Henry Clark Kribbens, white male, date of birth 9-18-1919, 2270 Cedarcrest Lane, Ebright, Virginia, make the following statement concerning the fire at the Tillery Warehouse to Fire Investigator Cedric Weehunt, Ebright Fire Department, and Investigator James Allen, of the State Fire Marshal's Office.
>
> On February 18, 1977, I left the Gutterball Bowling Alley at 1102 Through Street when it closed at 11:00 P.M. I walked down Main Street and passed the Tillery Warehouse. I guess it was about ten after 11:00 when I got there because it's only two blocks from the bowling alley which closes at 11:00 P.M. I saw a 1974 Lincoln Cosmopolitan, light tan, with wide whitewall tires, parked next to the warehouse. I passed within twenty feet of this car, and it was under a streetlight so I could see it good. I took notice because I had never seen a car there at night before. There wasn't anybody around the car and no lights I could see in the building. I don't know for sure whose car it was, but it looks just like the one that belongs to the owner of the warehouse, Jim Tillery.

I have read (had read to me) this statement of four pages. I have initialed all corrections and the bottom of each page. It is true and correct.

_____

                                                        Signed

Witness ——————————
Witness ——————————

Purposes

A statement given by a friendly witness may be used to refresh his or her memory immediately prior to the trial. At the time of the trial, if the witness shows no sign of changing testimony, it is used only as a refresher. If it appears, however, that the witness has second thoughts and may contradict the information given in the statements or introduce surprise testimony, the statement may have a stronger force. The witness should never be threatened in any manner, but reference to perjury and impeachment may help materially to refresh his memory.

The investigator must also take a statement from a prejudiced or hostile witness or a witness friendly to the defendant in order to prevent surprise testimony favorable to the accused. Use the same preamble employed when taking a statement from a friendly witness. The general content of the statement may be that the witness wasn't at home on the night of the fire, doesn't know anything at all about the fire, and hasn't heard any talk about it at all.

The hostile witness may refuse any request to sign the statement. If he says "I ain't signing a _____ thing. It's the _____ truth, and if you don't believe it, _____ you," write this explanation in the report. It may help the prosecutor impeach the witness in the event he should attempt to testify.

Mechanics

After talking to a witness and finding out that he has information significant to the investigation, the investigator employs a direct, businesslike approach with the witness, explaining why his knowledge of the case must be reduced to writing. The investigator establishes a relationship with the witness which influences him to convey certain facts, a relationship which must not be jeopardized. The statement must be taken by the investigator and reduced to writing, in narrative form, in the language of the witness as far as possible. Do not have the witness write the statement. Do not have him dictate to a stenographer. Do not use a tape recorder. Do not use a form with a printed heading. Do not give the witness a list of points to cover. Do not use a question-and-answer technique.

Reports

Definition

For our purposes a report may be defined as a formal communication conveying all pertinent information concerning a criminal investigation and the results thereof, from its inception up to the time of the report.

Purposes

First and foremost, a complete and comprehensive investigation report is invaluable to the prosecutor in preparing his case for court. Second, the investigator's supervisor, in reviewing the report, may note some areas of weakness in investigative techniques and procedures which can be reviewed with the officer to bring about more effective investigations. Furthermore, if the case is scheduled for trial, the supervisor may see the need for further investigative activity in certain areas. The reports are also essential to the maintenance of accurate records of previous fires in certain areas by individuals or families with a specific modus operandi. Meaningful figures on fire frequency and loss amounts are impossible without accurate reports from which this information can be obtained.

Mechanics

Why is report writing such a problem when investigators recognize the absolute necessity for clear, complete, concise, comprehensive investigation reports?

Getting the report written seems to be both an academic and a psychological problem. Academic because the investigator may lack formal education and grammatical knowledge or skill in composition, the ability to express thoughts clearly and accurately in writing. These problems can be overcome only through a dedicated effort by the investigator to correct the deficiency. Home study or attendance at the courses of adult study offered almost nationwide may solve the difficulty.

One of the psychological obstacles to satisfactory report writing is that initiating a "writing" of any kind is extremely difficult for most people. How many times have you put off writing a letter to someone because you just couldn't seem to get started? The plain truth is that the investigator must force himself to start and complete an investigation report.

The investigator may rationalize writing a brief, sketchy report of a minor fire because it is unimportant, but this is often the very case that ends up in court, much to the embarrassment of the investigator and the detriment of his organization. Following an unsuccessful investigation, the investigator may "let down" and not want any more to do with the case for the time being. At the completion of a successful investigation, he may suffer from physical and emotional exhaustion and not feel up to writing the report until later.

Whatever the reasons, they must be overcome, for the report must be written. What can be done to make this formidable task easier? First, there should be a format. The sample which follows is only a suggested report form which can be altered to meet local and departmental requirements.

Sample Report Form

Case No. _____
Place: _____
Date: _____

INVESTIGATION REPORT (Privileged and Confidential)

To:

From:

Re: Fire Losses: Tillery Warehouse, 1202 Main Street, Ebright, Virginia February 18, 1977, 1:00 A.M. and 4:00 A.M.

Property
Involved: One story frame warehouse building with metal roof and concrete foundation. Over 25 years old. Estimated size is 70 x 22 x 44 x 35. Building wired for electricity. No heaters or cooking stoves on premises. The part of the building where the fire first occurred was reported to be in a good state of repair, but the part of the building where the second fire originated was reported to be in a dilapidated condition.

Owner: J. H. Tillery, Ebright, Virginia

Occupants: None

Insurance: Insurance on building—$22,500, Policy No. VA-43027 with Milton Mutual of Bon Air, Virginia, effective September 16, 1974 through September 16, 1977. Insurance on contents—$55,000, Policy No. 901400 with Worth Insurance Company of New York. Agent: M. J. Rolt Agency of Killdevil, Virginia. Adjustor: G. Amant, Rolling Rock, Virginia.

Source of Request
for Investigation: Fire Marshal Charles German, Ebright

Reasons for
Investigation: Two fires, each in different parts of structure and at
                         different hours.

Persons Making
Investigation: Fire Investigator Cedric Weehunt, Ebright Fire Depart-
                         ment; Detective Henry N. Jones, Ebright Police Depart-
                         ment; Investigator James Allen, State Fire Marshal's Of-
                         fice

Dates of
Investigation: February 21, 22, and March 5, 6, 7, 1977.

Story of
the Fire: The first fire was discovered by Hank Jewett, white male,
                         Ebright, Virginia, who lives in a trailer which was within
                         50 yards of the warehouse that burned. Jewett stated that
                         he was sleeping when he was awakened by the barking
                         of his dog. He got up and looked out and saw a bright
                         reflection of light but did not see any flames. Jewett ran
                         up the hill and stopped a passing car and told the
                         occupants to call the fire department. The Ebright Volun-
                         teer Fire Department responded to the call. Fire Chief
                         Williams stated that when he arrived with the fire ap-
                         paratus he saw flames burning from the ground up on the
                         exterior of the building next to the door leading into the
                         east part of the warehouse. Nothing particularly unusual
                         was observed other than the fire being on the exterior.
                         The fire was extinguished without too much damage and
                         the entire building was checked to be sure that no fire
                         spread elsewhere. The building was rechecked again
                         about a half hour later. The part of the building first
                         subject to flame was completely saturated with water. At
                         the time of arrival at second fire, fire was in another part
                         of the building and seemed to be burning in several
                         different places.

Examination of
The Debris: An examination of this debris led the investigators to
                         believe that the fires had been started in three separate
                         and distinct places. This was due to the fact that in two
                         different places in the building the floor and subflooring
                         had burned through in addition to the fire on the exterior.

Witnesses:

Other Evidence:

Summary:

Obviously, some headings would be expanded significantly, in particular property involved, story of the fire, and examination of the debris.

Second, assemble and organize notes, statements, sketches, diagrams, daily activity log, and any other material pertinent to the investigation and sit down to a typewriter or dictating machine, in relatively quiet surroundings, for several hours of uninterrupted effort.

Third, keep in mind the ingredients of a good report—accuracy, conciseness, clarity, and completeness. Make every effort to spell and punctuate correctly, and do not write poor English unless it is a quotation from a witness. Likewise, profanity or obscenity should be avoided even when quoting a witness unless it is essential.

The investigation report is one of the most difficult but most important elements of an arson investigation. Completing this task effectively should give the investigator a keen sense of accomplishment, as a good investigation report reflects favorably on him and his department.

15 Interrogation

The history of man's methods of determining the guilt or innocence of accused persons is one in which he can take little pride. In fact, various methods might be cited as cardinal examples of man's inhumanity to man. Sorcery, trickery, and brutality are the words which best describe techniques used with the alleged objective of determining the truth. While the guilty person may have been revealed in many cases by these methods, innocent people confessed to and were convicted for crimes they did not commit. Let us take a closer look at some of these procedures.

Physical combat between the accused and a court-appointed adversary was used for many years to determine guilt or innocence. The rationale behind this procedure was that if a person was innocent of a crime he would fight with superhuman strength to prove this. Undoubtedly, many innocent losers were maimed or killed, while physically strong criminals could fight their way out of one crime after another.

One of the earliest examples of the use of logic and psychology to determine the truth of a matter goes back to King Solomon. Two women, each claiming to be the mother of a child, appeared before the king, and in an attempt to detect deception, Solomon announced he would cut the child in half with a sword and award half to each woman. One claimant readily agreed, while the other cried out in torment and begged that the child be given unharmed to the other woman. This act revealed to the King the true mother, to whom the child was awarded.

The ancient Hindus, believing that the donkey possessed supernatural powers, devised a simple test to determine guilt or innocence in which a donkey with soot on its tail was placed in a darkened stall, and suspects were told to pass by the stall and pull the donkey's tail, for it would bray only when the guilty party pulled its tail. The reasoning behind this procedure was quite basic: the guilty party, fearing the donkey's bray, would not pull the tail and therefore would be the only suspect with no soot on his hand.

While the two methods cited above have some slight merit, the physical endurance tests were absurd and cruel trials of guilt. Suspects were required to hold their hand in fire or icy water, or endure some other form of physical torture. People were placed in racks and stretched or pulled apart; bamboo shoots were driven under their fingernails; and other equally fiendish practices took place. Those who held out the longest were cleared because they were willing to suffer the most to prove their innocence.

Another trial procedure consisted of throwing suspects bound hand and foot into a pond of icy water. Supposedly the innocent parties would float to the top.

We are shocked at these examples of brutality and congratulate ourselves for progressing beyond such barbaric methods of extracting the truth. Review of some cases which have occurred in our times seems to indicate that we may not have progressed so far after all.

Three men were accused of murder. One accused, at the scene of the crime and in custody of law enforcement officials, denied participating in the crime. A mob gathered and hung him from a tree, cut him down, hung him again, and cut him down again. Still protesting his innocence, he was beaten and then allowed to return to his home. He was subsequently arrested, carried to another locality, and beaten until he confessed. The other two suspects were laid over chairs in jail before a mob and beaten with leather straps with buckles. As the beatings continued they confessed and even changed their statements to meet the demands of their torturers. They were told that if they changed their stories they would be beaten again.

Amazingly enough, this series of events took place in the United States of America in 1936! Even more astounding is the fact that the convictions went all the way to the U.S. Supreme Court before being reversed because the confessions were held inadmissible!

A mother of two children, ages three and four, was arrested in her apartment in the act of selling illegal drugs. She was questioned at that time and place and made an oral confession to the officers. At her trial, she testified that she had confessed, but only after she was told she would get ten years and that her children would be taken from her unless she "cooperated," in which case the officers would recommend leniency and see that her children were not taken from her. The officers did not deny her accusations, and, in fact, their testimony corroborated hers. Once again the Supreme Court in 1963 held the confession was inadmissible and the conviction was reversed.

A subject arrested and carried to the county jail was questioned for thirty-six consecutive hours by officers working in relays. During the entire period, the subject was never allowed to leave the interrogation room. At the trial the officers testified that the accused gave an oral confession, which he denied. In reversing the conviction in 1944, the Supreme Court said that whether he confessed or not was immaterial, for the confession was compelled, not voluntary, and therefore violated due process.

A man taken in custody was questioned by police for long periods day and night for four days without result. At this point, he was taken from the hotel where the questioning took place to the police station. The defendant, suffering from a severe sinus attack, had been promised medical help. At the police station, he was introduced to an individual under circumstances which indicated this person was a medical doctor. Actually, he was a state-employed psychiatrist with knowledge of hypnosis who then proceeded to "treat" the defendant, emphasizing that relief from his pain would come only through confession. After approximately two hours of this "treatment," the doctor called the police and the subject confessed. This confession was followed by two others, one to a business associate and another to two prosecutors. The Supreme Court in 1954 held all three confessions inadmissible; the first because it was obtained illegally, the second and third because they were the fruit of the first.

The cases cited above are flagrant violations of due process in criminal interrogation. Involuntary confessions have been inadmissible in criminal cases in federal and state courts since the founding of the Republic. In reaching a decision as to whether the conditions under which a confession was obtained were inherently coercive, the courts weighed the totality of circumstances in each case. The total weight of a number of improper circumstances was such that due process was violated and the confession was involuntary, although no single circumstance of police conduct toward the subject was flagrant enough to violate due process. The principal concern of the courts up to this point was whether the confession was voluntary.

Landmark Decision

A case which resulted in a landmark decision (*Escobedo* v. *Illinois,* U.S. Supreme Court, June 22, 1964) involved the arrest of the subject, Escobedo, on a felony charge. While in police custody and during questioning, he asked to see his lawyer and his lawyer asked to see him, which requests were refused. The Supreme Court ruled the confession was inadmissible and reversed the conviction. Until this decision it was the rule that no such absolute right existed—it was not automatically and in all cases a violation of due process for the officers to refuse to interrupt interrogation to allow the defendant to talk with a lawyer. While the apparent basis for reversal was refusal of the request of both the accused and his attorney to confer, the issue is somewhat clouded by the explanation accompanying the decision. In addition to denying the requests cited, the police and prosecutor failed to advise the accused of his right to remain silent and to answer no questions. The decision said in part, ''under the circumstances here, the accused must be permitted to consult with the lawyer.'' Which circumstances? The fact that the lawyer contact was refused or that the subject was not advised of his right to remain silent? The *Escobedo* case illustrates the truth that hard cases are the quicksands of sound law. In it, the Court considers the provision of the sixth amendment, which specifies that ''in all criminal prosecutions, the accused shall enjoy the right to have the assistance of counsel for his defense,'' and holds by a 5–4 vote that the right to have the assistance of counsel for one's defense antedates the beginning of a criminal prosecution and arises whenever a law enforcement officer begins to suspect that a person in his custody might be the perpetrator of an unsolved crime which he is investigating.

The exact intent of the court in the *Escobedo* decision soon became irrelevant because of another case decision which affected criminal interrogation to a degree unequaled in the history of our country. The case resulted in what is known as the *Miranda* decision. The following is quoted from the Supreme Court opinion in this case:

> On March 13, 1963, petitioner, Ernesto Miranda, was arrested at his home and taken in custody to a Phoenix police station. He was there identified by the complaining witness. The police then took him to ''Interrogation Room No. 2'' of the Dectective Bureau. There he was questioned by two police officers. The officers admitted at trial that Miranda was not advised that he had a right to have an attorney present. Two hours later, the officers emerged from the interrogation room with a written confession signed by Miranda. At the top of the statement was a typed paragraph stating that the confession was made voluntarily, without threats or promises of immunity and ''with full knowledge of my legal rights, understanding any statement I make may be used against me.''
>
> At his trial before a jury, the written confession was admitted into evidence over the objection of defense counsel, and the officers testified to the prior oral confession made by Miranda during the interrogation. Miranda was found guilty of kidnapping and rape. He was sentenced to 20 to 30 years' imprisonment on each count, the sentences to run concurrently. On appeal, the Supreme Court of Arizona held that Miranda's constitutional rights were not violated in obtaining the confession and affirmed the conviction. In reaching its decision, the court emphasized heavily the fact that Miranda did not specifically request counsel.
>
> We reverse. From the testimony of the officers and by the admission of respondent, it is clear that Miranda was not in any way apprised of

his right to consult with an attorney and to have one present during the interrogation, nor was his right not to be compelled to incriminate himself effectively protected in any other manner. Without these warnings the statements were inadmissible. The mere fact that he signed a statement which contained a typed-in clause stating that he had "full knowledge" of his "legal rights" does not approach the knowing and intelligent waiver required to relinquish constitutional rights.

The decision further says that when a person is "taken into custody or otherwise deprived of his freedom of action in any significant way" and undergoes "questioning initiated by law enforcement officers,"

he must be warned prior to any questioning that he has the right to remain silent, that anything he says can be used against him in a court of law, that he has the right to the presence of an attorney, and that if he cannot afford an attorney one will be appointed for him prior to any questioning if he so desires. Opportunity to exercise these rights must be afforded to him throughout the interrogation. After such warnings have been given, and such opportunity afforded him, the individual may knowingly and intelligently waive these rights and agree to answer questions or make a statement. But unless and until such warnings and waiver are demonstrated by the prosecution at trial, no evidence obtained as a result of interrogation can be used against him.

Interrogator Profile

It has been said that anyone who strives diligently to apply himself can become a good interrogator. It is true that anyone can learn to ask questions, but this does not make an interrogator. There are certain character and personality traits which a truly effective interrogator must possess. Additionally, the physical appearance of the interrogator has a definite bearing on his or her success.

The good interrogator, in our judgment, must be an extrovert, a forceful person with a personality which commands respect, a take-charge individual who immediately assumes a posture of leadership and control of any situation. If the investigator cannot "manage" the questioning, the subject will soon become aware of this and take over. Chances of success under these conditions are practically nil.

He must be an actor, able to feign anger, sympathy, or whatever emotion may be required under the circumstances. This may involve shedding real tears along with the subject.

He must be intelligent and possess a keen mind which reacts to any development during the questioning, for not only must he be constantly thinking ahead to the next question, but he must be able to alter the approach and procedure instantly when there is an unexpected answer to a question. Even though a line of questioning has been predetermined, there must be flexibility enough to change immediately if the subject's responses dictate. The interrogator must be constantly alert and thinking, thinking, thinking.

Interrogation requires an understanding of human nature and the ability to analyze people. Every person questioned is different; each individual has his own weaknesses, strengths, level of emotional stability and control, beliefs, and personality. If the interrogator has no empathy with this person, a fruitful relationship is never established.

In referring to the physical appearance of the interrogator, we do not mean to imply that no one under six feet tall or weighing less than 200 pounds can be successful. But we believe that extremes in appearance can be a definite handicap. For example, a small man will not command the same respect as one of average size. An extremely youthful looking woman will also have problems, particularly when dealing with people of middle age and beyond.

A person who lacks some of the qualities mentioned should not necessarily stop all efforts to be a good interrogator. However, if he or she has made a dedicated effort in this direction over a reasonable period of time and continues to be unsuccessful, it is highly probable that no amount of work, study, or training will bring success.

How does a person get training as an interrogator? This problem has perplexed investigation supervisors for many years, but one of their stock answers is "working with experienced investigators," which usually involves sitting in on a number of questioning sessions. There are definite risks in this procedure. Some officers work best alone, and, even though the trainee only observes, his presence disturbs the "teacher" and renders the interrogation ineffective. Additionally, an excellent interrogator may be a very poor instructor. If he does not, at the conclusion of each session, explain to the trainee why certain questions were asked or certain techniques employed, the value of this experience is questionable. Another possible pitfall is that the trainee may adopt methods and techniques of the teacher. Every individual's approach must be suited to his own personality and not altered or modified to conform to that of an instructor.

Actually, this training is multifaceted, consisting of study, attending seminars on the subject, and working with experienced people. Such a program presents several problems: How good is the study material? How effective are the seminar speakers? Most important, how good is the "experienced investigator"? Regardless of the problems encountered, this is the most effective means available at this time. The supervisor must evaluate the worth of any publication provided to trainees and of any seminars on the subject.

Meaning and Importance

There is a distinct difference between an interview and an interrogation, the key distinction being the atmosphere under which the two activities take place. An interview consists of asking questions to obtain information in an informal manner; an interrogation, on the other hand, consists of asking questions to obtain information in a formal atmosphere.

Other definitions refer to interrogation as the formal questioning of a person suspected of certain criminal activities or the legally acceptable verbal persuasion of a suspect to cause his confession of guilt in a crime or offense. Perhaps the most acceptable meaning is the shortest: "questioning a suspect to determine guilty knowledge."

Since the vast majority of arson convictions are based on confessions, it follows that a competent arson investigator must be a good interrogator. The nature of the crime involves the destruction of most physical evidence. Seldom are there fingerprints, pry marks, tools used in breaking and entering, or loot taken during commission of the crime. Seldom is there an eyewitness, and even when there is, the witness often has a lapse of memory in the courtroom and, under cross-examination, states that she "thought it was the accused, but really can't say for sure."

Although the interrogation plays a critical role in the investigative process, it does not replace any and all other investigative requirements. Following a cursory examination of the scene and a brief preliminary investigation, officers have been heard to suggest the following battle plan: "Let's bring all the suspects in, run them on the polygraph, and give me two hours with any that don't run clean. I'll get it out of them." This simply won't work.

The crime scene search is essential to the interrogation. Only after the investigator has determined to some degree the point of origin and the cause of a fire can he intelligently question anyone. Until the search is accomplished, the interrogator is not in a position to refute anything he is told. The suspect has a decided advantage and will soon realize that the officers know very little about the facts of the case. It is the crime scene search that provides the investigator with ammunition during the questioning. When the suspect is faced with the discovery of separate and unconnected fires, the presence of accelerants, possible evidence of breaking and entering, he then realizes that a thorough investigation has been conducted, and his defenses begin to crumble.

Interrogation does not take the place of physical evidence properly preserved and introduced with competence in the courtroom. An equally significant facet of the overall investigative process is the laboratory report which confirms the presence of and identifies an accelerant or incendiary device. In summary, the interrogation is a significant element of the investigation, but it is neither the whole investigation nor the solution to all problems.

Objectives

The primary objective of interrogation is to obtain a truthful confession. Ethical representatives of enforcement agencies most assuredly don't seek or want a confession from someone who didn't commit the crime. There are those who willingly confess to any crime when questioned. The investigator must be alert for this type of person and not just accept any confession at face value. Uppermost in his mind must be the search for truth, not just a confession.

A secondary but important objective is to obtain information which will allow the expansion of the investigation. Often, the suspect, in a recitation of events prior and subsequent to the fire, will mention names, places, and times. This information can be used effectively not only to check out any alibi, but also to pursue other investigative routes.

A significant objective is to determine the guilt of the suspect even though no confession may be obtained. In most cases at the conclusion of questioning the guilt or innocence of the suspect is apparent to the interrogator. While this is small consolation to those seeking a truthful confession, it at least enables the officers to direct further investigative efforts toward the suspect and not toward other persons with no involvement in the crime. On the other hand, if the suspect does not reveal symptoms of guilt the investigators must pursue other avenues.

Preparation for Interrogation

Generally speaking, preparation involves four areas: physical, mental and emotional, factual, and personal. Each of these is of utmost importance.

Physical

Any investigator who says that an interrogation is easy work and not really physically demanding is only going through the motions. Properly conducted, this is a demanding, exhausting job which leaves the investigator completely "wrung out." The investigator who has driven a long distance before daybreak to reach a fire scene, conducted a day-long scene search, and eaten only an "investigator's lunch" (a can or sardines, crackers, a big orange drink, and a moon pie) is not physically ready to take on the suspect. An investigator suffering from loss of sleep, exhaustion, or a massive hangover should postpone the activity until he is in top physical condition.

Mental and Emotional

The interrogator must have absolute confidence in his ability to get a truthful confession or his uncertainty will become evident during the course of the questioning and the probability of securing a confession will be minimal.

The emotional state of the officer is extremely important. Worry will definitely interfere with his concentration, which probably accounts for the fact that supervisors on occasion conduct mediocre interrogations, for they are anxious about problems connected with the overall operation of the organization, personnel and budget problems, reports, and other administrative and supervisory matters, and they simply cannot concentrate on the issue at hand. On occasion some event prior to the interrogation may put the officer in a highly emotional state—a quarrel at home, a "chewing out" by the boss, news of an accident or illness in his family—which will seriously diminish his ability to conduct an effective interrogation. Once again, it would be wise to delay the questioning until factors causing any emotional disturbance are resolved. Further, the interrogator must not be concerned about time. If he is subconsciously aware of an appointment or time deadline, he will not be able to concentrate fully.

Factual

The interrogator must know every detail of the case thoroughly enough to avoid any reference to his notes. Constantly referring to a notebook, thumbing through the pages, looking for certain items of information results in long pauses which give the suspect a chance to compose himself and realize, perhaps for the first time, that the investigator is not completely familiar with the case. Equally important, eye contact is lost with the subject, whose attention may be lost as he looks around the room, examines the furniture, and regains his confidence. During this pause another investigator who is present may jump in and ask a question which completely upsets the "game plan."

Another phase of factual preparation, often overlooked or ignored with disastrous results, consists of obtaining as much information as possible concerning the individual to be questioned. The interrogator should delve into his background and establish his prior criminal record, his attitude toward authority, his economic and social status, his emotional stability, the condition of his health, his religious orientation. Is he a good family man, does he work regularly, what is his general reputation for truthfulness, what are his interests and hobbies—all of these are important. It is foolish for an investigator to attempt to question an individual without making a sincere effort to find out as much as possible about him.

A failure to do such homework in one case placed the investigators in a very embarrassing position. An obviously set fire occurred in a farm home in a remote rural area. Investigation revealed that the house belonged to a man associated with an insulation business, and neighborhood interviews revealed that he had been observed in the general area approximately thirty minutes prior to discovery of the fire. The facts of the case were documented, physical evidence was gathered, and investigators were factually prepared for the questioning of the owner—so they thought. On arriving at the suspect's place of business with the express purpose of picking him up for questioning, the investigators were subjected to one shock after another. Upon inquiring about the subject, the investigators were escorted into an office big enough for several bowling alleys. Behind a desk four times the size of a standard pool table sat their quarry, the owner of a million-dollar-a-year business. After a partial recovery, the investigators told him the purpose of their visit. He offered his full cooperation, including the services of his firm's several attorneys and posting a $2,000 reward for information leading to the arrest and conviction of the fire setter.

Needless to say the "case" fell apart at this point, but two very sheepish investigators discussed (with each other) their lack of preparation for the interrogation, realizing they had gathered factual information on the fire while failing completely to gather vital facts on the subject.

Personal

The grooming and appearance of the interrogator are important considerations. Dress should be neat but conservative, not loud and flashy. Clothing should command respect but should not offend the subject or cause resentment because of its evidence of affluence. Such items as handkerchiefs protruding from chest pockets and excessive amounts of jewelry should be avoided.

There is disagreement about whether either police or fire officials should wear uniforms during an interrogation. Since the case has at this point reached the status of an investigation, plain clothes would seem to be more appropriate. Often departmental policy determines the dress during interrogation. If not, the prosecutor should be consulted and his recommendations followed. In the absence of guidelines, the interrogator must decide for himself how to dress, taking into consideration how he operates most effectively.

Another area of disagreement is the wearing of sidearms during questioning. Since this is normal equipment for most uniformed law enforcement officers and investigators, no valid argument seems to exist against wearing sidearms. A subject may claim he was intimidated by the sight of a weapon and confessed in fear of his safety, but a pistol is no more threatening than the handcuffs, mace, night sticks, and other equipment used as restraining devices. Again, departmental directives and the recommendations of the prosecutor may dictate policy in this area. If not, it is suggested that the interrogator wear whatever equipment, including a weapon, he uses in his normal day-to-day investigative routine.

The personal grooming of the investigator is critical to the success of the interrogation. Rules that were at one time quite inflexible have been softened to some extent. In the past there was little need for guidelines on hair length and beards, but hair lengths and styles which years ago might have been considered ridiculous are now generally accepted. In a recent arson trial involving a group classified as "hippies" because of their long hair and beards, the longest hair and heaviest beard belonged to the prosecuting attorney. It is suggested that the appearance of the investigator be suited to the type of person being questioned. A long-haired, bearded interrogator might relate very well to people of similar appearance; the same individual would command less respect from a conservative businessman or property owner.

The fact that the interrogation room will probably be small and intimate places certain personal grooming requirements on the investigators. Some amusing (but not really funny) testimony from persons subjected to questioning points out the need for personal cleanliness. One accused on the witness stand made the following statement concerning an interrogator: "To tell you the truth, judge, that man smelled so bad I would have admitted to anything just to get away from him."

During an interrogation, the investigator believed he was making real progress, having established a good relationship with the subject, and he was sure a confession was forthcoming. At this critical point the subject began, "I'm going to tell you something." The investigator's heart skipped a beat—this was it, a confession, or at least an admission. The subject continued, "You sure do have dirty teeth." Needless to say the whole interrogation collapsed.

Contact with Subject

The method in which the investigator first makes contact with the subject varies with localities and individual investigations. The subject may be brought into a station, or there may be a written or telephoned request that he come in. The most effective procedure consists of picking up the subject oneself. The circumstances under which this is done depend almost entirely on the background of the subject. A ring-wise criminal will probably say, "If you've got a warrant, arrest me. If you don't, I ain't going nowhere." Sometimes a subject will say, "I'll come on down after a while." In the first case if the investigator does not have a warrant he can't arrest the subject. In the second case, he must try to talk the person into coming along. The second person is probably stalling, with the specific purpose of contacting a lawyer to seek advice or to accompany him to the station. It is possible he has no intention of coming down later and will take off to parts unknown. If the individual specifically states that he wants to talk to a lawyer at this time, the investigator is on dangerous ground denying him this right or trying to talk him out of this. This is true even though no accusations of any kind have been made.

A factor which is an advantage in the investigation of arson is that the subject in many cases is not the ordinary criminal type. He may be a businessman or homeowner whose financial situation has caused him to commit arson, either directly or through the services of another party. His lack of experience in criminal matters does not give the investigator the privilege of abusing law enforcement powers, but he has an advantage in the fact that this may be the subject's first serious brush with the law.

The approach should be businesslike but not hard-nosed, identifying one-self, showing credentials, and stating the purpose of the visit. Shake hands with the subject firmly. A possible approach is, "We are looking into the fire which occurred on your property (or in your place of business) and would like you to come down to the station with us. We know you are anxious to get this matter straight and so are we. There are a few points we need to clear up and you can help us with these." The approach must be positive and affirmative, not "Would you be willing to accompany us," and most emphatically not "You wouldn't be willing to accompany us, would you?" When properly approached the subject has no valid reason for not going along, but he may resort to various excuses. If he is at work, he will say he can't get off, or will lose time from work, or will get fired. The investigator must take care of these matters with his supervisor prior to contacting the subject. The approach to his boss is similar to that used with the subject. In fairness to the employee the investigator must make it perfectly clear that he is completing an inquiry into the fire and that the employee is not accused or under suspicion. Any implications of possible guilt would be very damaging to the individual and might actually cause him to be fired. The subject should be relieved of any anxiety or worry by telling him truthfully that his employer has agreed to give him time off without loss of pay in order to accompany the investigator to the station.

If the subject is contacted at home, the approach is basically the same. The principal problem encountered here is that the subject feels he can be interrogated at his home. The investigator can state truthfully that he wants to talk in private, undisturbed, and further that he wants to spare the subject any embarrassment with the members of his family.

Regardless of whether the person is contacted at work or at home, it is absolutely essential that he be removed from the security of familiar sur-roundings, for otherwise an effective interrogation is impossible. A person in his living room, with one eye on the television, a small child sitting on his lap, his wife calling him to the telephone and other interruptions constantly occurring cannot be properly interrogated. If the subject refuses to come along willingly and cannot be arrested, no interrogation should be attempted. It is advisable to terminate the contact at this point and attempt to pick the subject up later under more favorable conditions. Do not attempt an interro-gation on a subject's "home grounds."

Let us assume that the individual has agreed to go to the station in the investigator's car. During the ten- or fifteen-minute ride, we suggest absolutely nothing should take place. If there is any conversation during the trip, it should not be in reference to the case. If the investigator knows anything about the background of the subject (and he should), they may talk about matters he is interested in, such as hunting, fishing, sports, and similar topics which can be discussed in general terms, rather than his job or home; he may be worried about these subconsciously. If he brings up the fire, the investigator should simply state that he would rather discuss this at the station. Most important, the person should be treated with courtesy, like an ordinary passenger in one's personal car. He is a citizen, not convicted or even accused (unless arrested) of committing a crime, and is entitled to the same rights, privileges, and decent treatment due any citizen.

Arrival at the Station

When using the term "station," we refer to police or fire department headquarters, a sheriff's office, or possibly local or regional headquarters of a state investigative agency. Regardless of what organization the investigators represent, optimum conditions for conducting the interrogation should be available. What are optimum conditions? Let us consider some requirements of the setting for this most important investigative process.

The most vital factory is privacy. There can be no successful interrogation in a room full of people, noise, and confusion; the room should be small, quiet, and soundproof. Temperature should be moderate, neither too hot nor too cold. Lighting should be adequate and even, with no bright lights directly on the subject. The room should contain chairs for whatever number of people are to be present. There should be no tables or desks between the interrogators and the subject. Ideally there should be no windows; if there is a window it should be "smoked" so no outside distractions interfere. Facilities for recording the questioning should be available, although not always used. The see-through two-way mirror on the wall is so well-known to the public now that the subject probably knows he is being observed through the mirror from another room. This may actually prove a detriment to the interrogators; even though no one is observing the activity, no amount of persuasion will convince the subject of this. Omit the mirror. To ensure privacy, the door must be locked and a prominently displayed sign on the door should read "Conference Room." Many departments have luminous signs which can be turned on when the room is in use. Others have a small red light which is activated by the closing of the door. Whatever system is employed, everyone should understand that the door is not to be opened except in emergencies. All the warning signs and lights in the world are of no avail if ignored. Individuals who are unfamiliar with interrogation procedures cannot comprehend the damage done when they knock on the door, come in, stay a few minutes, then get up and leave. Written messages handed in the door or messages delivered orally are equally disruptive. The necessity of absolute uninterrupted privacy must be clearly understood by all personnel.

There must be no radio in the interrogation room. Walkie-talkies, pagers, and similar units carried on the officer's person must be inactivated. Another source of interruption which must be eliminated is any speaker which may be hooked into a communication or paging system.

It is important to remove any distractions in the room. A telephone presents several problems. First, the phone may ring and interrupt the orderly process of interrogation. Second, the phone presents a constant opportunity for the subject to make calls, possibly to an attorney. There must be no pictures, calendars, or drawings on the wall or on any table in the room. Certificates, diplomas, and plaques may be a source of pride to the interrogator, but they are a source of distraction to the subject. No knickknacks or other objects which can be picked up should be visible, for handling such objects is a means of relieving nervousness. No water fountain should be in the room. A subject who begins to feel the pressure of lying to the interrogator will become thirsty, and constant trips to the water fountain, whether to quench thirst or to relieve tension, seriously interfere with the interrogation.

Interrogation Procedures

How many people there are in the conference room is a matter for the interrogator to decide. Some investigators insist that they can work more effectively alone. While this may be the case in some instances, it is generally accepted that two officers and no more provide the best chance of successful results. The mere presence of more than two interrogators always presents the possibility of courtroom claims of duress, coercion, and intimidation. Additionally, three or four people haphazardly questioning the subject make any interrogation continuity impossible. Another factor to be considered is the psychological effect on the subject. Can he reasonably be expected to confess to anything in front of three, four, or five people?

There is an old expression, "Two heads are better than one, even if one is a cabbage head." We hold this to be true in the case of interrogation, with the sincere hope that neither participant is a "cabbage head." Why two? At least one of the officers must be able to establish rapport with the subject. If only one person is present and an immediate clash develops between the interrogator and subject, this rapport will not be forthcoming. One investigator may pick up a discrepancy in the subject's story which the other missed completely. On occasion a lone investigator may reach a point in the questioning where he doesn't know where to go, what question to ask, what avenue to follow. At this time another interrogator may take over. In summary, one interrogator is acceptable, two is ideal, three or more is illogical and ineffective.

One final word of warning concerning the number of people present: if a pair of officers start out with the interrogation, the same two must continue the entire process. One cannot get up and leave the room, go to the restroom, or have a cup of coffee while the other continues the questioning. Admittedly a relay procedure is an advantage to the interrogators, but it may well result in a court ruling that the confession is inadmissible.

A good rule of thumb to follow is to afford the subject the opportunity to do whatever the investigators do. If they need restroom privileges, ask him if he needs to go to the toilet. If they must have a cup of coffee, offer him the same. If they have food brought in, ask him what he would like. Even if he says he doesn't want coffee or anything to eat, bring it in anyway and place it in front of him. Why? To anticipate claims such as "They wouldn't let me go to the toilet" or "They drank coffee and ate and I hadn't had anything to eat or drink for twelve hours." These may seem inconsequential considerations, but the interrogator who follows these basic guidelines is on solid ground during cross-examination on conditions under which the confession was obtained.

Assuming that at this time the two investigators and the subject have entered the interrogation room, they ask the subject to take a seat and reidentify themselves. It is not necessary to display credentials if this has been done on initial contact. During these activities, the subject should be treated decently. If this is his first encounter with law enforcement, as it may well be, it is a very traumatic experience. Investigators should gain the individual's respect by conducting themselves properly, in a serious, professional manner—firm, but at the same time courteous. Before proceeding further, they should again identify the matter under investigation.

Legal Rights

Up to this point in the investigation the subject has not been advised of his rights under the *Miranda* decision. But no question in reference to the case at hand has been asked, so there has been no requirement for the *Miranda* warning.

A huge volume could be written on the *Miranda* decision and its effect on law enforcement. All investigators have read page after page of material and listened to hour after hour of lectures and discussions on this subject. The biggest hangup is not *that* the *Miranda* warning is required, but *when* in the investigation it is required. That "the individual must be advised of his rights when the questioning changes from being investigatory to accusatory" implies that during the course of an interview the probable involvement of the subject in the commission of the crime becomes evident. We must at this point cease the questioning and advise the person of his rights.

The key words in the court decision are (1) custodial or in-custody interrogation and (2) deprived of his freedom of action in any significant way. Concerning the first item, the court stated in the *Miranda* opinion.

General on-the-scene questioning as to facts surrounding a crime or other general questioning of citizens in the fact-finding process is not affected by our holding. It is an act of responsible citizenship for individuals to give whatever information they may have to aid in law enforcement. In such situations the compelling atmosphere inherent in the process of in-custody interrogation is not necessarily present.

Concerning the second item, we note that the word *significant* was not repeated in later portions of the court's decision. This has led to a broad interpretation: if a person is prevented from coming or going as he pleases, he has been taken into custody, and the rules of custodial interrogation apply.

All law enforcement officers have been lectured, instructed, and so thoroughly indoctrinated in all phases of the requirement under the *Miranda* decision that they have adjusted to these requirements and learned to live with them. Arguments over technical phases of the warning continue unabated among police officers, prosecutors, and others affected by this landmark decision. As a general rule of thumb, when in doubt, advise the individual of his rights under the terms of the *Miranda* decision. The following basic form is suggested.

YOUR RIGHTS

Place _____

Date _____

Time _____

Before we ask you any questions, you must understand your rights.

You have the right to remain silent.

Anything you say can be used against you in court.

You have the right to talk to a lawyer for advice before we ask you any questions and to have him with you during questioning.

If you cannot afford a lawyer, one will be appointed for you before any questioning if you wish.

If you decide to answer questions now without a lawyer present, you will still have the right to stop answering at any time. You also have the right to stop answering at any time until you talk to a lawyer.

Waiver of Rights

I have read this statement of my rights and I understand what my rights are. I am willing to make a statement and answer questions. I do not want a lawyer at this time. I understand and know what I am doing. No promises or threats have been made to me and no pressure or coercion of any kind has been used against me.

Signed _____

Witness _____

Witness _____

Time _____

This form is fairly simple and requires no elaborate explanation by the investigators, with the possible exception of some explanation of the meaning of *coercion*. The individual may be an illiterate who can only sign his name with an "x" mark, and his defense attorney will have a field day in court if it cannot be proved beyond any doubt that the individual fully understood what was said to him.

There is a tendency on the part of some local prosecutors to add to the basic form, and this may result in real trouble. Additions such as "I holistically comprehend the ramifications of affixing my signature to any and all portions of the heretofore included documentation, etc., etc." will surely cause problems for the investigators when they try to prove in the courtroom that a subject with a third-grade education understood this verbal garbage. If the local prosecutor believes any additions are necessary to protect the officers and himself, these should be plainly worded in language that any subject can understand.

The entire matter of the *Miranda* decision may soon be resolved by the U.S. Supreme Court in a recent decision modifying the stand taken by the Warren Court of the 1960s. In a minority opinion in a late 1975 decision, Justice William J. Brennan wrote, "Today's distortion of *Miranda*'s constitutional principles can be viewed only as yet another step toward the erosion and, I suppose, ultimate overruling of *Miranda*'s enforcement of the privilege against self-incrimination."

The facts of the case referred to are these. A subject taken in custody on a robbery charge, when given the *Miranda* warning, exercised his privilege to remain silent and answer no further questions. As a result the interrogation was stopped immediately. Several hours later, the subject was questioned by another detective (not involved in the previous questioning) about a murder. The subject was again advised of his rights under the *Miranda* rule and made statements which led to his conviction on the murder charge. The state court of appeals upset the conviction, contending that since the accused had said earlier he wished to remain silent, the second interrogation violated his rights. The U.S. Supreme Court reversed the appeals court decision, saying that it would be "absurd" to hold that once a suspect exercised his right to remain silent, he could never be questioned again. Since the man had subsequently been advised of his *Miranda* rights, the second questioning two hours after the first was reasonable.

There are other cases now on appeal which may result in additional erosion of the *Miranda* rule. Until the decision is overruled, however, we must continue to adhere to its requirements.

Having explained his rights and secured his signature on an acceptable document, the investigators now proceed with the interrogation. The subject is seated in a chair directly in front of them, with no desk or table between the suspect and them to serve as a protective shield for him and create an unwanted psychological barrier. He should have nothing to play with, such as a hat, gloves, or cigarette lighter.

This is the point at which to establish rapport with this individual by asking him what his friends call him and addressing him by that name, asking him general questions to which the answers are known to see if he will lie. This is a "get-acquainted" period for all parties; they get accustomed to the surroundings, to each other's voices. Is the subject a talker or will his answers be short and crisp? Is he reasonably calm or will he fly off the handle? The investigators are analyzing the suspect, making a determination as to the type of person he is. This analysis will help them decide what their approach will be.

The following interrogation procedure is suggested, but the procedure will vary with each case. Ask the individual to tell everything he knows about the fire. During this recitation, listen carefully for any discrepancies from information developed during the investigation. Keep the suspect on the subject and do not allow him to "take over." Be in control of the situation. During this time do not thumb through notes but give the subject undivided attention, looking him in the eye and requesting that he look at you. If there are any areas that are not clear, ask the subject to repeat these portions of his story.

Following this recitation ask direct questions to further clarify pertinent points. Do not create a hostile attitude in the suspect. Questions should be plainly stated and easily understood. Ask questions one at a time which require only one answer, and allow the subject time to answer each question. At the conclusion of this direct examination summarize all that has been covered and have the suspect verify the information.

The third and most important phase of the interrogation is cross-examining the suspect. Begin to bear down, pointing out that his version of his activities is refuted by known facts developed during the investigation. In the case of an insurance fraud fire involving a business, the suspect may have made certain statements concerning the healthy financial state of his operation. Point out to him known facts concerning his losses, his indebtedness, his generally poor financial condition. During this process two things are accomplished: (1) the suspect realizes that a thorough investigation has been made, and (2) his defenses begin to weaken. Be absolutely certain of facts and do not get caught in an error, as this will bolster the confidence of the suspect, and he may feel that he is actually in control of the situation.

The Confession

At this stage of the interrogation, the critical point is reached at which the investigator goes after the confession in earnest. The approach will vary with the type of suspect. Keep in mind that the subject is probably not a hard-nosed criminal, but rather an ordinary citizen in a financial bind. Even in the case of non-fraud fires, often the only crime ever committed by this person is setting a fire or fires. Point out to the subject that this investigation is just seeking the truth. Appeal to his common decency, emphasizing positive factors, that he is a good worker, a family man, a good provider. He has no previous criminal record and is generally a good citizen. What he has done is wrong, but anyone might have been driven to do the same thing under the circumstances. Minimize the seriousness of the crime, emphasizing that he has not assaulted another person with a knife or gun or committed a crime of violence. Everybody makes mistakes but it takes a real man to admit these mistakes.

During this time, if he lowers his head or looks away, insist that he look you in the eye. A good interrogator can sense when the subject is ready to confess. Put yourself in the man's position—he is about to confess to something that may result in disgrace to him and his family, separation from his loved ones, and a prison sentence. This is a critical point and you must not let it get away from you. Point out that you know what he is going through, how hard it is to tell the truth. Offer to have only one interrogator stay in the room. Pat him on the leg or put your hand on his shoulder.

At this time he may throw up his last defense: "You want me to tell you I did something I didn't do." State emphatically that you are seeking the truth, and you know and he knows what the truth is. You may have to review some of the evidence against him, pointing out how the whole case will look in the courtroom. Display an attitude of confidence in his guilt and explain that he is butting his head against a stone wall.

Now he may ask the question, "What will happen to me if I say I did this?" Be very cautious about making any promises you cannot keep. You cannot promise leniency or a light or suspended sentence. You can, however, cite the outcome of previous cases in which an individual has been man enough to tell the truth, to admit that he made a mistake. You can truthfully say that you will tell the prosecuting attorney that he was cooperative. You can truthfully say that you will testify in the courtroom that he was cooperative and seemed to be generally sorry for what he had done. Do not make such statements as "I'm going to help you."

You may have to prod the suspect along at this point and ask him, "Are you sorry you burned the house (or store)?'' An affirmative answer may be the first actual admission on his part that he did in fact commit the crime. Following this admission, it is a mistake to say, ''Tell us all about it.'' The interrogator must assist the suspect by taking him through his actions connected with the commission, being cautious at the same time not to lead him. For example, you might say, ''After leaving the tavern at 11:00, you drove around for a while (a known fact). Then what did you do?''

At the beginning of and during his oral confession, do not bring out a pad and start writing. Go through the entire fire-setting activity, listening carefully, prodding when necessary. When this has been completed, don't show any change in attitude toward the subject. Any contempt you may feel for him must not be reflected by word or deed. Having gotten this burden of guilt off his back he will feel a sense of relief. On most occasions when a subject is asked if he doesn't feel better now that he has told the truth, the response is affirmative. Often individuals will go into a lengthy recitation of how this thing has been eating their insides, that they have been worried half out of their mind, etc.

Various other approaches may be employed from time to time, the choice depending mainly on the suspect. In dealing with a subject who has had frequent brushes with the law, it is a waste of time to appeal to his sense of decency, good reputation, and so forth. The only approach that may succeed with this type of individual is ''laying it on the line.'' He must be convinced the evidence against him is so overwhelming that resistance is futile.

Another approach which may succeed on occasion is a forceful, aggressive one. The danger in this is that it may end up in a shouting contest with the subject and accomplish very little except making him angry. The chances of reestablishing rapport after such a scene are slim. But this tactic may be effective for the bad guy during a good guy–bad guy routine in which the bad guy deliberately baits the subject, wanting the subject to dislike him intensely so the nice guy has an even more favorable image. There are dozens of other tricks in the trade, but these do not replace good interrogation techniques on a day-to-day basis.

Suspect Reaction

During the course of the interrogation, suspects will react in a variety of ways when things are getting tight. A subject may swear constantly and may make such statements as ''I swear to God I'm telling the truth.'' Use of profanity must be nipped in the bud. Investigators advise the subject that they are not going to curse and don't expect him to. To handle the ''swearing to God'' routine, they tell him he doesn't need to do this, that they will know when he is telling the truth.

One reaction from the suspect when a question puts him in a bind is feigned loss of memory: ''I can't recall'' or ''Not that I remember.'' This can be countered by asking how it is he can remember minor details of the case but now pretends he can't recall a major event connected with it. This is a copout. Don't let him get away with it.

On occasion a subject will emphasize his excellent reputation, his pillar of the church and community status, and possibly his connections with people of influence. He can be told the investigators are aware of this and therefore anticipate that he will be an honorable and truthful person.

There are certain activities to which the subject resorts in an effort to relieve his tension. One of these is some physical action, such as combing his hair, clipping his fingernails, picking hair off the back of his hand or arm. If the subject is wearing a sweater he may pick each sleeve completely bare of imaginary fuzz up to the elbow. These actions can be curtailed by insisting that the subject look at the investigators. If he continually drops his eyes or lowers his head, they can point out that not being able to look them in the eye is another indication of guilt.

A subterfuge to which a suspect sometimes resorts is a pretense of boredom. He will slouch down in the chair and yawn continuously. This is strictly a pretense. Insist that he sit up in the chair and respond to questions.

A few requests which the subject may make are excuses for leaving the interrogation room. He will claim to be thirsty, and probably he is, for dryness of the mouth is a genuine sign of nervousness and guilt. When he asks for water, point this fact out to him. "I need to go to the toilet" or "I am hungry" are standard escape statements. These things should have been taken care of prior to the start of the interrogation. If they were not, the individual must be allowed bathroom privileges. If he is hungry, ask him what he wants and send out for it. It is advisable not to start an interrogation within an hour or so of normal meal time.

Indications of Guilt

Very few of us can claim to have gone through life without telling even one little white lie to get out of a tight spot. Certain physical reactions which we could not control accompanied this deceit, the intensity of the reaction being governed by the seriousness of the situation. These same physical reactions take place with the subject and investigators must be constantly looking for them and pointing them out to him as an indication of his guilt.

As noted previously, dryness of the mouth is a sign of guilt. The subject will constantly lick his lips and try to do something about his mouthful of cotton. He will swallow repeatedly when there is no saliva to swallow. Another physical condition which he cannot control is excessive sweating, particularly the hands. The subject's face may become flushed and perspiration may break out on his forehead even though the room is cool and comfortable. Watch the arteries in the neck closely; if they are pulsing this is a clear indication of tension in the subject.

Summary

During the entire interrogation process the investigator is the epitome of professional competence. He is a listener, a thinker, in complete control of his emotions; he can feign anger, sympathy; he is flexible, adjusting to changes and pursuing any opening; he does not curse; he does not abuse; he does not lie. Unfortunately, in spite of his best efforts, he is not going to win them all. He must try to profit by each interrogation, analyzing mistakes, and discussing them with his partner.

One case involved interrogation of a subject for burning his car. The investigators had good circumstantial evidence, but not enough hard evidence to charge the subject. The interrogation went well; the suspect's story was refuted repeatedly. A confession seemed only a matter of time when the suspect leaned back in the car seat, smiled, and said, "Fellas, I know you want me to tell you that I burned my car. I ain't saying I did and I ain't saying I didn't, but I'm just not ever going to tell you I did. You're wasting your time and mine. So now let's don't have no hard feeling about this thing. Let's be friends. Just to show you I don't have no hard feelings, I'm asking you fellas to come on in the house and share a mess of beans with me and my family."

Every last one of us, more often than we like, will be invited at some time in some way, "to share a mess of beans."

16 Presenting Your Case

Many hours, days, or weeks of investigation may be wasted if the case is not properly presented in the courtroom. In the majority of arson cases the success or failure of the prosecution's case hinges on the investigator and his competence. This is not to diminish the importance of the prosecutor, but he can only offer the evidence that has been developed by the investigator. Furthermore, he must rely on the investigator in most cases as the key witness, who will by effective testimony convince the judge or jury of the guilt of the defendant.

There are no hard and fast rules for being a good witness. Generally speaking, testifying impressively requires understanding the basic rules of evidence, knowledge of the case at hand, and proper conduct in the courtroom. This chapter contains suggestions for overcoming the problems which the investigator faces as a witness.

Evidence

Definition

Evidence may be defined as a statement of a witness, physical object, or document pertinent to the point in question legally offered to a court.

Types of Admissible Evidence

Physical evidence is tangible material which has been obtained legally and which will be introduced as evidence at the trial by the investigating officer or other competent witness or witnesses. Usually this evidence consists of items, articles, or material found in the vicinity of the crime scene, such as cans, jars, footprints, and the like.

The investigator must assure that the evidence is properly identified as to when, where, and by whom it was found. There must be no possible doubt that this is the same evidence which the investigator originally discovered. The whereabouts of this evidence from the time of its discovery until its introduction in the courtroom must be established so as to resist successfully any attack by the defense attorney concerning its admissibility. The fact that it is still in its original condition must be substantiated. A possible exception exists when the evidence is altered as a result of laboratory examination.

Written evidence is statements and confessions, as well as leases, deeds, insurance policies, and other documents. After the initial problem of getting such papers admitted is overcome, these make very effective evidence which speak for themselves.

Oral evidence is the type of evidence the investigator is most commonly involved with, including what he observed through seeing, hearing, feeling, smelling, or tasting. Unfortunately, it is also the most unreliable evidence, because of honest mistakes, unconscious bias, lapse of memory, or improper observations. It is advisable for the investigator to refer to his original notes on the witness stand to avoid inaccuracies as far as possible. Requirements which must be met before these notes can be used in the courtroom are explained in Chapter 14.

Types of Inadmissible Evidence

Opinions and conclusions are one kind of inadmissible evidence. With the exception of the expert, a witness may testify only to facts, not to their effect or result, nor to conclusions based on the facts. It is the function of the judge or jury to interpret the facts and reach conclusions.

The fire Chief may testify, "Immediately after we (the fire department) extinguished the fire, I found in the living room a five-gallon can with gasoline in it which was used to set the fire." This is questionable on two counts. First, while the fire chief may be positive that the liquid is gasoline, the laboratory report will make this identification more effective. Second, the witness expresses an opinion and reaches a conclusion concerning the use of the gasoline which is not within his prerogative.

A witness may testify, "The flames were about twenty feet high, bright red, with black smoke, so a flammable liquid was present." Again an opinion and a conclusion by this witness are unacceptable. This testimony would be proper until the last phrase in the sentence, as a lay witness may testify on matters of common observation.

Hearsay is also inadmissible evidence. This is a type of testimony which seems to confuse many investigating officers. Simply stated, a witness may not testify to what he hears someone else say, other than the defendant. He cannot testify to what people told him about what they saw, or what they heard, or what they observed.

The investigator may testify, "Fire Fighter Weehunt told me . . ." This is not acceptable testimony because the judge, jury, and defendant are entitled to hear this evidence directly from Fire Fighter Weehunt. Only in this way can the witness be subjected to cross-examination and his credibility be evaluated.

There are a few notable exceptions to the hearsay exclusion, such as dying declarations, res gestiae, and statements made in the presence of the defendant. As a general guideline, however, the investigator should operate on the premise that he cannot testify to what is told to him by anyone other than the defendant.

Preparation for Court

At the inception of the investigation, it must be assumed that every case will go to trial. The very cases on which the investigator takes a shortcut are those that end up in the courtroom, with an aggressive, well-prepared defense attorney ripping him to shreds simply because he failed to prepare himself. A poorly conducted investigation cannot be salvaged in the courtroom regardless of how convincing and forceful a witness the officer may be.

During the investigation, a daily log of all activities should be kept, noting the dates and times of beginning and ending of all interviews and interrogations. Information about the fire scene examination or examinations should be recorded—dates, times, and also those present. An activity log of this nature will help the officer keep organized during the investigation and will be invaluable in the courtroom if and when the defense counsel attempts to confuse the witness by switching dates, times, and places.

At the conclusion of the investigation, a complete and comprehensive report must be prepared *without delay*. If several days pass before this task is started, both the memory and the notes of the officer will cool and writing the report will become an extremely difficult undertaking. At this time all notes must be assembled and organized, physical evidence must be collected and arrangements made for its custody and storage, photographs, charts, diagrams, and sketches must be properly identified and labeled.

It is also appropriate at this point to discuss the case with the prosecuting attorney and assist in the preparation of the case for trial if requested to do so. In some jurisdictions, lines of communication between investigator and prosecutor are established early in the probe and continue on an almost daily basis. In other localities no such liaison exists. Under any circumstances, the prosecutor must be advised of the outcome of the investigation as soon as possible.

At some time prior to the trial, the investigator must conduct a pretrial conference with the prosecuting attorney. The entire case is reviewed to ensure that he knows all of the facts of the case, favorable and unfavorable. The testimony of the investigator is discussed, including the general line of questioning the prosecutor will pursue. Possibly, the prosecutor will direct that certain key witnesses be recontacted, to assure their availability and to determine their present attitude concerning appearance in court.

Prior to the actual day of trial, the witness/investigator should refresh his memory on the facts of the case. Original notes must be reviewed; maps, diagrams, and photographs must be studied; if feasible, the fire scene should be reexamined.

The Investigator in Court

On arrival at the site of the trial, the investigator should inform the prosecuting attorney of his presence. Any late developments in the case should be discussed, along with the "court plan" which will be followed. The prosecutor may direct the investigator to locate other state witnesses.

The officer should enter the courtroom quietly, without fanfare. The inexperienced individual who makes a production of his initial appearance in the courtroom may alienate prospective jury members before the trial even begins. Most judges want the atmosphere of their courtroom to be one of dignity. Action on the part of anyone which detracts from this atmosphere will certainly not be appreciated.

The witness should not discuss any phase of the case at this time with anyone, even with fellow investigators. It is probable that those seated in the courtroom are prospective jurors, witnesses, both friendly and hostile, and family or friends of the defendant. Any conversation concerning the case which may be overheard could come back to haunt the investigator later in the trial.

There are several methods of administering the oath to witnesses. In some courts all the witnesses, prosecution and defense, are called to the bench prior to any proceedings and sworn in as a group. On other occasions, each witness is called and administered the oath separately.

Regardless of what procedure is followed, this first impression is most important. The witness must be serious and leave no doubt that he believes in the oath itself and respects the solemnity of the occasion. He should stand erect before the clerk of the court, look him in the eye, and raise the right hand to shoulder level, with the wrist straight and fingers extended and joined. Response to the question of the oath to tell the truth should be a firm and positive "I do."

At this point, the witness may be instructed to proceed directly to the witness stand. If so, he should walk briskly to the stand, with dignity which commands respect. If he is to be the first witness to testify, he should find out where the witness stand is located and by what route it is reached. This may sound trivial, but the witness who takes a chair at the defense table or wanders uncertainly about the courtroom makes himself an object of ridicule and leaves a poor impression on the members of the jury.

An important point which should be brought out at this time relates to excluding, separating, or sequestering witnesses. Exclusion means that the witness is excluded from the courtroom except when he or she is testifying. Witnesses may be grouped in one room outside the courtroom, but the normal procedure is to place prosecution and defense witnesses in separate rooms. Usually exclusion is requested by counsel for the defendant to prevent witnesses from hearing testimony given by others.

When excluded, under no circumstances discuss the case with other witnesses. A person may be called to the stand, testify, and return to the witness room. There must be absolutely no conversation of any kind under these circumstances. The average lay witness is not aware of these restrictions and may, in relief over finishing his turn on the stand, give the entire group a blow-by-blow description of his testimony. At some point during the trial, defense counsel may ask a witness, "Have you heard any discussion of the proceedings in the courtroom from a previous witness?" If the answer is "Yes," the judge may declare a mistrial.

Furthermore, excluded prosecution witnesses must not discuss courtroom activities with *anyone* other than the prosecutor during breaks, recesses for meals, or overnight adjournments. Again, this might result in a mistrial if brought out.

Complete isolation, or sequestration, of witnesses is a rather unusual maneuver but is occasionally done, particularly with prosecution witnesses who may qualify as experts. Such witnesses are sometimes assigned hotel or motel rooms near the trial site and must be prepared to respond on short notice to a call to the stand. During this period of isolation, which may last for hours or days, the witness should not listen to the radio, watch television, or read the newspaper or any publication with any reference to the case at hand. There must be no discussion of this case with anyone except the prosecutor without the prosecutor's approval. Again, violation of these provisions could result in a mistrial.

The appearance of an investigator on the witness stand is extremely important. Dress neatly and conservatively, in a manner proper for the locale. Clothes should not prejudice the members of the jury against the witness because of their style, color, design, or apparent cost. Although men's styles may lean to bright, colorful suits and jackets, shirts, ties, and even shoes, in certain localities such dress would prove highly offensive to most residents, and the jury is made up of these residents. For the same reason ostentatious jewelry must not be worn. Women should dress modestly in styles acceptable to the community.

On occasion, defense counsel will attempt to influence the jury by linking the investigator, by inference at least, with the rich and ruthless insurance company which is trying to escape paying the poor, helpless, defendant who had a fire. An overdressed investigator will make it much easier for the defense attorney to establish this close association between the insurance company and the witness.

Wear a uniform if appropriate. Determine from the prosecutor his wishes on this matter. If the uniform is worn, be sure it conforms to regulations, fits, and is pressed. Unless regulations specifically require it, which is unlikely, do not wear white or colored socks with a dark blue uniform, and do not roll the socks down to the ankle bone. Western-style boots might be appropriate in some sections of the country, but in others they make the witness appear ridiculous. If possible, avoid wearing a gun in court, as it may create the wrong impression and arouse criticism.

Be well groomed. Clothes should be pressed and shoes shined. Male witnesses must be clean shaven, and their hair should not be unusually long. In spite of the fact that long hair is gaining limited acceptance, many individuals frown on shoulder-length locks.

Do not offend. The investigator should not display lodge or club emblems or jewelry. This may be interpreted as an attempt to appeal to a member of the jury who belongs to such an organization. Worse yet, a juror may have been refused membership in the same lodge or club.

The witness should not have cigarettes or paper sticking out of his pockets. This may convey the impression that he is slipshod and probably his investigation is also.

The manner in which a person conducts himself on the witness stand is critical and will determine to a large extent the impact of his testimony. Important evidence may be rendered valueless if not properly presented.

Sit erect but be relaxed and comfortable. Casually cross the legs, but do not repeat crossing and uncrossing. Hands should be folded in the lap or placed on the arms of the witness chair. Do not display nervousness by pulling at an ear lobe, twisting hands, fiddling with a button or shoelace (if legs are crossed), or constantly squirming.

Speak clearly and distinctly, in a conversational tone, loud enough for the judge and jury to hear every word. A good witness relates the facts clearly, concisely, and audibly. Do not put hands over the mouth or face when answering questions. A witness who cannot be heard or understood often irritates the jury and infuriates the judge, especially if this continues after the judge has warned the witness to speak up. Do not nod the head to indicate a yes answer, for this cannot be entered on the trial transcript by the court reporter.

Use plain, simple everyday language that can be understood by the jury. Do not try to impress the jury or courtroom audience with your knowledge by using technical terms or a vocabulary which is peculiar to the fire or arson field, such as *tetrahedron of fire* or *alligatoring*. The judge and jury are not interested in how brilliant the witness may be, but in what he can tell them about the case at hand. Do not use underworld terms, such as *busting, making,* and the like.

Be strictly impartial and fair. Tell the truth even if it hurts. Defense counsel may ask, "Was the defendant cooperative?" If he was, say so; but do not lean over backward or go overboard or the testimony and witness will appear phony. Do not appear anxious to convict. Do not scowl at the defendant or indicate prejudice against him by word or deed.

Be respectful to the court and both attorneys. Address the judge as "your honor" and the attorneys by name. Answer questions which require only an affirmative answer by *Yes,* not *Yeah, Right,* or *That's correct.* Such answers may convey by emphasis or inflection an impression that the witness did not intend.

Be serious. Do not be casual, cute, or smart alecky on the stand. Do not attempt to be funny or make wisecracks. Remember that this is a serious matter and that a person's liberty may be at stake. The defense may attempt to make the atmosphere as frivolous as possible, as if the case amounted to nothing. Do not help him accomplish this by displaying a nonchalant attitude.

Be professional. The witness must not be self-satisfied or arrogant and convey the impression that it is fortunate for the cause of justice that he is present and available to testify.

Keep your head up. While the question is being asked, look at the questioner. If the answer is brief, address it to the questioner, whether judge, prosecutor, or defense attorney. If the response is lengthy, speak to the jury or, in case of a trial without jury, to the judge.

Keep cool. During cross-examination, defense counsel will make every effort to cause the witness to lose his temper. Badgering the witness is a technique as old as the hills. Do not fall into a trap and get into a heated argument or shouting contest with the defense attorney. He knows the investigator cannot think and respond logically while angry.

Do not volunteer additional information, particularly on cross-examination. On direct examination it is up to the prosecuting attorney to bring out all the facts by additional questioning. The exception, of course, is when the witness is instructed "to tell his own story." On cross-examination, by voluntarily giving additional information, the investigator provides the defense attorney with questions which might never have occurred to him otherwise.

Do not mind saying "I don't know" or "I don't recall." No witness knows everything. It is better to say "I don't know" or "I don't recall" to a question on cross-examination concerning some phase of the case than to guess at an answer and subject oneself to a ruthless raking over. However, the investigator must not use this as a smoke screen for not answering those questions which he does not want to answer.

Pause before answering questions. The investigator should develop a routine in answering all questions. If he answers questions immediately on direct examination but pauses ten seconds on cross-examination, he conveys the impression that he is in trouble and unsure. A slight pause is not harmful, unless the question is so elementary that any hesitation would be ridiculous. This pause gives the witness an opportunity to compose his thoughts and answer and provides counsel with time to object. Do not answer any questions until the court rules on the objection.

Seek relief. On occasion the prosecutor will apparently abandon the witness to be torn apart piece by piece by the defense counsel. The prosecutor realizes that if he constantly comes to the rescue of the "star" witness, this person may seem to be weak and unable to stand on his own. At such times the investigator must attempt to protect himself. If defense counsel insists that the response to a question be "Yes" or "No," advise the court that the question cannot be answered in this manner and request permission to elaborate on the answer. Normally the judge will grant the request, since there are no legal grounds for requiring a "Yes" or "No" answer.

Do not guess or express opinions and conclusions. No witness should guess at distances or times. If he has not measured and noted this information, he should say, "about ten feet," or "approximately five minutes." If the measurement is critical to the case, it should have been accurately determined beforehand. Only witnesses who have qualified as experts may express opinions and reach conclusions. The non-expert witness must be careful to confine testimony to reporting observations and not to express opinions or reach conclusions based on these observations.

Watch for trick questions. Although these take many forms, there are a few used fairly consistently by defense attorneys:

1. "Do you know who started the fire?" Reply, "Not of my own knowledge, but my investigation shows the defendant started it."

2. "Do you think the defendant should be convicted?" Reply either "Yes" or "I am here to testify to the facts as I know them; the jury will make this determination."

3. "Have you discussed this case with anyone?" Defense counsel wants you to say "No." Reply, "Yes." If asked to name these people, do so. Hopefully, this list will include only a very limited number of people who have some official connection with the matter under investigation.

The Expert Witness

The matter of the expert witness is a large subject to which many pages could be devoted. In the paragraphs which follow, only essentials concerning expert testimony will be covered.

Definition

The expert witness is one whose experience in a special calling gives him or her knowledge of a subject beyond that of persons of common intelligence and ordinary experience.

The Qualification Process

The prosecuting attorney has the responsibility for qualifying an individual as an expert. To assist in this effort, the witness should inform the prosecutor fully concerning his education, special training courses, description of duties connected with present employment, experience in years, and approximate number of fires attended or investigated. This will normally suffice, but additional information concerning articles published, lectures delivered, awards received, and membership in professional organizations can be offered. The investigator should not furnish false information in an effort to qualify. If it can be shown that he is lying, a perjury charge may follow. In the event the facts cited are found to be false later, his professional career may very well be jeopardized.

A note of caution must be sounded concerning attendance at fire and arson seminars. Generally speaking, the only requirement for satisfactory completion of such courses is attendance—and often these records, if any, are loosely kept. There is a definite risk in citing the completion of such courses to assist in qualifying a witness. The defense attorney may point out that no requirements were placed on enrollees, no test or examination of any kind was administered, and every person registering and paying a fee received a certificate.

Purpose of Qualification

Assuming that an individual qualifies as an expert in the opinion of the presiding judge, what special purpose does this witness serve? The ordinary witness can testify only to things that he saw, heard, tasted, smelled, or felt, while the expert can state opinions and conclusions reached by reason of his expertise. The expert witness cannot, however, expect his testimony to be accepted without question. He must be able to explain in terms understandable to the jury the technical reason or logic behind this conclusion.

Need for Qualification

When should a person be qualified as an expert witness? As a general rule, only when it is absolutely necessary. He may fail in the effort to qualify, which is embarrassing to his organization and to him and almost destroys his value as a non-expert witness. By qualifying, the witness makes available to counsel many avenues of attack on cross-examination which do not exist with ordinary witnesses.

In a typical arson case, does the fire fighter need to qualify to testify that when he entered the structure there were three separate fires? Probably not, because he is testifying only to what he saw. However, if he states the fire reacted strangely when water was applied and it appeared a flammable liquid was burning, he must then qualify as an expert in the fire-fighting field and must establish his expertise, particularly as it relates to extinguishing flammable liquid fires.

What about the fire chief? When he is asked questions concerning time of arrival at the fire, number of pieces of apparatus responding, total length of hose laid, quantity of water used, there is no particular need for expertise, as the information is routine on most fire calls. If he testifies that the fire originated in the vicinity of an oil space heater, this is based on observation of the actual burning and examination of the debris, and he will probably not be required to qualify. However, if he testifies that the fire was caused by failure of the carburetor on the space heater, he must qualify not only as an expert in determining origin and cause, but also in the field of oil space heaters—and oil space heater carburetors specifically! If he does not possess this expertise, he will need the hide of an alligator to withstand the assaults of counsel for whichever side has been damaged by this testimony.

A professional arson investigator will normally be required to qualify as an expert witness. He is the witness on whom the prosecutor counts to "pull the case together." He must, by means of his testimony, render significant the observations of previous witnesses and must describe the fire scene examination, not only what was found, but the conclusion derived from such findings.

For example, let us assume that several witnesses, including fire fighters, testify that there was a hole burned in the hardwood floor in the center of a bedroom. This testimony is only a fact based on observation, with no opinion expressed or conclusions reached as a result. The investigator, as an expert, must give meaning and significance to the hole in the floor, based primarily on his own examination of the area. From the shape, size, location, pattern, dimensions, and characteristics of the hole, which he describes in detail, supplemented with photographs and diagrams, he may conclude that this hole originated as the result of the burning of a flammable liquid at this point. He would probably further testify that there was no logical explanation for the presence of such a liquid in this area.

Now the witness has offered testimony very damaging to the defendant, and defense counsel is obligated to attempt to destroy his credibility. The initial attack may suggest that in spite of the investigator's experience, his knowledge relative to examination of floors is limited. Failing in this effort, counsel may attempt to discredit the investigator by showing that he reached conclusions without even considering other possible causes for the hole: "How does he know the fire did not burn through from underneath the floor?" "Is he aware of the fact that people walked through this area during and after the fire?" "Couldn't burning objects falling from above cause the condition described?" "Would not the floor at this point have been worn from constant usage more than the area around it, and thus burn through more readily?" "What would you say if I told you that a sewing machine was located in this area of the room and this machine was oiled frequently?" "Couldn't termites attacking this point in the floor break down the composition of the wood fibers and accelerate the burning?"

These are only samples of the most obvious lines of questioning. During all of the cross-examination, defense counsel has been badgering, baiting, and browbeating the witness within acceptable limits. If the expert cannot handle these simple questions, his first mistake was showing up for court, and his second was qualifying as an expert. If the expert does not possess knowledge, skill, experience, patience, and character, he should not enter the courtroom, where only the strong survive.

Appendix A

Building Construction Terminology and Definitions

Abutment: That part of a pier from which the arch springs.

Alteration: Any change or modification in construction or occupancy.

Anchor: An iron bolt embedded into the foundation wall by means of which the sill is made secure; a "T"-shaped iron through a brick wall to which is secured a floor beam; the means by which a brick veneering is secured to a frame wall.

Approved: Approved by the appropriate agency in the authority having jurisdiction.

Arch: A segmental or concave arrangement of building materials supported by piers or abutments to carry loads.

Arch-buttress: An arch, springing from a buttress or pier against a wall, called a flying buttress.

Area: As applied to the dimensions of a building, means the area of the building.

Asbestos boards: Asbestos fiber and cement, rolled and pressed into sheets about one-fourth inch thick.

Attic: Attic story means any story situated wholly or partly in the roof; so designated, arranged, or built as to be used for business storage or habitation.

Automatic: As applied to a fire door or other opening protection, means normally held in open position and automatically closed by a releasing device actuated by abnormal high temperature, or by a predetermined rate of rise in temperature.

Baluster: The uprights supporting a handrail.

Basement: That portion of a building between floor and ceiling which is partly below and partly above grade.

Batten: A flat, narrow piece of wood usually placed over joints between boards; thus, boards and battens.

Bay: The ceiling area of space between supporting floor beams or girders, measured center to center of the supporting members.

Beam: A beam is usually a horizontal structural member subjected to shear and bending only. The load carried by a beam may be either uniform or concentrated or both. Beams may be classified as simple, fixed, cantilevered, or continuous, depending on the condition of their end supports. A *simple* beam is one that is supported at its ends and is free to rotate at the supports. A *fixed* beam is one that is supported at its ends but is restrained at the supports so that rotation will not occur. A *cantilevered* beam is one that has one of its ends supported and fixed against rotation while its opposite end is not supported and is free to deflect under load. A *continuous* beam is one that is supported on more than two supports.

Beam ceiling: A ceiling marked off with projections resembling beams.

Bearing wall: A wall which supports any load in addition to its own weight.

Brace: A connection between structural members to strengthen the structure.

Bracket: A projection built from or as part of the wall and designed to support a load.

Bridging: A structural member that is used to stiffen wood floor joists, wood studding, and steel bar joists used in floor and roof construction. Bridgings usually take the form of cross members, horizontal rods, or solid blocking.

Building: Any structure built for the support, shelter, or enclosure of persons, animals, chattels, or property of any kind which has enclosing walls for 50% of its perimeter.

Building line: The line, established by law, beyond which a building shall not extend, except as specifically provided by law.

Building official: The officer or other person charged with the administration and enforcement of appropriate ordinances, or a duly authorized representative.

Bulkhead: The enclosure of a stair, elevator, or other shaft above the roof line; or, the deep extension of a cornice extending above the roof.

Buttress: A projection built against a wall to resist lateral thrust, usually made of stone or brickwork.

Casement window: A sash hinged at the side.

Cast stone: A building stone manufactured from cement concrete precast and used as a trim, veneer, or facing on or in buildings or structures.

Cellar: That portion of a building, the ceiling of which is entirely below grade or less than four feet six inches above grade.

Cement blocks: Made of sand, cement, and water, molded or pressed, and generally with cores.

Cement-lime mortar: One part portland cement, one part slaked lime, three parts sand.

Cement mortar: One part portland cement and three parts sharp sand.

Centering: The temporary framing upon which a floor arch is laid.

Chord: The outermost structural member of a truss. Each truss has a top and bottom chord.

Coaming: The raised curbing surrounding a floor opening or skylight, also called curbing.

Collar beam: A beam used to support a principal roof rafter.

Column: A column, strut, or post is a structural member subjected to compression.

Combustible material: A material which cannot be classified as noncombustible in accordance with that definition.

Common-property line: A line dividing one lot from another when said lots are not of one ownership.

Concrete blocks: Same as cement blocks with the addition of gravel.

Contour: The outline or form of an object, as for example, covering the beams of a floor so completely as to cover all accessible parts of the beams and flooring.

Coping: The masonry cap on top of a wall or parapet.

Cornice: An ornamental projection from the front of a building at the roof or immediately above a store window.

Counterbalanced door: A vertical sliding door with two opposing leaves meeting horizontally. When opening door, the upper leaf slides upward and the lower leaf slides downward.

Court: An interior open space (larger than a light shaft) enclosed on three or four sides by building walls.

Curb level: Referring to a building, means the elevation at that point of the street grade that is opposite the center of the wall nearest to and facing the street line.

Curtain walls: A wall built on the outside of steel skeleton frames which carries only its own weight and merely keeps out the elements. No structural parts depend upon these walls.

Deadening: The insulation material placed on walls or ceilings to deaden sounds.

Dead load: The weight of all permanent construction.

Door frame: The case in which a door opens or shuts, consisting of two uprights and one horizontal piece connected together by mortise and tenon.

Dormer: A vertical window projecting from a sloping roof.

Double-action door: A door which swings both ways from a closed position.

Dwarf wall: A wall that has less height than that of a story in which it is used.

Eave: That part of a roof projecting beyond the exterior walls.

Facade: The face or front of a building.

Finish: The ceiling and inside covering of walls or partitions, such as lath and plaster.

Fire door: A door and its assembly, so constructed and assembled in place as to give the specified protection against the passage of fire.

Fire partition: A partition of construction which subdivides a building to restrict the spread of fire or to provide areas of refuge, but is not necessarily continuous through all stories nor extended through the roof, and which has a fire resistance rating as required by appropriate regulations.

Fireproof construction: Structure in which all exterior walls are of masonry or reinforced concrete and in which all the structural members are of noncombustible material and provide not less than the required fire resistance.

Fire resistance rating: The time in hours that the material or construction will withstand the standard fire exposure.

Fire retardant: Wood chemically impregnated so as to meet specified flame spread ratings.

Fire tower: A brick or other masonry tower or shaft enclosing a stairway of fireproof material, with an indirect entrance from each floor of the building and with an unobstructed exit to the street.

Fire wall: A wall of incombustible construction which subdivides a building or separates buildings to restrict the spread of fire and which starts at the foundation and extends continuously through all stories to and above the roof, except where the roof is of fireproof or fire resistive construction and the wall is carried up tightly against the underside of the roof slab.

Flame spread rating: Numerical value assigned to a material tested in accordance with recognized testing procedures.

Flashing: Pieces of metal placed around roof openings, or where the roof covering abuts a parapet wall, to insure water tightness.

Floor arches: Fireproof material between steel beams.

Floor area: The area included within surrounding walls of a building exclusive of vent shafts and courts.

Floor lights: Heavy glass in wood or iron frames inserted into the flooring to give light to the floor below.

Flue: The opening through a chimney by means of which the smoke and gases of combustion pass out of the building.

Footing: The part of the foundation of a building which transmits the building loads to the ground.

Foundation: The walls, piers, piling of a building below the first or grade floor.

Gable: The upright triangular end of a building at end of a roof and shaped like an inverted V.

Gambrel roof: A roof with two sides each having a double slope.

Girder: The largest timber or steel member in a floor, which supports the floor joists or steel beams.

Girts: Horizontal timbers laid on top of frame wall studding and on which rests the floor joists.

Grade: With reference to lumber, the division of sawn lumber into quality classes with respect to its physical and mechanical properties as defined in published lumber manufacturers' standard grading rules.

Groin: The angle formed by the junction of two arches.

Grout: A mixture of cement and sand and water used for filling cavities in concrete work.

Gypsum blocks: Made of gypsum mortar and a binder.

Half-story: Similar to an attic, but being a finished form of a room and flooring and having side walls at least four feet high.

Hatchway: A small opening, hand trapped, opening onto a roof.

Header: A joist cut in between other joists and running at a square angle and to which are fastened shorter joists to form a floor opening for a stairway or fireplace hearth.

Height: As applied to a building, height in stories does not include basements and cellars, except as specifically provided otherwise. As applied to a story, means the vertical distance from top to top of two successive finished floor surfaces. As applied to a wall, means the vertical distance to the top measured from the foundation wall, or from a girder or other immediate support of such wall.

Hip roof: A roof having the same pitch on all four sides.

Horizontal exit: The connection of any two floor areas, either in the same building or not, by means of a vestibule, open air balcony or bridge, or through a fire partition.

Independent wall: Supports an individual structure and differs from a party wall.

Inner court: An open unoccupied space bounded by the walls of the building, but located within the exterior walls of the building.

Iron fronts: Hollow cast-iron structural material forming the front of a building.

Jack rafter: A short roof rafter.

Jambs: The side pieces of an opening in a wall, such as door posts, and the uprights at the sides of window frames.

Joist: A joist is a light beam. Joists are usually spaced closer together than are beams.

Keystone: The center stone, wedge-shaped, in the crown or top of a segmental arch.

King post: The center post or vertical member connecting the apex of a triangular truss with the base.

Knee: A piece of timber bent to receive some weight or to relieve a strain.

Lally columns: Steel columns filled with cement.

Laminated floor: A flooring made by laying joists spiked together with no interval or space between.

Lantern skylight: A long rectangular roof structure, open to the floor below, and having a solid roof and glass sash sides.

Lath: A groundwork for plaster or slates, usually a thin strip of wood nailed to studs, joists, or rafters.

Lean-to roof: A sloping as found on sheds adjoining a larger building.

Lintel: The beam or girder placed over an opening in a wall which supports the wall construction above.

Lock-jointed: Metal, blind-nailed.

Mansard roof: A flat-topped roof with two or more sloping sides and forming an additional story; usually has combustible concealed spaces, difficult to locate fire if started within them.

Masonry: That form of construction composed of stone, brick, concrete, gypsum, hollow clay tile, concrete block or tile, or other similar building units or materials or a combination of these materials laid up unit by unit and set in mortar. Plain monolithic concrete may be considered as masonry.

Solid masonry: Masonry built without hollow spaces.

Metal lath: Expanded, slit, or perforated sheets of metal.

Mezzanine or mezzanine floor: An intermediate floor placed in any story or room.

Monolithic building: One entirely constructed of reinforced concrete.

Mortise: A rectangular opening made in a piece of timber to receive a tenon.

Mushroom: A type of column (umbrella-shaped on top) used to reinforce concrete structures. The term mushroom sometimes is used to denote the spread of a fire going up a shaft and "mushrooming" into the various floors.

Nosing: That part of stair tread which projects out from the riser.

O. C. (on centers): A building term referring to distance between wood beams or joists, as measured from center to center of the beams.

Occupancy: The purpose for which a building is used or intended to be used. Change of occupancy is not intended to include change of tenants or proprietors.

Oriel: A window structure projecting from the outside walls of a building and usually supported on brackets.

Parapet: That portion of a wall extending above the roof.

Partition: An interior wall other than folding or portable which subdivides spaces within any story.

Party wall: A bearing wall between two buildings used to support the floor beams of both buildings.

Pebble dash: A rough surface wall finish.

Penthouse: An enclosed structure other than a roof structure located on the roof, extending not more than twelve feet above a roof.

Pier: A column of masonry used to strengthen or support a building.

Pilaster: A built-out brick pillar of a wall, usually extended outward to support a girder.

Piles: Large timbers driven into the ground for the purpose of providing a foundation in unstable soil. Piling may be precast concrete, or cast at the site.

Pintle: An iron pin or bar, wider at the top than at the base, set on the post cap and supporting the next upper story post in a mill constructed building.

Pivoted window: One having a single sash moving on a pivot.

Plate: A horizontal timber upon which rests the lower end of the rafters.

Post caps: An iron cap imposed on the upper end of a post on which rests the floor timber.

Posts: Square or round timbers set on end to support beams or girders.

Poured concrete: Concrete cast without reinforcing.

Public place: Normally means an unoccupied open space adjoining a building and on the same property, which is permanently maintained accessible to the fire department and free of all encumbrances that might interfere with its use by the fire department.

Rabbet: A groove or channel cut or formed in or near the edge of a board or other material to unite the edges, as in a rabbet joint; for instance, fire doors are sometimes rabbetted.

Rafters: The sloping timbers which form the pitched sides of a peaked roof to which roof boarding is nailed.

Rail: The horizontal pieces of framing, such as in a door frame.

Railing: The top piece of a balustrade.

Ramp: An inclined runway from one floor to another, usually in garage construction.

Reinforced concrete: Concrete in which are inserted bars of steel or heavy wire mesh.

Ribbon board: In balloon framing, the horizontal board nailed to the stud frame as the bearing for the second floor joists; the horizontal bracing for studding or rafters.

Ridge: The highest part of a pitched roof; the horizontal timber against which rests the upper ends of the rafters.

Rigid frame: A rigid frame consists of vertical column members and horizontal beam members rigidly attached at their intersections in such a manner that no change in the angles between the pieces is possible.

Riser: The vertical board or part of the stair under the tread or step.

Roof structure: A structure above a roof or any part of a building enclosing a stairway, tank, elevator machinery, or ventilating apparatus, or such part of a shaft as extends above the roof.

Sash: The framework which holds the glass in a window.

Sash frame: The frame which receives the sash.

Scuppers: Holes or pipes by which water can be drained from a floor. Flush or pipe scuppers are inside drain pipes. Outside scuppers are openings through the outer wall at floor level.

Self-closing: As applied to a fire door or other opening protectives, means normally closed and equipped with an approved device which will insure closing after having been opened for use.

Self-releasing: Beveling the ends of timbers so that in case of fire or rupture, they will release or fall out without damaging the wall.

Setbacks: Horizontal ledges formed on a vertical wall by an offset or recession of an upper story of fire resistive "tall" buildings. This is for the purpose of limiting the height and bulk of buildings to conserve the light and air for lower buildings and streets surrounding it.

Shaft: Vertical opening extending through one or more stories of a building.

Sheathing: The base or first outside covering over studding.

Sill: The horizontal piece, such as at the bottom of doors or windows; the horizontal timber laid on a foundation wall.

Skirting: The baseboard or narrow board placed on a wall at the floor level.

Sleepers: Pieces of timber placed on top of fireproof floor arches and to which the top flooring is nailed.

Soffit: The underside of the structural members of a building. A stair soffit is the underpart of a stairway.

Spall: To chip, crack, break, or otherwise disintegrate. Term used in connection with heat and fire on stonework of buildings.

Span: The horizontal distance between supports.

Spandrel: An exterior beam or girder that frames over an opening, such as a window or doorway.

Sprinklered: Equipped with an approved automatic sprinkler system properly maintained.

Stage, general: A partially enclosed portion of an assembly building, cut off from the audience section by a proscenium wall, which is designed or used for the presentation of plays, demonstrations, or other entertainment.

Stairway: One or more flights of stairs and the necessary landings and platforms connecting them.

Stile: The upright piece in framing or paneling. The vertical member in a door or window frame.

Story: That portion of a building included between the upper surface of any floor and the upper surface of the floor next above, except that the topmost story shall be that portion of a building included between the upper surface of the topmost floor and the ceiling or roof above.

Stretcher course: Brick or stone laid lengthwise in the direction of the wall.

Structure: That which is built or constructed, an edifice or building of any kind, or any piece of work artificially built up or composed of parts joined together in some definite manner.

Struts: Pieces of timber used principally to support rafters.

Studs: Upright pieces of timber, 2″ × 4″ or larger, used for partitions or the outer framework of frame buildings.

Substructure: That part of the building below the grade, or below the top of the foundation; in piers, the piling or supports of the "deck" or floor.

Superstructure: That part of a building above the foundation; in piers, the shed or structure above the "deck" or main floor.

Tenon: A piece of wood cut so as to fit into a hole in another piece called a mortise.

Terra cotta: Called tile, molded and burned clays. For porous tile a small amount of sawdust is added to the mixture which is burned out in the kiln.

Tie: A beam, post, rod, or strut connecting two or more structural members.

Tilting sash: A window sash in several pieces, each on a horizontal pivot.

Tin-clad: As applying to a fire door, means the metal covering with lap or lock joints.

Tongue: A projection or rib on one edge of a board, formed to fit into a groove.

Top flooring: The upper layer of floor boards, sometimes called wearing floor.

Transom: A sash window (usually made to open) over a doorway.

Trap door: A door set flush with a ceiling or floor.

Trim, inside: The baseboard, moldings, door and window frames or other similar ornamentations.

Trimmers: Pieces of timbers from and at right angles to the joists for chimneys and the well holes for stairs.

Truss: An assemblage of structural members, as beams, rods, bars, forming a framework to carry loads and which is supported at both ends.

Unbroken area: An area with no subdivision walls or fire resistive partitions, where fire could have a clean sweep.

Unprotected iron: Structural metal work with no insulating covering such as concrete or tile.

Valley: The space between two inclined sides of a roof.

Vaults: Underground rooms, usually brick or concrete floors and ceilings.

Vault lights: Usually small, heavy bull's-eye glass in heavy iron frames.

Veneer: A facing of brick, concrete, metal, stone, tile, or similar material attached to a wall for the purpose of providing ornamentation, protection, or insulation, but not counted as adding strength.

Ventilating shaft: A masonry shaft by means of which air, gas, or smoke is exhausted to the outer air.

Wainscoting: The lower trim or facing on walls and much higher than a baseboard, usually of wood or tile.

Wall, bearing: A wall which supports any vertical load in addition to its own weight.

Wallboard: A manufactured plaster and fiber board made in sheets and used for ceilings or facing of walls.

Wall box: An iron box set into a brick wall to receive the end of a floor timber.

Wall, cavity: A wall built of masonry units or of plain concrete, or a combination of these materials so arranged as to provide an air space within the wall, and in which the inner and outer parts of the wall are tied together with metal ties.

Wall, curtain: A nonbearing wall between columns or piers, and which is not supported by girders or beams, but is supported on the ground.

Wall, exterior: A wall, bearing or nonbearing, which is used as an enclosing wall for a building, but which is not necessarily suitable for use as a party wall or fire wall.

Wall, faced: A wall in which the masonry facing and backing are so bonded as to exert common action under load.

Wall, fire: A wall of incombustible construction which subdivides a building or separates buildings to restrict the spread of fire and which starts at the foundation and extends continuously through all stories to and above the roof, except where the roof is of fireproof or fire resistive construction and the wall is carried up tightly against the underside of the roof slab.

Wall, foundation: A wall below the first floor extending below the adjacent ground level and serving as support for a wall, pier, column, or other structural part of a building.

Wall, nonbearing: A wall which supports no load other than its own weight.

Wall of masonry, hollow: A wall built of masonry units so arranged as to provide an air space within the wall.

Wall, panel: A nonbearing wall in skeleton or framed construction, built between columns or piers and wholly supported at each story.

Wall, parapet: That part of any wall entirely above the roof line.

Wall, party: A wall used or adapted for joint service between two buildings.

Wall plate: An iron plate embedded in a wall on which rests the end of a floor member.

Wall, retaining: Any wall used to resist the lateral displacement of any material.

Weatherboards: Boards adapted for sliding to form lapped joints with boards above and below and to shed water.

Well or well hole: An opening larger than an ordinary light or ventilating shaft, piercing a floor or floors for purposes of light and ventilation.

Wing: A building projecting from the main building.

Winged wall: A fire wall which projects at right angles from the face of the main wall.

(Compiled by William Miles, St. Petersburg Junior College, Clearwater, Fla., from portions of the following building codes: National Building Code, published by the American Insurance Association (New York); Southern Standard Code, published by the Southern Building Code Congress (Birmingham, Ala.).)

Appendix B

A Glossary of Insurance Terms

Actual cash value: The sum of money it will take to replace property destroyed, less depreciation due to age and wear.

Additional living expense clause: A provision in some insurance policies to cover the cost to the insured of living away from his residence because of fire damage. This amount depends on the amount stipulated in the policy.

Adjustor: A representative of the insurance company to work with the assured in discussing the amount of loss and to advise the insured what the insurance company's liabilities are. An adjustor who works directly for the insurance company on the company's permanent payroll is known as a "staff adjustor." An adjustor working for an independent firm who is hired by the insurance company to adjust the loss is known as an "independent adjustor." Neither of the two aforementioned adjustors is the same as the "public adjustor" who represents the insured only. Staff adjustors and independent adjustors work for the insurance companies and are not hired by the insured, as is the public adjustor.

Adjustment: The determination of the amount of loss, the cause of the loss, and what the final settlement in cash value shall be after all factors have been considered.

Agent, insurance: A seller of an insurance policy who represents the company in this capacity. The agent, paid on a commission basis, is licensed to operate in the state in which he conducts his business. He is not to be confused with an adjustor, and his powers are limited by the terms of his contract and state laws.

Appraisal: This term appears in that part of a fire insurance policy known as the Appraisal Clause, which stipulates that if it appears neither the company nor the insured can agree upon a settlement and loss figure, either or both may ask for an appraisal by an outside firm.

Assigned risk: A parcel of property on which various company underwriters will not write insurance coverage is placed into a pool by state law requiring such coverage. Then the coverage is handled by a lottery system to ascertain which company or companies will underwrite the insurance.

Assignment of interest: Occasionally when one party sells a dwelling to another and the seller has insurance coverage, he will with the approval of the insurance company assign his interest over to the new owner, and the insurance policy is then considered as being held by the new owner of the dwelling.

Assured: The same as "insured."

Binder: The contract entered into between an insurance company and the party seeking insurance through an agent. The "binder" protects the party desiring insurance from the time a request is made for insurance until the policy actually is received.

Broker: The insurance "broker" does not represent the insurance company as does the insurance agent, but generally solicits business and then places the coverage through companies of his own choosing. He may also place the coverage with insurance companies that the insured may desire to do business with.

Business interruption insurance: The main purpose of this coverage is to reimburse the insured for loss of earnings which he sustains due to a fire which prevents his continuing in business. The amount varies with the coverage stipulated in the policy.

Cancellation of policy: The cancellation or termination of a policy prior to the expiration date can be done either by the insured or the company covering the risk. Most policies have a section covering cancellation and how the notice of cancellation shall be handled.

Civil authority clause: This clause in an insurance policy protects the insured against damages which may result when firemen, policemen, or other civil authorities control a fire.

Claim: A demand upon the insurance company to pay for a loss which occurred and is covered under the contract of the insurance policy.

Co-insurance clause: This clause in a policy deals with a contract between the property owner or insured and the insurance company. The insured agrees to keep himself insured up to a percentage of the value of his property and/or contents, and in return he pays a lower premium for his coverage. Usually this coverage amounts to about 80 percent of the value.

Concealment clause: This term refers to the direct withholding of any fact of information regarding the nature of the loss and the property to be insured.

Concurrent insurance coverage: When two or more insurance policies cover the same interest in the identical manner and to the identical amount. It is important that policies on a risk be concurrent so that in case of loss, each policy has the same terms and conditions which affect the extent of liability by the insurance companies.

Consequential loss: Almost all fire policies cover the insured only against "direct" losses resulting from the peril they are insured against. Indirect losses, such as moving expenses when a home or business burns, are considered "consequential losses" and not "direct" losses or expenses.

Coverage: The insurance policy term which specifically spells out what losses will be covered and to what extent.

Daily report: Referred to as the "daily" or "application" which is made out by the "agent" and submitted to the insurance company's home office to inform them of the insured's desires and what amount has been agreed upon between the agent and the insured.

Debris removal: This clause is not in all policies, but when it is, it simply states that the insurance company assumes the tasks for removal of debris resulting in damage to property covered in the policy.

Demolition clause: In the standard fire policy, there is a clause which excludes the company from any liability of loss to property which is caused by "law requiring construction or repair," such as urban renewal programs, ordinance violations, etc.

Depreciation: The decrease in the value of property due to wear and tear over the years and poor upkeep; also may be due to the obsolescence of the property.

Effective date: The date on which a policy or "binder" goes into effect and the time in which protection is furnished under the policy.

Examination under oath: Many insurance companies now include this section in their policies. This gives the insurance company the right to have any insured examined under oath in connection with a claim to ascertain that no misstatements have been made in the insured's claim. It is believed that this clause helps reduce the possibility of an insured giving wrong information on a claim, since there is the possibility of a perjury conviction.

Expiration date: The date when the policy expires.

Exposure: A dwelling or business located in a highly congested area or in a dangerous business operation in the area has a greater "exposure" hazard to fire than one located away from such conditions.

Extra living expenses: *See* Additional living expense clause.

Face of policy: The front page or first page of the insurance policy. It normally shows the name of the company, the policy number, effective dates of the policy, the coverage, and the amounts of coverage.

Fire department service clause: A clause in the fire insurance policy that will reimburse the insured for charges a fire department makes for services rendered.

Foreign insurance company: Any insurance company which writes insurance in any state or country other than the one in which it is chartered.

Fraud: Deception, cunning, or artifice used by the insured to deceive or cheat. Proof of willful fraud voids a policy.

Homeowner's policy: An insurance contract between the insurance company and a homeowner. The contract provides a comprehensive coverage designed to supply in one package the insurance coverage which is generally purchased by a homeowner.

Improvements and betterments: Additions or changes which are made by a tenant, at his own cost, to a building he is leasing which increase the value of the property. Once the betterments have been accomplished and they become part of the realty, special insurance consideration is required.

Inherent explosion: Explosion caused by any hazard which arises naturally from the occupancy of a structure. An explosion of a hot water heater in a dwelling is classified as an inherent explosion and generally is covered in the fire insurance policy.

Insurance: A contractual relationship between two parties in which an agreement is made for one party to reimburse the other party for losses caused by hazards covered. The first party collects a premium, and is known as the company, while the second party, who pays the premium, is known as the insured, and the contract is called the insurance policy.

Insurance carrier: The insurance company is called the "insurance carrier," since the company assumes the responsibility in a financial way and carries the risks of the policyholder or insured.

Insurance company: An organization that is chartered or allowed to operate under state or provincial laws to act as an insurer. In the United States they must register in every state in which they desire to do business.

Insurance policy: The written contract of insurance to which the insurance carrier agrees and which details what is expected of the insured in the event of a loss.

Insured: Sometimes called the "assured." The insured is the person and/or persons, partners, partnerships, corporations, trusts, or associations named as having an interest insurable under the terms of the policy.

Lapsed policy: A policy which is terminated due to nonpayment of premiums; also, failure for the insured to renew a policy after its expiration date.

Lessee: A person or group of people acting as one who lease a building for a definite period of time; more commonly known as the tenant.

Lessor: A person or group of people acting as one who grant a lease of a building to another person or group of people; more commonly known as the landlord.

Liability: In the broad sense, means the legal responsibility and enforceable obligation of a contract. The term *liability* is commonly used in a monetary sense in the insurance industry.

Limits of liability: Limit means maximum or tops. In an insurance policy, this means the maximum amount an insurance company agrees to pay in case of a loss under the terms of the policy.

Loss: The amount of damage resulting from a fire which is covered under the terms of the insurance policy.

Loss ratio: An insurance term meaning the comparison between premiums written and losses on a percentage basis.

Manual: A book published by insurance companies or rating bureaus that rates, classifies, and sets up rules for underwriting insurance on various types of business.

Moral hazard: Not to be confused with the physical hazard. This refers to the possibility of a loss being caused by dishonesty or general carelessness of the insured, his agents, or employees. It may arise out of the character and circumstances of the insured, which is apart from the nature of the interest or property covered.

Mortgage clause: If there is a mortgage on the property, a clause in the policy stipulates that proceeds of the policy are payable to the holder of a mortgage to the extent of his interest.

Mutual insurance company: An insurance organization which is owned by its policyholders and operates solely through premiums paid in by them. A stock insurance company, however, operates and derives its capital funds from contributions by stockholders.

Named insured: The person, firm, or corporation named specifically on the policy as being protected under the terms of the policy.

Nonconcurrency: When more than one policy has been written to cover the same property against the same hazard, but they are not identical as to the amount and extent of coverage. Although both policies are valid, adjustment becomes difficult due to unlike coverage.

Nonwaiver agreements: When an insurance company is making an investigation of a loss, it must be careful not to indicate by any of its actions, especially by its adjustors, that the company is admitting liability. A nonwaiver agreement is simply a legal statement by which both parties have agreed that the investigation of the loss shall in no way be construed as an admission of liability on the part of the insurance company.

Off premises clause: Applies to household goods which are covered in the standard fire insurance policy and may be off premises at time of loss, i.e., being transported in an automobile from a vacation when a fire in the automobile caused the household contents to be destroyed.

Other insurance clause: In practically all insurance policies there is a provision stating what is to be done in the event it is learned that more than one policy is found to be covering the same property. It is stated that each carrier will divide the loss on a prorated basis. Note: Although the insured may have two policies, he is not allowed to collect total loss value from each carrier. In other words, if he had two $5,000 policies and his loss was $5,000, he can only collect $2,500 from each of the carriers, and not a total of $10,000.

Overinsurance: A condition when the insured has purchased more coverage than is necessary to protect his property and contents. This is a poor practice since the carriers only have to pay its fair and reasonable value at the time of a loss.

Policy: The written or printed contract of coverage between the insurance company and the policyholder.

Policyholder: The insured, the person or people named on the policy.

Proof of loss: A statement sworn to by the insured and submitted to the insurance company advising them of the property lost or destroyed by a fire.

Pro-rata liability: If the insured has purchased fire coverage with more than one company, each company will pay only its pro-rata share of any loss. Fire insurance companies do not have to pay equal amounts or face value of their policies which would allow the insured to make a profit from the insurance.

Rate: The base set by the rating bureau to be charged in premiums for insurance coverage.

Renewal: When an insurance policy is about to expire, the insured may request that the policy be continued, and this would take effect upon the expiration of the old policy, providing the carrier desired to continue underwriting the risk.

Rent insurance: A landlord or lessor obtains insurance to guarantee against a loss of income in the event of fire or other hazard.

Reserve: When a loss occurs, and the adjustor has made an appraisal of the loss, he notifies the carrier of the loss and suggests that funds be set aside to cover the loss. These funds are called reserves.

Risk: The property that is covered under the policy.

Salvage: After a fire, property or contents which has been partially damaged is subject to salvage and repair.

Smoke damage insurance: Coverage under this type of insurance is collectable when smoke is caused by the sudden, faulty, and unusual operation of a heating or cooking apparatus. However, this apparatus must be connected to a chimney by means of a smoke pipe and be on the premises outlined in the policy. Fireplaces and industrial apparatus are excluded in the policies.

Sound value: The value of the insured property just prior to fire damage.

Standard form: Many of the leading insurance companies have adopted an insurance policy form which has been approved by most state insurance boards or departments.

Stock insurance company: This type of company is controlled by stockholders and is conducted on a profit-making basis. Profits made from collection of the premiums and investments are paid to the stockholders in the same manner as owners of a business.

Subrogation: The right of the insurance company, upon paying the insured's loss in full, to take over all his legal rights against third parties. In the event of any payment under the policy, the insurance company can and does have the right to subrogate for recovery any and all losses sustained where it can be proven a third party is responsible.

Term: Dates between which time the policy is in effect; from the effective date to the date of expiration.

Underwriter: The person within the insurance company who is responsible for accepting risks and determines how much coverage his company will accept on a given location.

Unoccupied: A building or dwelling which is furnished with furniture and/or fixtures, but not lived in or used. This is different from vacant, where the building or dwelling is void of furniture and/or fixtures. The standard fire insurance policy does prohibit the continuance of unoccupied or vacant dwellings and buildings beyond a specific period of time. Special permission must be obtained to continue insurance on vacant property over an extended period of time.

Vacant: Not lived in or used and void of furniture and/or fixtures.

(*From* James Thomas, ''A Glossary of Insurance Terms,'' *Fire and Arson Investigator* 26 (January–March 1976): 40–47. Reprinted by permission.)

Index

A

Accelerant, indications of, 40, 84, 85, 90, 91, 92, 93

Arson vs. general crime, 7–8

Arson investigation by fire chief, 35

Arson motives. *See* Motives for arson

Arson Pattern Recognition System (APRS), 103–109

Arson problem, the, 1–17
  causes of increase in, 7–17
  courtroom contribution to, 12–15
  failure to convict, 12–13
  insurance industry's lack of concern, 15–17
  International Association of Arson Investigators resolution on, 2–3
  judicial decisions and, 14–15
  lack of records of known arsonists, 15
  law enforcement agency lack of recognition of, 7–12
    local level, 10–12
    national level, 7–8
    state level, 8–10
  National Commission on Fire Prevention and Control comments on, 1–2

National Fire Data Center, 5

National Fire Protection Association
  annual reports, 4
  comments on arson, 3
  methods of compiling data, 5

National Fire Protection and Control Administration, 5

need for accurate reporting, 4–6

reluctant witnesses, 13–14

seriousness of, 1, 4–6

statistics, table of, 4

studies of, 1–4

Arson suppression, fire department's role in, 35–44

Automobile fires, 153–182
  burning to defraud insurance company, charge of, 158
  car burning methods, 156–157
  car burning not criminal offense per se, 158
  catalytic converters, hazards of, 160–61
  damage to evidence in extinguishing fire, 157
  false theft report, 156
  frequency of incendiary auto fires, 154
  gas tank explosions, 157–158

Automobile fires, continued
  insurance adjustor role, 168–172
  investigative procedure, 157–168
    area search, 167
    contact with owner/operator at
      scene, 159–160
    conduct and physical appearance
      of owner/operator, noting,
      161–162
    footprints in area, checking, 162
    general terrain, noting, 160–161
    interrogation of owner/operator,
      182
    interviewing witnesses, 167–
      168, 182
    notifying insurance carrier and
      state arson investigation
      agency, 168
    observations at scene, 160–168
    reviewing case to determine ac-
      tion, 181
    road marks, observing, 163–164
    time of fire, recording, 159
    vehicle tire tracks, observing,
      162
    weather conditions, observing,
      161
  motives, 155–156
  National Automobile Theft Bureau,
      problem of incendiary auto
      fires, 154
  National Fire Protection Association
      estimates of auto fires, 154
  salvage examination, 172–181
    accelerant, evidence of, 179
    burn patterns on vehicle, 181
    containers, evidence of, 179
    contents, 179
    electrical system, 173–174
    exterior, 180–182
    fuel system, 172–173
    glass, 179
    indications of excessive heat,
      178
    interior, '76–180
    jack and lug wrench, 180
    keys, 179–180
    missing accessories, 180
    motor compartment, 174–176

    radio, heater, tape deck, 179
    spare wheel and tire, 180
    tires and wheels, 180
    trunk area, 180
    underside, 180
  vehicle examination, immediate,
      160–167
    absence of parts or accessories,
      166–167
    accelerants, evidence of, 162–
      163
    collision damage, 164
    containers, accelerant, 162
    contents of vehicle, 167
    gas cap and drain plug, 165–166
    indications of stolen vehicle,
      165
    location of vehicle, 161
    nature of burning, 161
    obvious mechanical defects, 166
    proximity to combustibles, 160
    tires and wheels switched,
      164–165

B
Barn fires, 54
Burn patterns, 53, 69, 80, 84, 85, 86,
      87
Business fraud fires, motives in, 20–23
  disposal of undesirable property, 22
  dissolution of partnership, 22
  liquidation of failing business,
      20–23
  relocation of business, 23
  sale of land without building, 23
  settlement of estate, 22
  termination of lease, 23

C
Cause of fire, determining, 35, 59–80.
      See also Fire scene search
  authority to search scene, 65

case histories, 64, 70, 77–79, 80
effect of fire-fighting operations on,
    68–71
factors affecting accurate determina-
    tion of, 60–61
    cleanup operations, 61
    overhaul operations, 43, 60–61
    salvage operations, 43, 61
fire causes, accuracy of figures on,
    59–60
guidelines for suspecting arson, 62
inaccuracy in classifying, 59–60
investigator at fire scene, 65–80
    arrival of, 71–72
    keeping an open mind, 67–68
    key areas of knowledge re-
        quired, 68–71
    mental attitude of, 65–66
    outside information sources, 77,
        78
    physical condition of, 67
    steps in fire scene examination,
        72–77
    tools and equipment needed by,
        71
    use of photographs and movie
        footage, 79
search warrant for, 65
security measures at fire scene, 43,
    62–64, 72
unreasonable search, 65
Chemistry of fire, 45–58
classes of fires, 51
combustion, definition of, 46
explosive range
    of common vapors, 48
    definition of, 47–48
fire, definition of, 45–46
fire point of liquids, 47
fire triangle, 48–50
    fuels, 49
    heat source, 49
    oxygen, 49–50
flammable range
    of common vapors, 48
    definition of, 47–48
flash point
    of common liquids, 47
    definition of, 47

heat transfer methods, 51–53
    conduction, 51
    convection, 52–53
    direct flame contact, 51, 53
    falling burning material, 53
    flashover, 52
    radiation, 53
    superheated gases, 52
ignition source, 46, 49
ignition temperature
    of common substances, 47
    definition of, 46–47
oxidation, definition of, 46
spontaneous heating, 54–58
    of charcoal, 56
    by chemical action, 56
    definition of, 54
    fermentation, 54–55, 56
    of hazardous substances, 56
    ignition temperature, 54
    oxidation heating, 55, 56
    in painting operations, 56
    spontaneous combustion, 54
    spontaneous ignition, 54–55
    of wood in pyrophoric carbon
        state, 56–57
vapor density
    of common vapors, 48
    definition of, 48
Chronic fire setter, 32–34
    development stages of, 32–33
    pattern of operation, 33–34
Classes of fires, 51
Combustible Gas Detector (Sniffer),
    109–110
Combustion, definition of, 46
Concealment of other crime by arson,
    26–27
Courtroom failures in arson prosecu-
    tion, 12–15

D
Delirium tremens, 32
Dwelling fraud fires
    motives in, 19–20
    rural, 132–139

E

Electrical system fires, 114–123
  aluminum wiring, hazards of,
      120–122
    fire scene examination of, 122
    trouble signals, 122
  circuit breakers, 116–117
    case histories, 116
    location of, 115
    operating principle of, 115
  copper wiring, 120
  diagram of circuits, 117
  electrical wiring checkout, 117–118
  electrical wiring codes, 121
  fuse boxes, 115
  fuses, 115
  guidelines for investigation, 123
  hazardous circuit conditions, 121
  meter, 115
  overload on circuits, 118
  panel board, 114–115
  short circuit, 118–119
  voltages, 114
Epilepsy, 32
Escobedo decision, 226–228
Evidence of arson, 246–248
  admissible, 246–247
  inadmissible, 65, 247–248
  photographing, 43
  preservation of, 44, 89, 90
Explosions, 183–194
  definition of, 183
  dust, 190
  chemical, 187–190
    black powder, 188–189
    dynamite, 189
  gaseous, 185–187
    LP gas, 187
    natural gas, 185–186
  investigative procedure, 190–194
    detailed search of scene, 193–
        194
    establishing motive for criminal
        act, 194
    immediate examination of scene,
        191
    interviewing witnesses, 191–193
    tracing explosives to their
        source, 194

  verifying explosion, 190–191
  mechanical, 184–185
  terms relating to, 183–184
  unstable materials, 190
Explosive range
  of common vapors, 48
  definition, 47–48

F

Failure to convict in arson cases,
    12–13
Federal Bureau of Investigation Uni-
    form Crime Report, 7
Fermentation, 54–55, 56
Fire, definition of, 45–46
Fire cause determining. *See* Cause of
    fire, determining
Fire causes, accuracy of figures on,
    59–60
Fire classifications, 51
Fire department's role in arson sup-
    pression, 35–44
  enroute to fire, observations, 37–38
    general weather conditions, 37
    man-made barriers or obstruc-
        tions, 37
    people leaving scene of fire,
        37–38
    unusual natural conditions, 37
    wind conditions, 37
  fire chief assuming responsibility
      for arson investigation, 35
  at fire scene, making note of,
      38–41
    accelerant, evidence of, 40
    behavior of fire, 40
    color of smoke, 39
    exact location of fire, 38
    in house fires, presence or ab-
        sence of furniture, etc., 40,
        42
    manner and dress of occupants,
        40–41
    means of gaining entry, by fire
        personnel, 38
    in mercantile or manufacturing
        fires, absence of stock, fix-
        tures, etc., 40, 42

separate and unconnected fires, 39
streamers or other devices to hasten spread of fire, 40
time of arrival, 38
unusual flame color, 39
unusual manner of individuals present, 41
following extinguishment, 41–44
evidence of arson, photographing and preservation of, 43–44
examination to determine origin and cause, 41
fire prevention bureau examination, 44
heating system, examination of, 41
interviewing owner and occupants, 43
indications of incendiary fire, detecting, 41
location of vehicles, noting, 42
securing exact state at scene after extinguishment, 43
suspicious circumstances, noting, 42–43
wiring system and fuse boxes, examination of, 42
key actions at fire scene, 35
determining origin and cause of fire, 35, 41
observation and detection, 35, 36–44
motivation factor, 36
observations as courtroom testimony, 36
police cooperation, 44
requesting investigation, responsibility for, 36, 44
at station, making note of, 36–37
how fire was reported, 36–37
identity of person reporting fire, 37
recording telephone conversation, 37
time fire was reported, 36
training in arson detection, 36
Fire point of liquids, 47

Fire prevention bureau examination at fire scene, 44, 65
Fire scene search, 81–102. *See also* Cause of fire, determining
for fuel sources, 88–93
accelerant, indications of, 40, 62, 84, 85, 90, 91, 92, 93
categories of, 88
combustible solids, 88–89
containers for flammable liquids, 89
examining debris layer by layer, 88, 90
flammable liquids, detection of, 89, 90, 91
preserving evidence of, 89
for heat sources, 93–102
candles, 94–96
cigarettes, 96–98
cooking stoves, 98–99
electric irons, 101
heating devices, 99–100
hot surfaces, 101
light bulbs, 101–102
matches, 93–94
open flames, 93
pilot lights, 98
soldering irons, 101
welding and blowtorches, 100–101
for point of origin, 81–88
burn patterns, 84, 85, 86, 87
case history as example, 85–86
ceiling examination, 81
deep charring, 84
example of search procedure, 82–83
lowest point of burning, 83
scene reconstruction, 82
tracing fire flow downward, 81–82
Fire setters, mentally afflicted, 27–34
chronic fire setter, patterns of behavior, 32–34
the delirium tremens victim, 32
development stages of, 32–34
investigative interrogation of, 34
investigative procedures for apprehension of, 32–34

Fire setters, continued
  the epileptic, 32
  the mental defective, 29
  patterns of operation, 32–34
  the psychoneurotic or neurotic, 31
  the psychopath or sociopath, 31
  the psychotic or insane, 30–31
  the pyromaniac, 27, 28, 31
  the senile, 32
Fire triangle, 48–50
  fuels, 49
  heat source, 49
  oxygen, 49–50
Flammable range
  of common vapors, 48
  definition, 47–48
Flash point
  of common liquids, 47
  definition, 47
Fuel sources, 88–93
Fuels, physical states of, 49

G
Gas liquid chromatography, 111
Guidelines for suspecting arson, 62

H
Hazardous substances, 56
Heat sources, 93–102
Heat transfer methods, 51–53
  conduction, 51
  convection, 52–53
  direct flame contact, 51, 53
  falling burning material, 53
  flashover, 52
  radiation, 53
  superheated gases, 52

I
Ignition sources, 93–102
Ignition, spontaneous, 54–55, 56
Ignition temperature

of common substances, 47
definition, 46–47
Incendiary or suspicious fires, table of
  statistics on, 4
Insanity, 30–31
Insurance fraud fires
  motives for, 19–23
  rural, 132–139
Insurance industry's lack of concern,
  15–17
International Association of Arson Investigators 1975 resolution,
  2–3
Interrogation, 224–245
  contacting subject for interrogation,
    234–236
  definition of, 230
  early methods of determining guilt
    or innocence, 224–225
  Escobedo decision, 226–228
  important role in investigation, 230
  interrogation room, 236–237
  interrogation vs. interview, 230
  interrogator qualifications, 228–229
    appearance, 229
    character and personality traits,
      228–229
    dress during interrogation, 233
    mental and emotional state,
      231–232
    personal grooming, 233–234
    physical requirements, 231
  landmark Supreme Court Decisions,
    226–228
  of mentally afflicted fire-setters, 34
  Miranda decision, 227–228, 238–
    241
  modern-day violations of due pro-
    cess, case histories, 225–226
  objectives of, 231
  preparation for, 231–237
    information about individual to
      be questioned, 232
    factual information about case,
      232–233
  procedures, 237–245
    conduct in interrogation room,
      238

confession, obtaining, 242–243
cross-examination, 241–242
indications of guilt, noting, 244
establishing rapport with subject, 241
legal rights, informing subject of, 238–241
Miranda decision requirements, 238–241
number of people present, 237
questioning subject, 241
suspect reaction, noting, 243–244
training in, 229
U.S. Supreme Court rulings on criminal interrogation, 226–228
Interviewing witnesses, 209, 210–215. *See also* Notes, taking; Statements of witnesses
average witness, 210
definition of interview, 210
discoverer of fire, 210–211
fire department personnel, 210
friendly witness, 210
hostile witness, 210
insurance adjustor, 213
insurance agent, 212–213
investigator etiquette, 214–215
neighbors, 211–212
supplementary sources of information, 213–214
traits of good interviewer, 214–215
types of witnesses, 210
Investigative procedures with mentally defective fire setters, 32–34
Investigative process, motive for arson essential to, 18
Investigator in court. *See* Presenting case in court
Investigator at fire scene, 65–80. *See also* Fire scene search
arrival of, 71–72
authority to search scene, 65
crawling through close quarters, 67
digging through debris, 67
guidelines for suspecting arson, 62
keeping an open mind, 67–68

key areas of knowledge required, 68–71
building construction and materials, 68
chemistry of fire, 68
fire behavior, 68
fire-fighting operations, 68–71
fire streams, 69, 70
ventilation, effects of, 69
mental attitude of, 65–66
outside information sources, 77, 78
discoverer of fire, 79
fire department personnel, 77
insurance adjustor, 77
neighborhood check, 77
photos and movie footage, 79
physical requirements of, 67
steps in fire scene examination, 72–77
in complete destruction, 74, 76, 77
overhead view, 74–76
in partial destruction, 73–74, 76
time-consuming task, 73
tools and equipment needed by, 71

J
Judicial decisions in arson cases, 14–15
Juvenile fire problem, 195–207
adolescent fire setter, 206–207
factors leading to antisocial behavior, 206–207
motives, 206
childhood development factors, 195–197
guidelines for dealing with juvenile suspects, 207–208
infant fire setter, 198–199
motives, 198
special problems, 199
trademarks, 198–199
juvenile age groups, classification of, 197
preadolescent fire setter, 199–206
case history, 203–206

Juvenile fire problem, continued
    emotional disturbance of, 199
    group activity motive, 199
    motives, 199–200
    special problems, 203
    trademarks, 200–203
    vandalism and destruction, 200

L
Law Enforcement Assistance Administration, 13
Law enforcement agency lack of recognition of arson problem, 7–12
Local fire marshal, 65

M
Malicious destruction, 26–27
Manic depression, 30
Mental affliction and arson. *See* Fire setters, mentally afflicted
Mental defective, the, 29
Miranda decision, 227–228, 238–241
Motives for arson, 19–34
    aiding a cause, 24–25
    in automobile fires, 155–156
    in business fraud fires, 20–23
        disposal of undesirable property, 22
        dissolution of partnership, 22
        liquidation of failing business, 20–23
        relocation of business, 23
        sale of land without building, 23
        settlement of estate, 22
        termination of lease, 23
    to conceal or commit another crime, 26–27
    conflicts between groups, 25–26
    definition of, 2
    to divert attention from other crimes, 26

    domestic quarrel, 25
    in dwelling fraud fires, 19–20
    to escape from jail or other institution, 26
    insurance fraud, 19–23, 132–139
    investigative process and, 18, 28, 29
    labor disputes and strikes, 24
    malicious destruction, 26–27
    mentally afflicted fire setters, 27–34
        the delirium tremens victim, 32
        the epileptic, 32
        investigative interrogation of, 34
        investigative procedures for apprehension of, 32–34
        the mental defective, 29
        psychiatrist's and psychologist's aid to investigative team, 28–29
        the psychoneurotic or neurotic, 31
        the psychopath or sociopath, 31
        the psychotic or insane, 30–31
        the pyromaniac, 27, 28, 31
        the senile, 32
    to obliterate evidence, 26
    personal grudge, 26
    personal goals, financial, 23
        building contractor, 24
        conspiracy, 24
        competitors, 24
        insurance adjustor, 23, 24
        insurance agent, 23–24
        watchmen and security personnel, 24
    personal goals, nonfinancial, 24
        defendant in impending trial, 24
        fire fighters, 24
        police personnel, 24
        security personnel, 24
        students, 24
    protest, 25
    racial conflict, 24–25
    revenge, spite, or anger, 25
    vandalism, 26
Municipal arson investigation, 10–12

arson squad, 11
fire chief responsibility, 65
fire marshal, 65
fire prevention officer, 65
lack of communication between
    police and fire personnel, 11,
    12
police power and, 11

N
National Automobile Theft Bureau,
    154
National Commission on Fire Preven-
    tion and Control on arson,
    1–2
National Fire Data Center, 5
National Fire Protection Association on
    incendiary and suspicious
    fires, 3–4
fire causes, annual report policy on,
    59
method of compiling data on fires
    and fire losses, 5
motor vehicle fires, estimates of,
    154
statistics of incendiary or suspicious
    fires, table of, 4
National Fire Protection and Control
    Administration, 5
National law enforcement agencies'
    lack of recognition of arson
    problems, 7–8
New York State District Attorneys'
    Association, 13
Notes, taking, 216–217
definition of, 216
mechanics of, 216–217
purposes of, 216
suggestions on, 217

O
Observations of Fire personnel as
    courtroom testimony, 36

Oxidation, definition of, 46
Oxidation heating, 55, 56
Oxygen
    burning rates, 49–50
    life-sustaining level, 49

P
Paranoid psychosis, 30–31
Paranoid schizophrenia, 30
Pathological fire setting, 28–29
Personal goals as motive for arson,
    23–24
Point of origin of fire, 81–88
Police power for investigative person-
    nel, 9
Presenting case in court, 246–256
admissible evidence, 246–247
    oral, 247
    physical, 246–247
    written, 247
evidence, 246–248
    definition of, 246
expert witness, 253–256
    definition of, 254
    investigator as expert, 255–256
    qualification of, 254–255
inadmissible evidence, 247–248
    hearsay, 247–248
    opinions and conclusions, 247
investigator in court, 249–253
    administering of oath, 249
    conduct during questioning,
        252–253
    dress and manner, 250–252
    excluded witness conduct, 250
    isolation of witnesses, 250
    trick questions, 253
preparation for, 248–249
    daily log of investigation, 248
    comprehensive report, 248
    assembling all information on
        case, 248
    pretrial conference with pros-
        ecuting attorney, 248–249

Psychoneurosis, 31
Psychopathic personality, 31–32
Psychosis, 30–31
Pyromaniac, 27, 28, 31
Pyrophoric carbon state of wood, 56–57, 99

R
Records and reports of incendiary fires
  inaccuracy in, 4–6
  National Fire Data Center for, 5
  NFPA method of compiling, 5
  need for accurate system of, 5
Reluctant witnesses, 13–14
Reporting arson, inaccuracy in, 4–6
Reports, investigation, 220–223
  definition of, 220
  pointers on, 223
  purposes of, 220
  sample report form, 221–222
  writing the report, 220–221
Revenge, spite, or anger as motive for arson, 25, 125–128
Rural fires, 124–140
  goals of investigation, 139–140
    criminal prosecution, 139
    deterrent effect, 139–140
    reducing false claims, 140
  fires in series, investigative procedures in, 128–132
    checking neighborhood changes, 13
    conference of fire and police agencies, 128–130
    cruising in general fire area, 128
    establishing pattern of fires, 130
    observing crowd, 128
    persons released from state institutions as possible suspects, 131
    physical evidence of arson, searching for, 128
    photographs of crowd, obtaining, 128

surveillance or stakeout, conducting, 130–131
insurance fraud fires, investigative procedures in, 132–139
  court records, examining, 138
  difficulties of investigation, 132–133
  financial information on claimant, sources of, 137–138
  fire scene examination, conducting, 137
  information from insurance adjustor, requesting, 134–136
  interrogation, planning, 139
  interviewing witnesses, 136–137
  investigation at fire scene, 133–134
  neighborhood checkout, 136–137
  prosecuting attorney, consulting, 138–139
  report, writing, 139
  reviewing evidence, 138
revenge or spite fires, investigative procedures in, 125–128
  conditions favorable to investigation, 125
  developing and questioning possible suspects, 127–128
  footprints, searching for, 126
  physical evidence of arson, searching for, 126–127
  tire tracks, checking, 126
  tracking with dogs, 126
today's rural scene, 124–125

S
Schizophrenia, 30
Scientific aids, 103–113
  Arson Pattern Recognition System (APRS), 103–109
    applications, 107–108
    computer-assisted analysis, 105
    data elements, 105–106, 107 (Table 7-1)
    linkage of data bases, 106

Combustible Gas Detector (Sniffer), 109–110
Gas liquid chromatography, 111
ultraviolet light (UVL), 111–113
Security measures at fire scene, 43, 62–64, 72
case histories, 64
fire chief's authority, 62
fire fighters' procedure, 62
keeping unauthorized persons away, 62, 72
posting guards, 64
roping off areas, 64
Senility, 32
Sex psychopath, 31–32
Sociopath, 31–32
Spontaneous combustion, 54
Spontaneous heating, 54–58
of charcoal, 56
by chemical action, 56
definition of, 54
fermentation, 54–55, 56
of hazardous substances, 56
ignition temperature, 54
oxidation heating, 55, 56
in painting operations, 56
spontaneous combustion, 54
spontaneous ignition, 54–55, 56
of wood in pyrophoric carbon state, 56–57
Spontaneous ignition, 54–55, 56
State bureau of investigation, 10
State fire marshal's office investigative responsibilities, 9, 10, 65
State law enforcement agencies' lack of recognition of arson problem, 8–10
State police agency investigative responsibility, 10–11
Statements of witnesses, 217–220. See also Interviewing witnesses
definition of, 218–219
purposes of, 219
taking down the statement, 219–220
vital to investigation report, 217
Statistics on incendiary fires, table of, 4

Streamers or other devices to hasten spread of fire, 40, 90

T
Testimony of fire department personnel in court, 36
Tetrahedron of fire, 48–50
Training of fire personnel in arson detection, 36
Training in interrogation, 229

U
Ultraviolet light (UVL) as investigative aid, 111–113
Uniform Crime Report, FBI, 7
United States Supreme Court rulings on criminal interrogation, 226–228
Urban fires, 141–152
arson investigation organization, 146–147
authority for, 143–144
combined police and fire department responsibility, 147
equipment and vehicles for investigators, 147
fire department responsibility, 146
full time arson squad, 143
personnel qualifications, 143
police department responsibility, 146–147
training in arson investigation, 144–146, 150
ideal investigation procedures, 141–142
increase in urban incendiary fires, 142–143, 148
patterns in, 141
public education in arson suppression, 150–152
arson squad roving patrol, 152
arson task force, 152
citizenry in general, 151

Urban fires, continued
    city officials, 150
    fire and police departments, 150
    judges, 151
    lending institutions, 150–151
    prosecutor's office, coordination with, 151
    real estate and insurance agents, 150–151
  records and data, 149–150
  urban blight, problems of, 148–149
    "buy and burn" conspiracies, 148–149, 151
    federal housing, effect of, 149
    increase in incendiary fires, 148
    vandalism and looting, 148, 149

V
Vandalism, 26, 148, 149
Vapor density
    of common vapors, 48
    definition of, 48

W
Witnesses, interviewing. *See* Interviewing witnesses
Witnesses' statements. *See* Statements of witnesses
Witnesses, types of, 210